MONET

OTHER BIOGRAPHIES FROM NBM GRAPHIC NOVELS
GIRL IN DIOR
MARIE ANTOINETTE, PHANTOM QUEEN
BY ANNIE GOETZINGER
THOREAU, A SUBLIME LIFE
BY A. DAN, MAXIMILIEN LE ROY
GHETTO BROTHER- WARRIOR TO PEACEMAKER
BY JULIAN VOLOJ, CLAUDIA AHLERING
GLENN GOULD, A LIFE OFF TEMPO
BY SANDRINE REVEL
ELVIS
BY PHILIPPE CHANOINAT AND FABRICE LE HENANFF
SARTRE
BY MATHILDE RAMADIER & ANAIS DEPOMMIER
BILLIE HOLIDAY
BY JOSÉ MUÑOZ, CARLOS SAMPAYO

MONET

Itinerant of Light

SALVA RUBIO
Writer

EFA
Art

nbm GRAPHIC NOVELS

Nantier • Beall • Minoustchine
NEW YORK

To the amazing people from Lombard: Julie, Rebekah, Éric, Camille, Geneviève, Clémentine and the rest of the team: thank you for all the hard work, for being available, for being so patient and so generous with me.

Thank you to Gauthier Van Meerbeeck and François Pernot who made a dream come true for me.

Thank you to Ricard for his work, his talent, his inspiration, his determination, his patience, his creativity and his availability.

Thank you to Óscar Valiente and Luis Fernández from Norma Comics for believing in this project from the get-go and for welcoming me into their home.

Thank you to Rubén del Rincón, Santi Arcas, Roger, Raule, Homs, Oriol Hernández, Ibán Coello, Rafa Sandoval, Jordi Tarragona, David García, Jaime Martín, Ikna, Javi Rey, Diego Olmos, Josep María Polls, Juan Bernardo Muñoz, Pau, Toni Fejzula, Francis Portela, Mery Cuesta, Octavio Botana, and all the teachers, students and administrative staff at the Joso School for their warm welcome.

Thank you to Alberto Jiménez Alburquerque, Gabor, Montse Martín, Antonio Navarro, Juan Díaz Canales, Teresa Valero, Angux, Kosen, Edu Ocaña, Guillermo Mogorrón, Jesús Alonso Iglesias, Kenny Ruiz, Mateo Guerrero, Pedro J. Colombo, Raúl Arnáiz, Tirso Cons and all the comic book artists in Madrid who accepted me as one of their own from the very start.

Thank you to Master Munuera for his advice.

And a very special thank you to Antoine Maurel for believing in me, for giving me this opportunity, and, ultimately, for changing my life.

Salva Rubio

Thank you to Antoine Maurel, for that night in Barcelona and the quest for the city's best burger.

Thank you to Camille Blin for all her support, attention, patience, positive attitude, and virtual hugs.

Thank you to Salva, of course.

Thank you to my mother, Montserrat, who gave us a love for drawing early on, for her unwavering support and her unconditional love.

Thank you to Marta, my love three times over. I love you.

Thank you to Hug and Guiu: I learn so much watching you draw, talk, paint, live. I will never be as good as you.

Ricard Efa

ISBN 9781681121390
Library of Congress Control Number: 22017910452
© EFA/RUBIO/Editions du Lombard
(Dargaud-Lombard S.A.) 2017
© 2017 NBM for the English translation
Translation by Montana Kane
Lettering by Ortho
Printed in China
First printed October 2017

Also available wherever E-Books are sold

Preface

Of all his contemporaries and painter friends, Monet was the one who put in the most effort to advance the cause of new painting. So much so that today, his name goes hand in hand with the Impressionist movement, which probably wouldn't have seen the light of day without his involvement. Like all revolutions, his began with the reevaluation and calling into question of centuries-old painting traditions. What Monet wanted was not to represent reality, nor to idealize the model as the Old Masters did, but to paint a visual feeling, to the detriment of details. To paint emotions and impressions, to represent only one thing: his perception— "The motif is something that's secondary; what I want to reproduce is what's between the motif and me." Impressionism, therefore, owes its existence to Monet's gaze. "My God, what an eye!" Cezanne used to say.

No upheaval of such magnitude can be accomplished in one day. From the early break with tradition--painting outdoors? Why, what a ridiculous idea!-- to the critical disaster of the Salon of the Rejected--Monet's first impression--the slavish faithfulness to atmosphere and light and the quest for the spontaneity of the moment— akin to the one found in the then new art form known a photography--was a lifelong journey.

And it is this journey that Salva Rubio and Ricard Efa show us here, focusing on the human being behind the icon: the vagaries of this quest, the trials and errors, the reflections, everything that led him to become the painter everybody knows today. By shifting the focus, by painting the artist's works and those of his friends from a different point of view, Salva Rubio and Ricard Efa help us see Monet's art in a new light. Using a subtle mirror effect in which the painter and his works become the models, they enable us to enter the space that Monet was so fond of, the space between the motif and the canvas. Under their brushes, we witness the birth of a painter.

Hugues Gall
Director of the Claude Monet Foundation and the Giverny Museum

"My instincts lead me, in spite of myself, to reckless activity that swallows up my day-to-day life. Like a beast grinding at the mill. Feel sorry for me, my friend."

Claude Monet

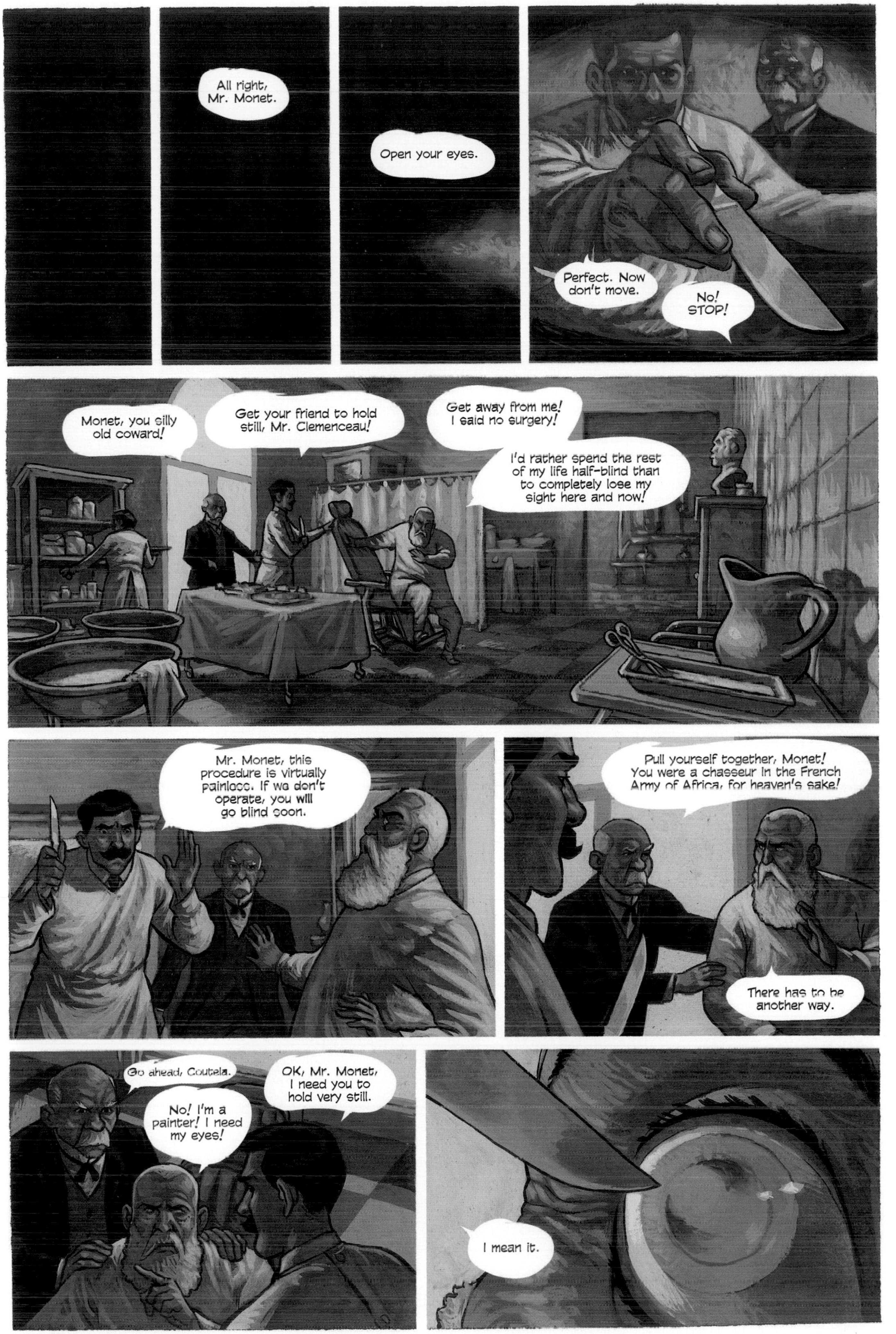
All right, Mr. Monet.
Open your eyes.
Perfect. Now don't move.
No! STOP!
Monet, you silly old coward!
Get your friend to hold still, Mr. Clemenceau!
Get away from me! I said no surgery!
I'd rather spend the rest of my life half-blind than to completely lose my sight here and now!
Mr. Monet, this procedure is virtually painless. If we don't operate, you will go blind soon.
Pull yourself together, Monet! You were a chasseur in the French Army of Africa, for heaven's sake!
There has to be another way.
Go ahead, Coutela.
No! I'm a painter! I need my eyes!
OK, Mr. Monet, I need you to hold very still.
I mean it.

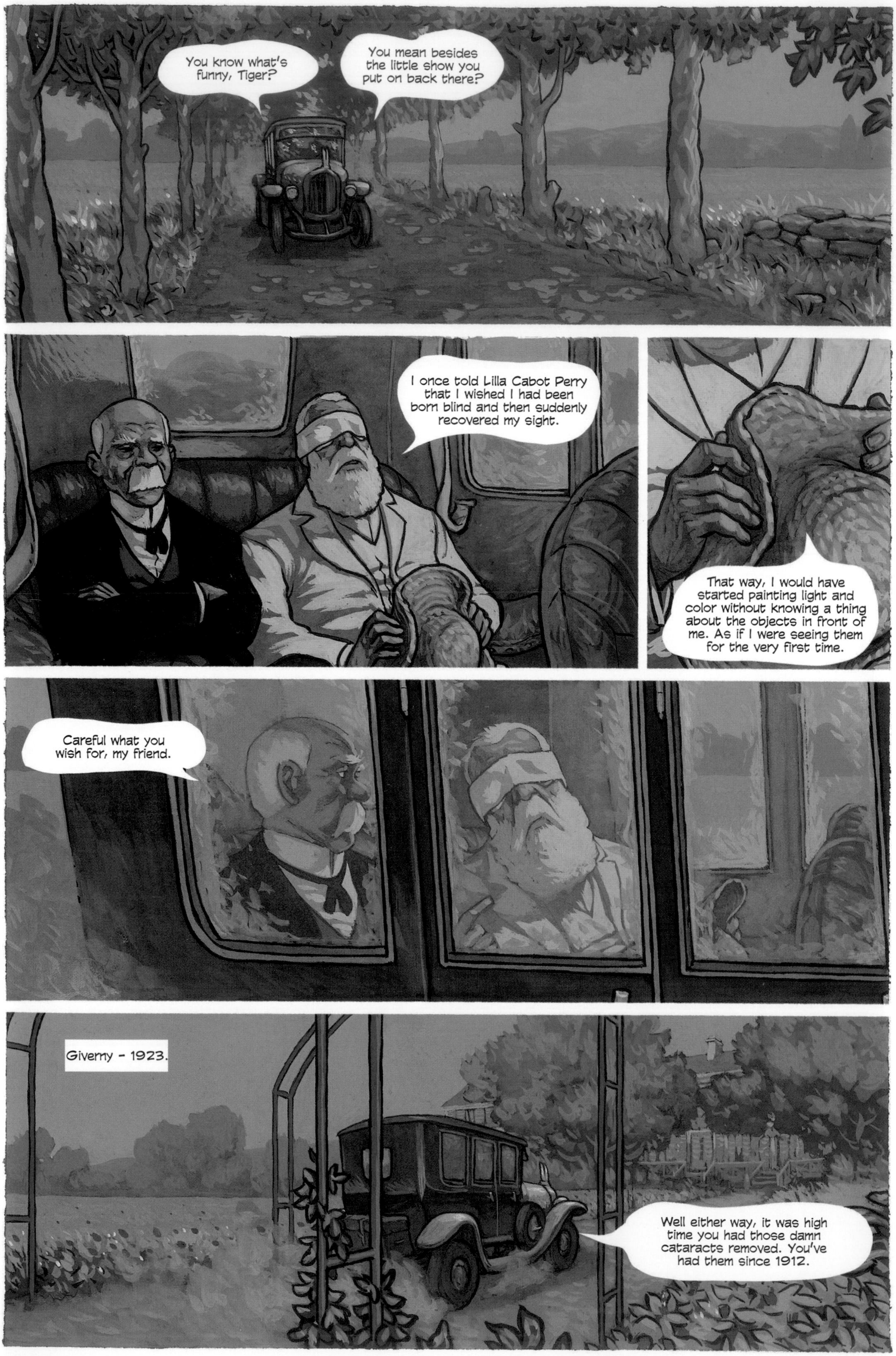
You know what's funny, Tiger?
You mean besides the little show you put on back there?
I once told Lilla Cabot Perry that I wished I had been born blind and then suddenly recovered my sight.
That way, I would have started painting light and color without knowing a thing about the objects in front of me. As if I were seeing them for the very first time.
Careful what you wish for, my friend.
Giverny - 1923.
Well either way, it was high time you had those damn cataracts removed. You've had them since 1912.

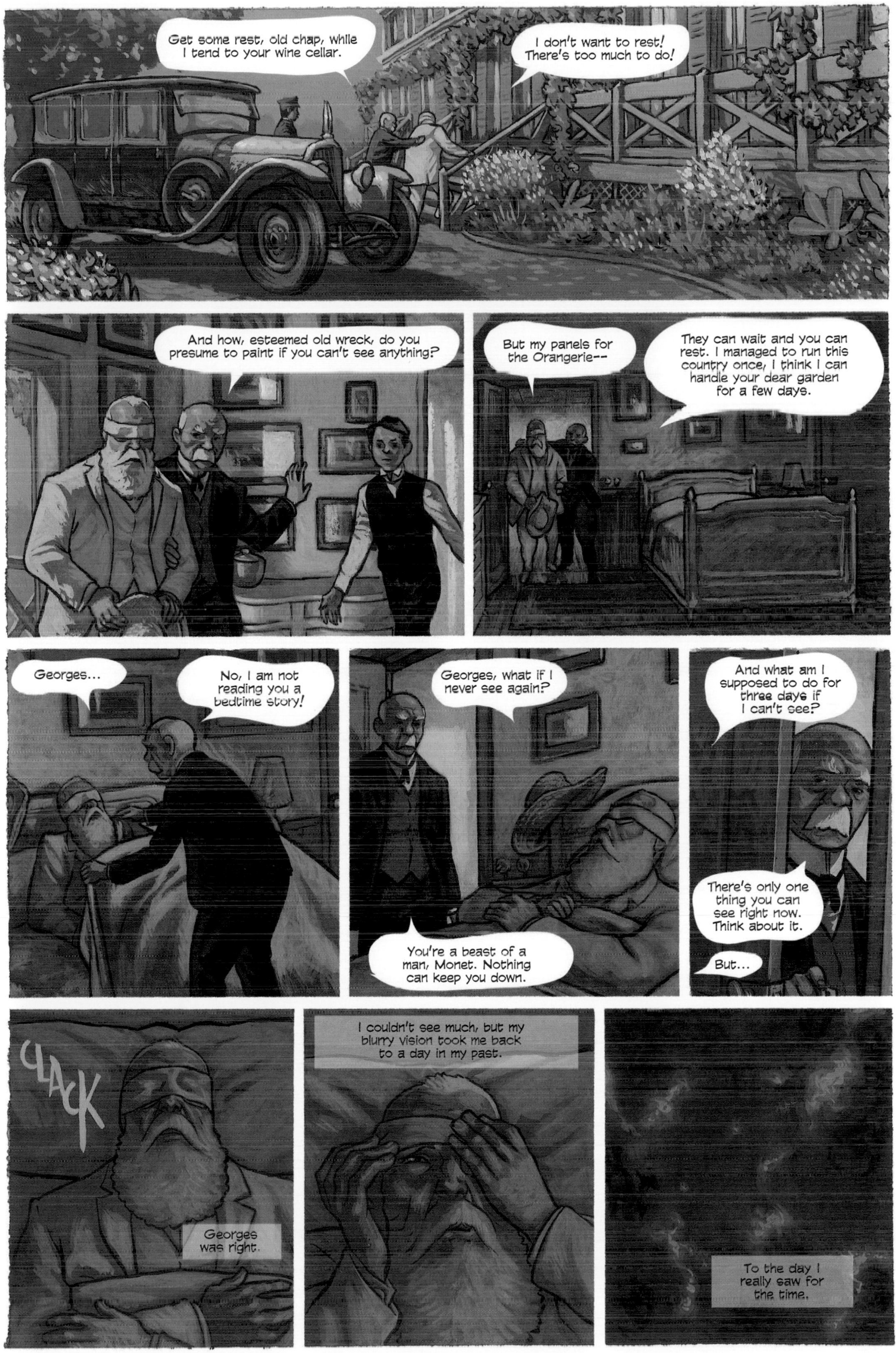
Get some rest, old chap, while I tend to your wine cellar.
I don't want to rest! There's too much to do!
And how, esteemed old wreck, do you presume to paint if you can't see anything?
But my panels for the Orangerie--
They can wait and you can rest. I managed to run this country once, I think I can handle your dear garden for a few days.
Georges...
No, I am not reading you a bedtime story!
Georges, what if I never see again?
You're a beast of a man, Monet. Nothing can keep you down.
And what am I supposed to do for three days if I can't see?
There's only one thing you can see right now. Think about it.
But...
CLACK
Georges was right.
I couldn't see much, but my blurry vision took me back to a day in my past.
To the day I really saw for the time.

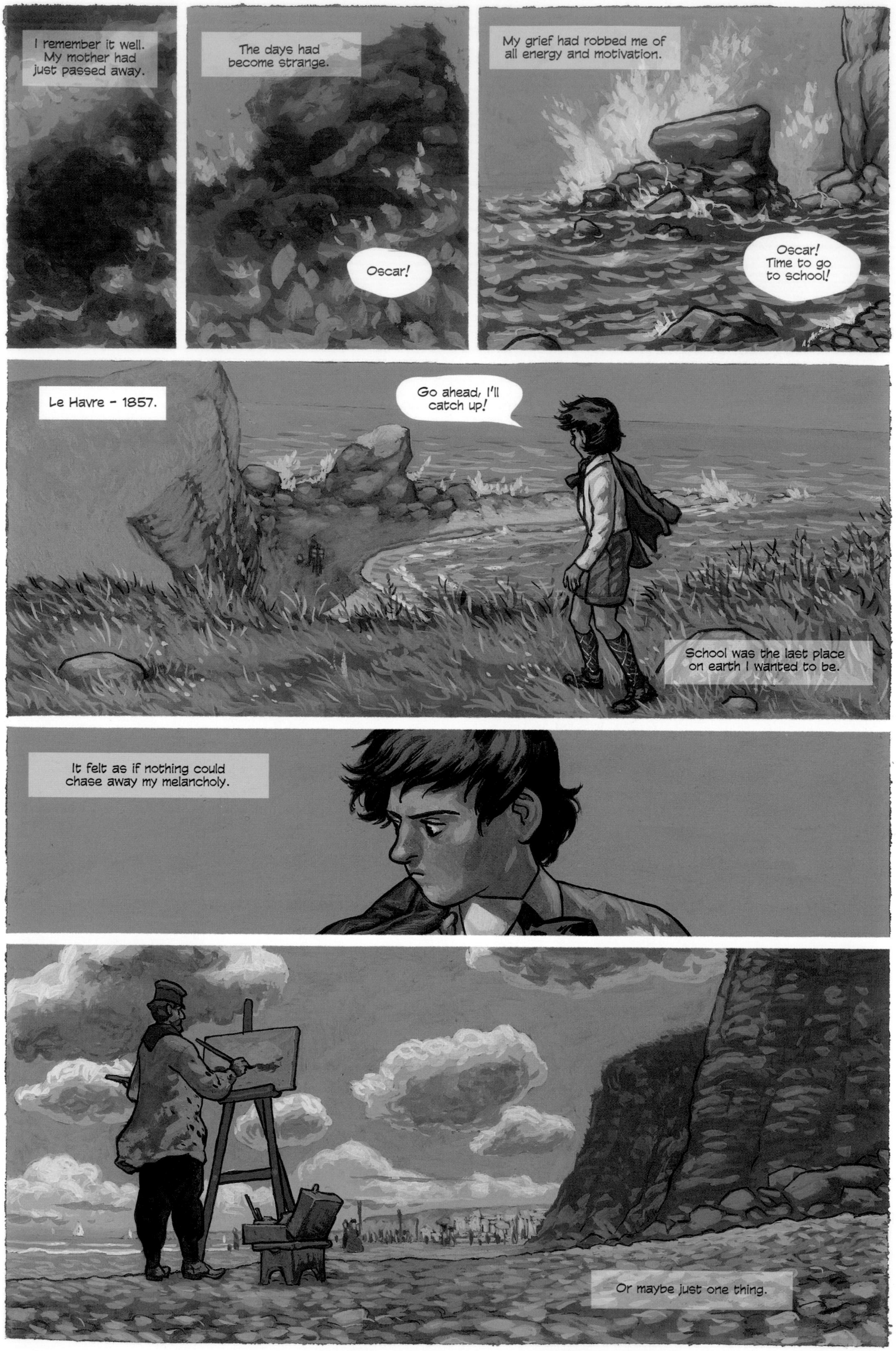
I remember it well. My mother had just passed away.
The days had become strange.
Oscar!
My grief had robbed me of all energy and motivation.
Oscar! Time to go to school!
Le Havre - 1857.
Go ahead, I'll catch up!
School was the last place on earth I wanted to be.
It felt as if nothing could chase away my melancholy.
Or maybe just one thing.

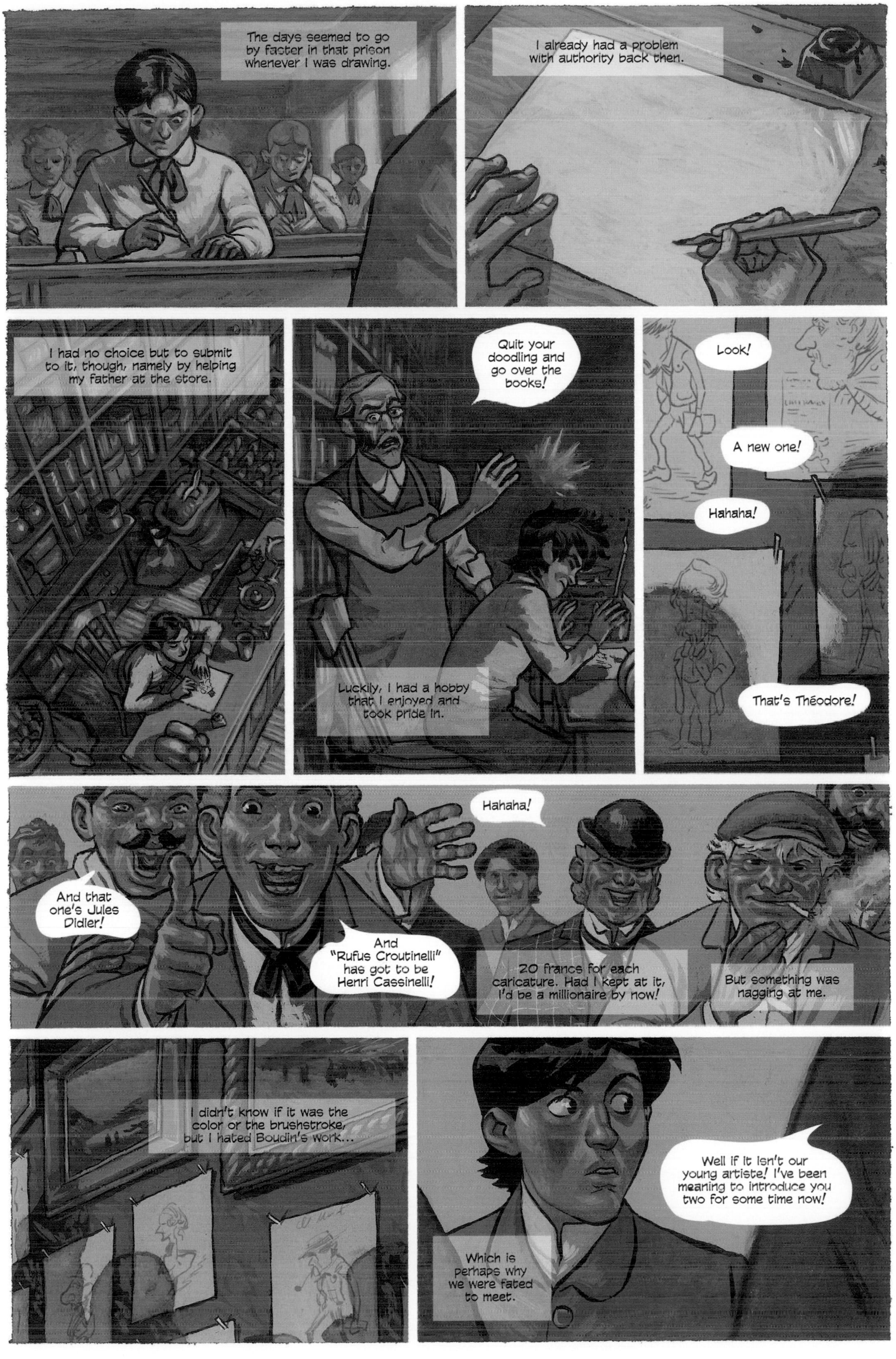
The days seemed to go by faster in that prison whenever I was drawing.
I already had a problem with authority back then.
I had no choice but to submit to it, though, namely by helping my father at the store.
Quit your doodling and go over the books!
Luckily, I had a hobby that I enjoyed and took pride in.
Look!
A new one!
Hahaha!
That's Théodore!
Hahaha!
And that one's Jules Didier!
And "Rufus Croutinelli" has got to be Henri Cassinelli!
20 francs for each caricature. Had I kept at it, I'd be a millionaire by now!
But something was nagging at me.
I didn't know if it was the color or the brushstroke, but I hated Boudin's work...
Well if it isn't our young artiste! I've been meaning to introduce you two for some time now!
Which is perhaps why we were fated to meet.

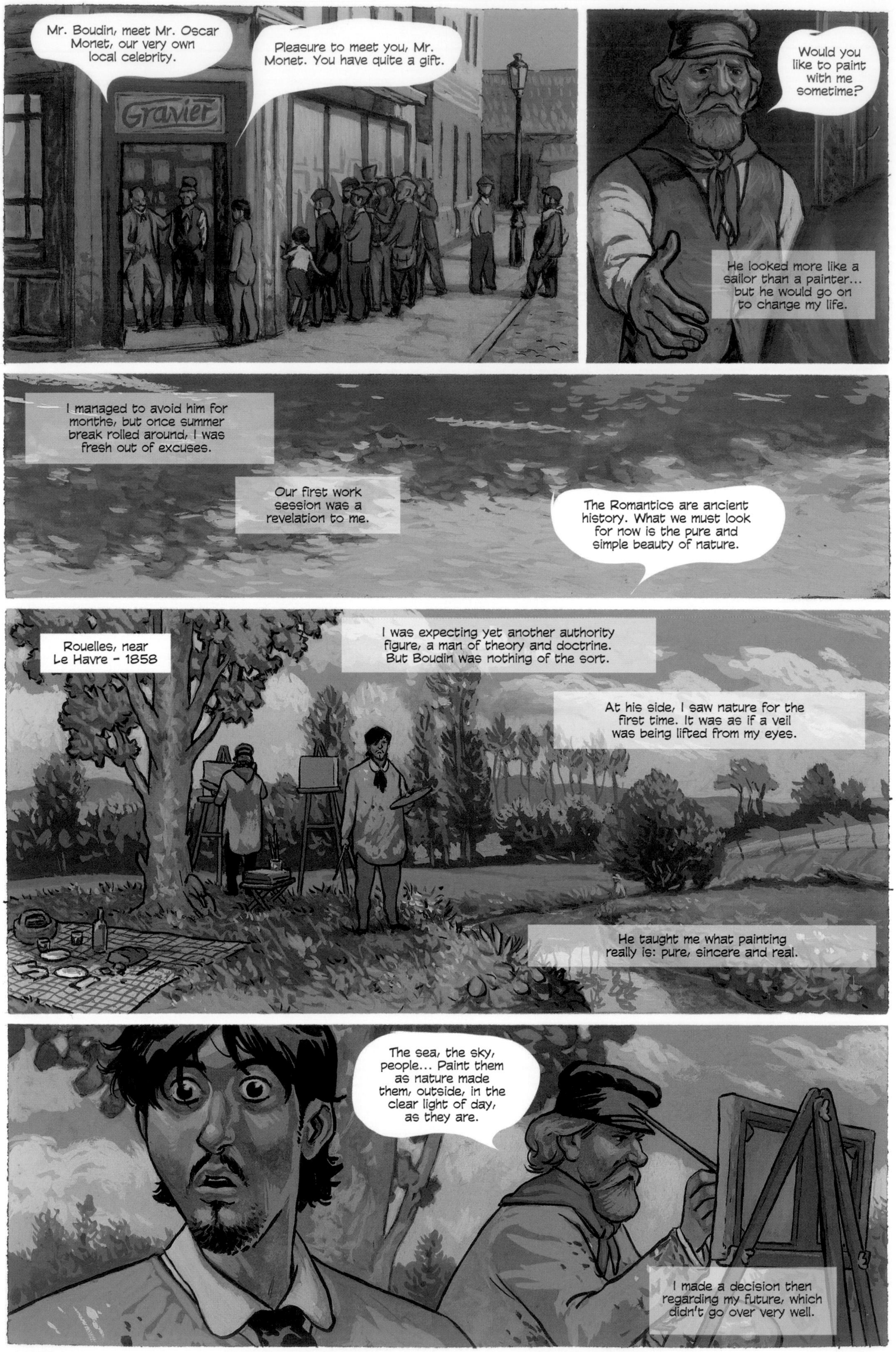
Mr. Boudin, meet Mr. Oscar Monet, our very own local celebrity.
Pleasure to meet you, Mr. Monet. You have quite a gift.
Gravier
Would you like to paint with me sometime?
He looked more like a sailor than a painter... but he would go on to change my life.
I managed to avoid him for months, but once summer break rolled around, I was fresh out of excuses.
Our first work session was a revelation to me.
The Romantics are ancient history. What we must look for now is the pure and simple beauty of nature.
Rouelles, near Le Havre - 1858
I was expecting yet another authority figure, a man of theory and doctrine. But Boudin was nothing of the sort.
At his side, I saw nature for the first time. It was as if a veil was being lifted from my eyes.
He taught me what painting really is: pure, sincere and real.
The sea, the sky, people... Paint them as nature made them, outside, in the clear light of day, as they are.
I made a decision then regarding my future, which didn't go over very well.

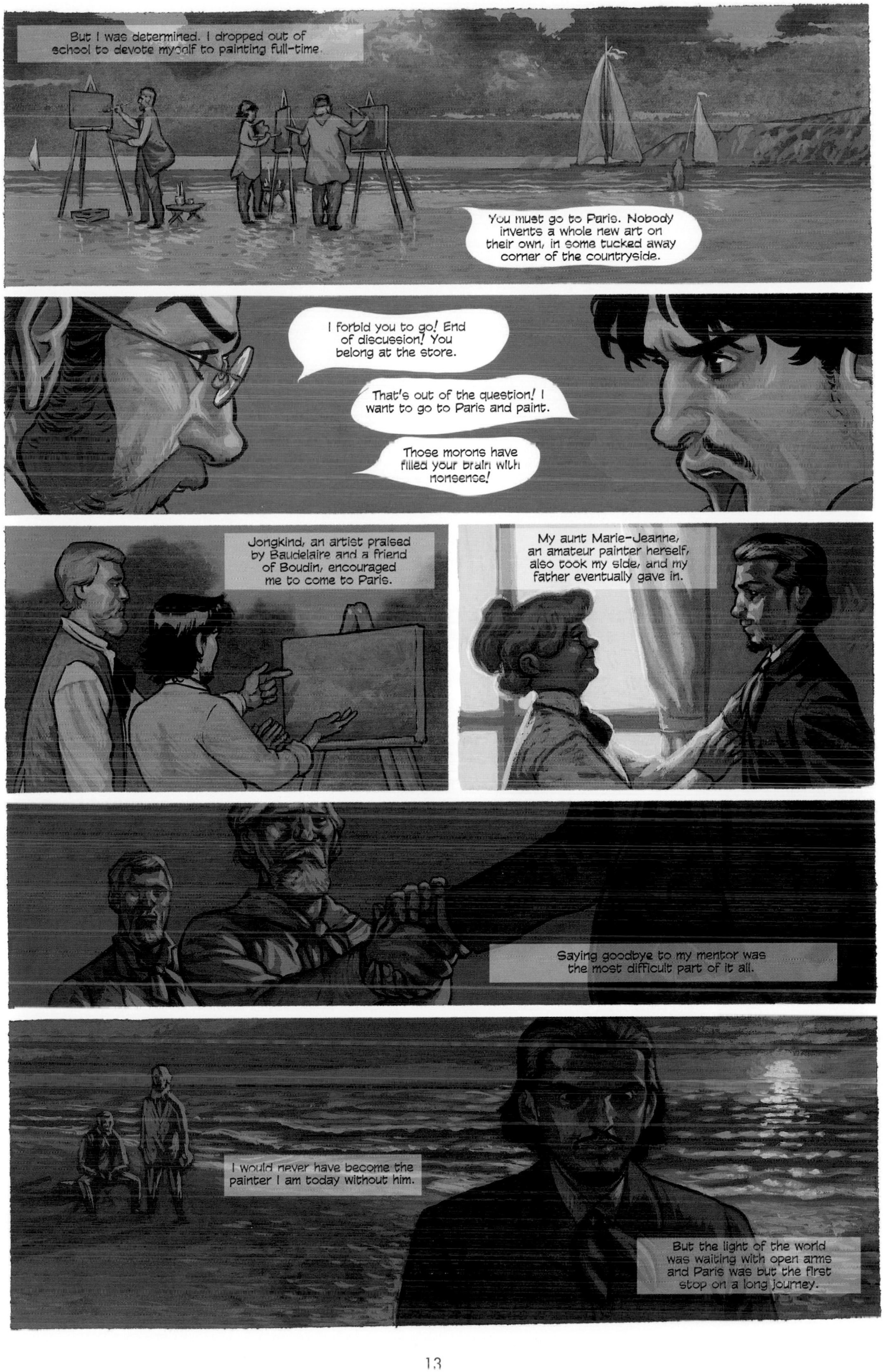
But I was determined. I dropped out of school to devote myself to painting full-time.
You must go to Paris. Nobody invents a whole new art on their own, in some tucked away corner of the countryside.
I forbid you to go! End of discussion! You belong at the store.
That's out of the question! I want to go to Paris and paint.
Those morons have filled your brain with nonsense!
Jongkind, an artist praised by Baudelaire and a friend of Boudin, encouraged me to come to Paris.
My aunt Marie-Jeanne, an amateur painter herself, also took my side, and my father eventually gave in.
Saying goodbye to my mentor was the most difficult part of it all.
I would never have become the painter I am today without him.
But the light of the world was waiting with open arms and Paris was but the first stop on a long journey.

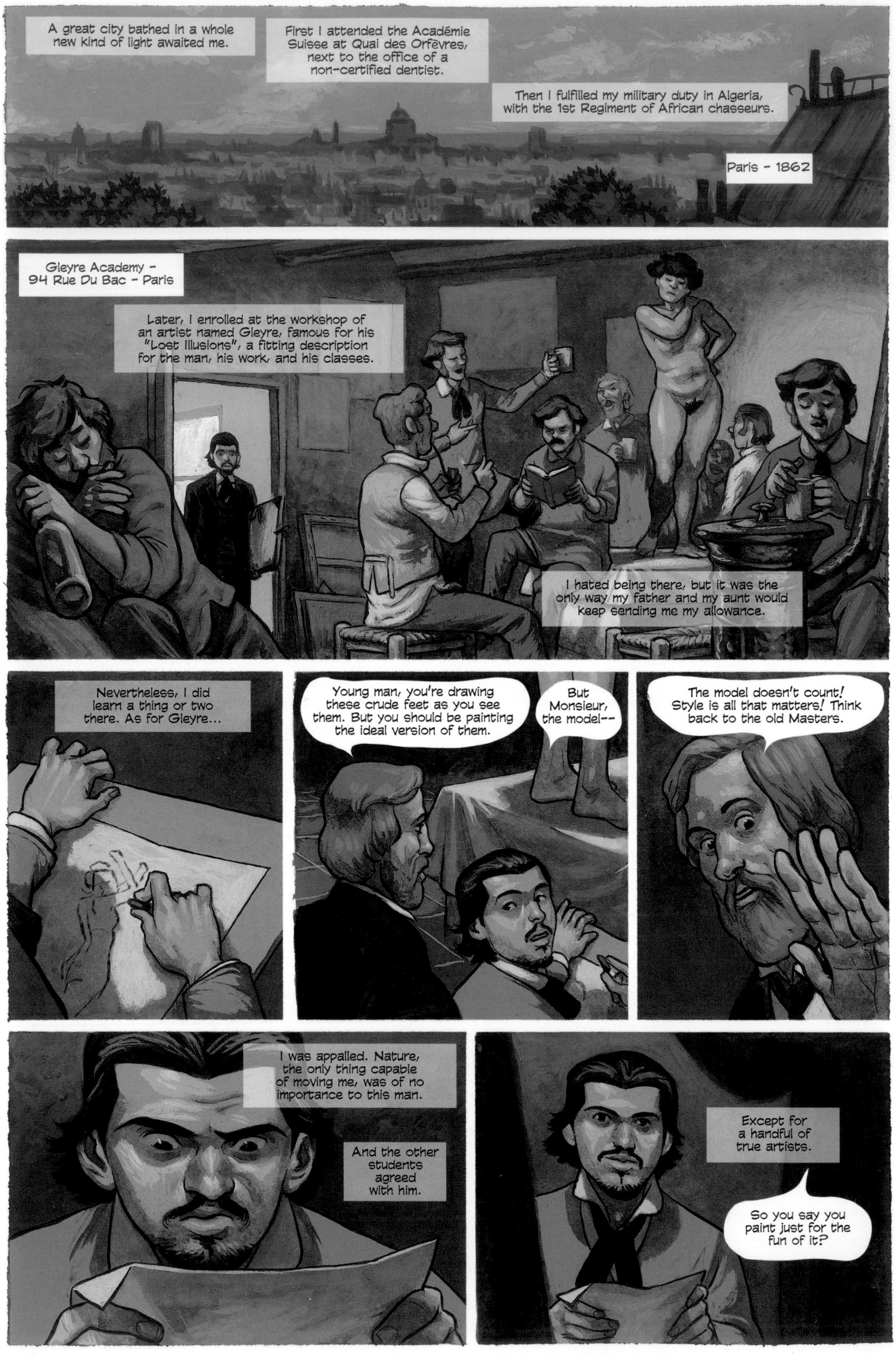
A great city bathed in a whole new kind of light awaited me.
First I attended the Académie Suisse at Quai des Orfèvres, next to the office of a non-certified dentist.
Then I fulfilled my military duty in Algeria, with the 1st Regiment of African chasseurs.
Paris - 1862
Gleyre Academy - 94 Rue Du Bac - Paris
Later, I enrolled at the workshop of an artist named Gleyre, famous for his "Lost Illusions", a fitting description for the man, his work, and his classes.
I hated being there, but it was the only way my father and my aunt would keep sending me my allowance.
Nevertheless, I did learn a thing or two there. As for Gleyre...
Young man, you're drawing these crude feet as you see them. But you should be painting the ideal version of them.
But Monsieur, the model--
The model doesn't count! Style is all that matters! Think back to the old Masters.
I was appalled. Nature, the only thing capable of moving me, was of no importance to this man.
And the other students agreed with him.
Except for a handful of true artists.
So you say you paint just for the fun of it?

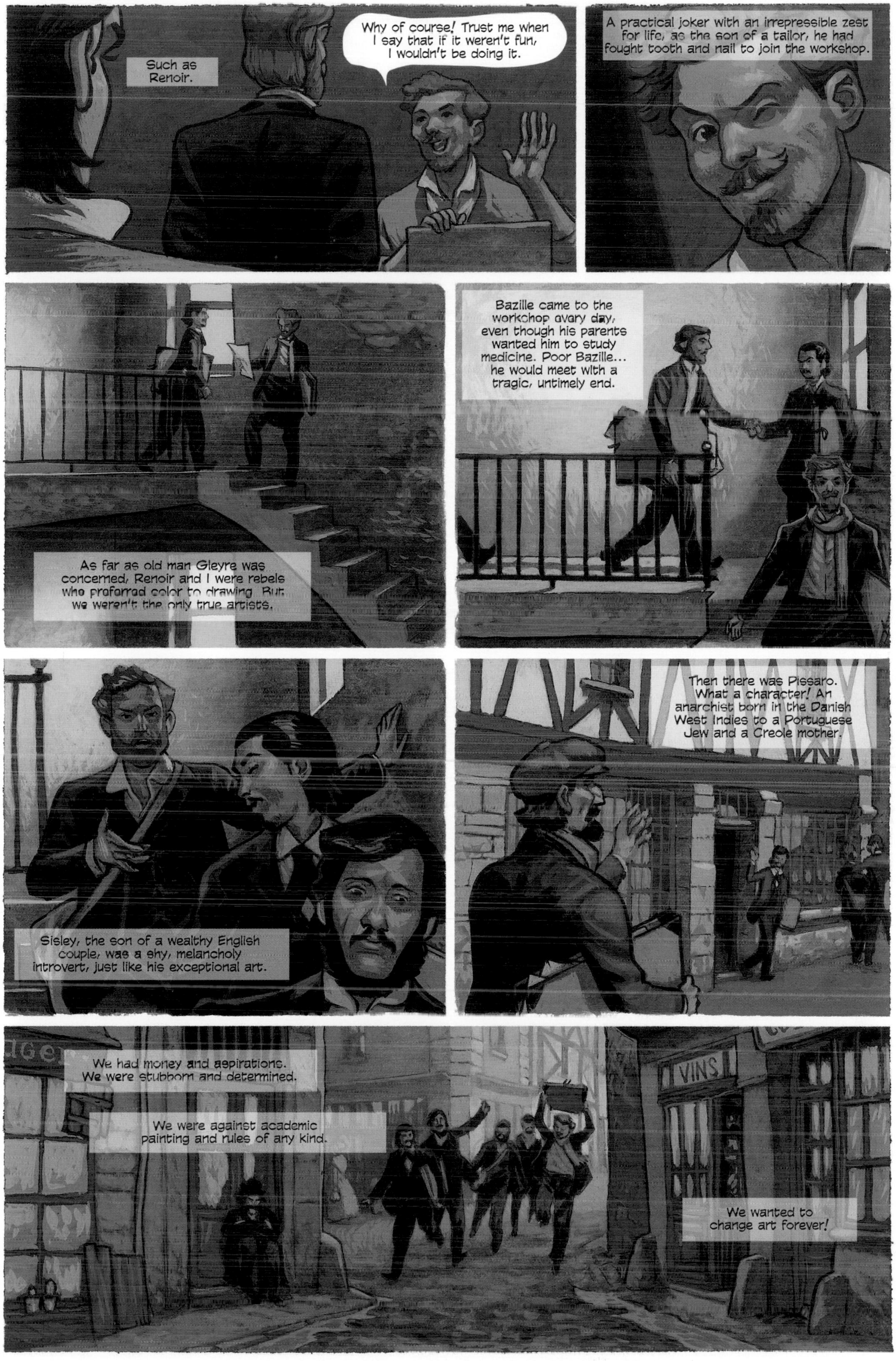
Such as Renoir.
Why of course! Trust me when I say that if it weren't fun, I wouldn't be doing it.
A practical joker with an irrepressible zest for life, as the son of a tailor, he had fought tooth and nail to join the workshop.
As far as old man Gleyre was concerned, Renoir and I were rebels who preferred color to drawing. But we weren't the only true artists.
Bazille came to the workshop every day, even though his parents wanted him to study medicine. Poor Bazille... he would meet with a tragic, untimely end.
Sisley, the son of a wealthy English couple, was a shy, melancholy introvert, just like his exceptional art.
Then there was Pissaro. What a character! An anarchist born in the Danish West Indies to a Portuguese Jew and a Creole mother.
We had money and aspirations. We were stubborn and determined.
We were against academic painting and rules of any kind.
VINS
We wanted to change art forever!

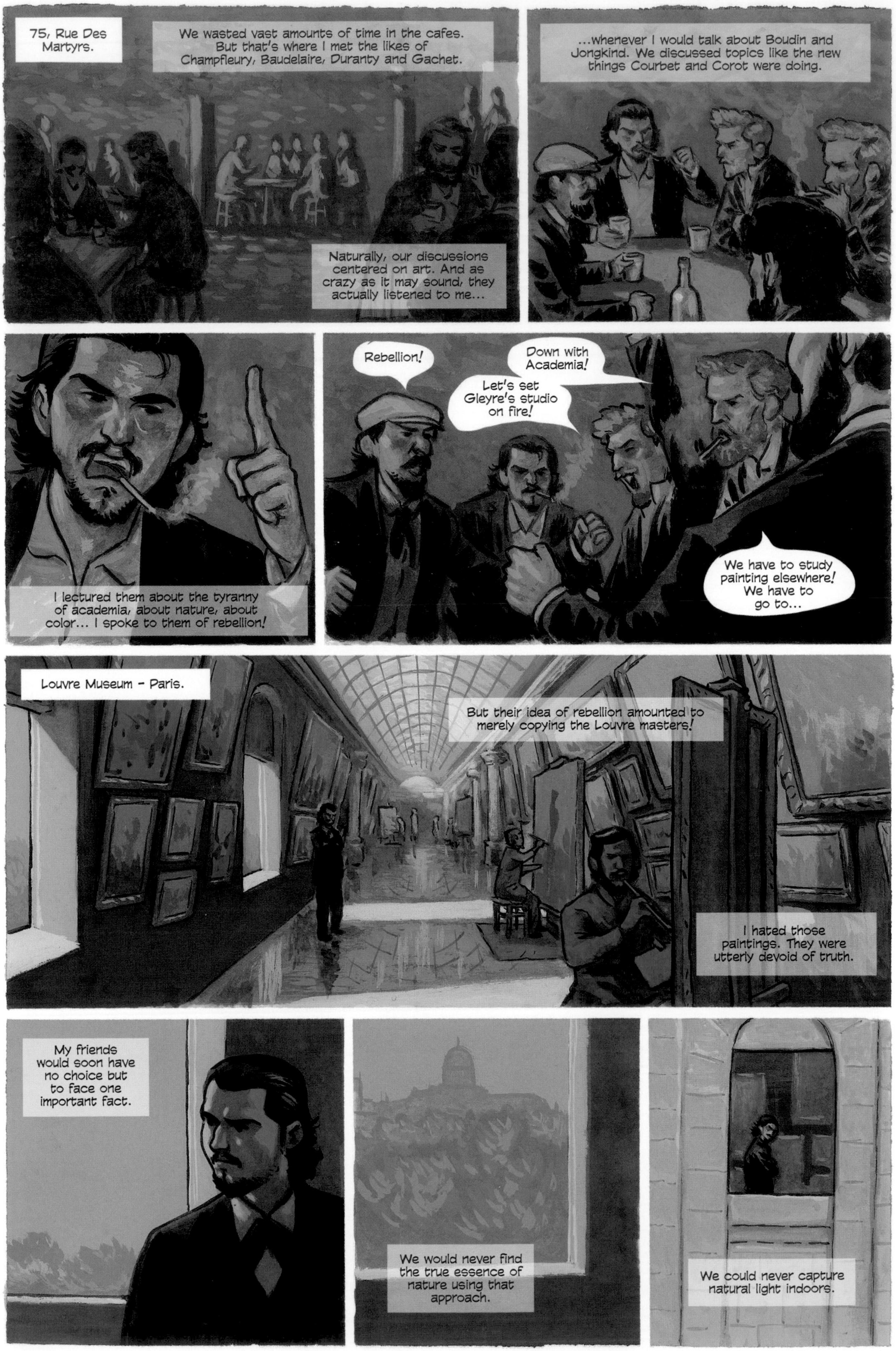
75, Rue Des Martyrs.
We wasted vast amounts of time in the cafes. But that's where I met the likes of Champfleury, Baudelaire, Duranty and Gachet.
Naturally, our discussions centered on art. And as crazy as it may sound, they actually listened to me...
...whenever I would talk about Boudin and Jongkind. We discussed topics like the new things Courbet and Corot were doing.
I lectured them about the tyranny of academia, about nature, about color... I spoke to them of rebellion!
Rebellion!
Down with Academia!
Let's set Gleyre's studio on fire!
We have to study painting elsewhere! We have to go to...
Louvre Museum - Paris.
But their idea of rebellion amounted to merely copying the Louvre masters!
I hated those paintings. They were utterly devoid of truth.
My friends would soon have no choice but to face one important fact.
We would never find the true essence of nature using that approach.
We could never capture natural light indoors.

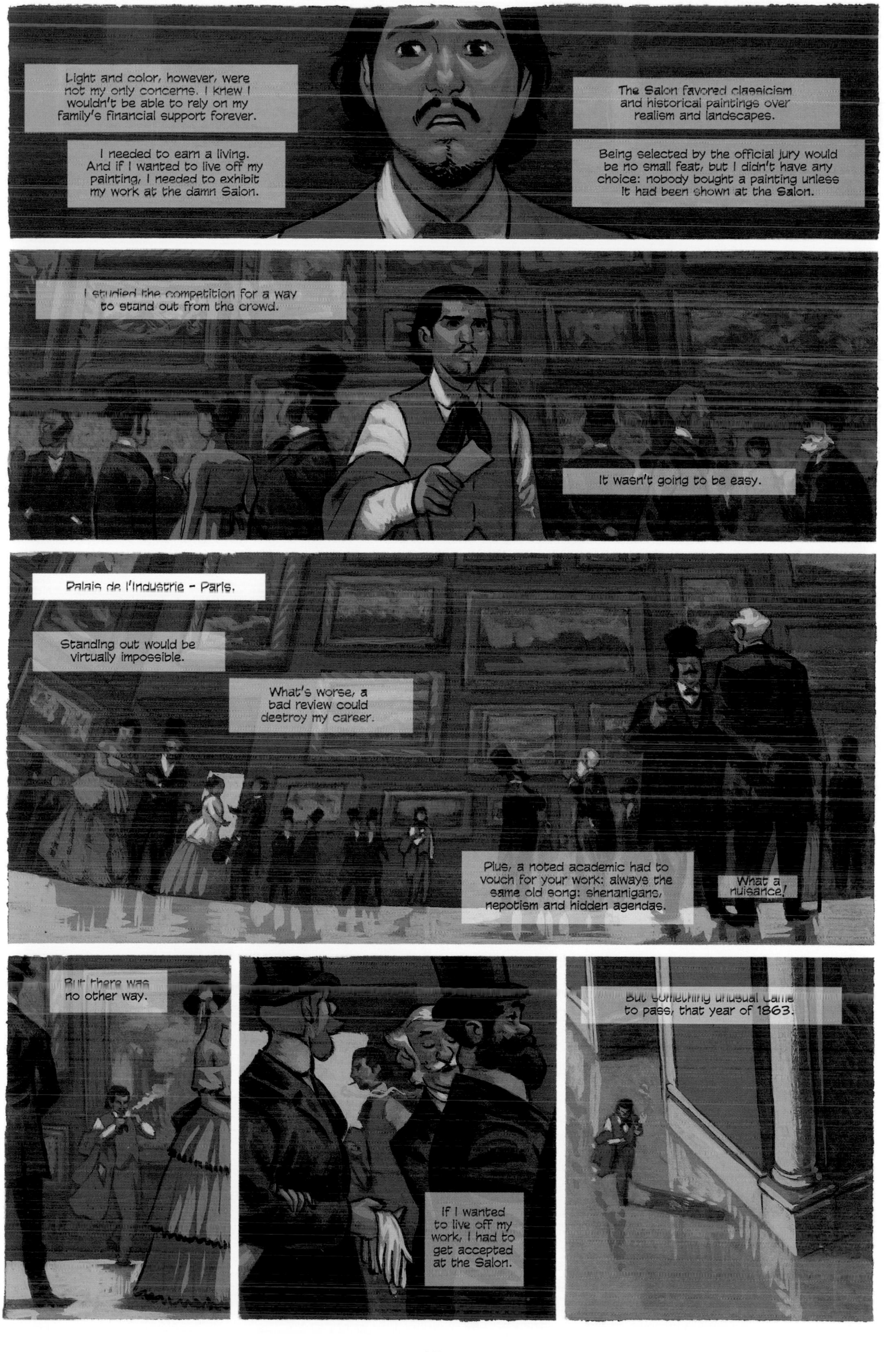
Light and color, however, were not my only concerns. I knew I wouldn't be able to rely on my family's financial support forever.
I needed to earn a living. And if I wanted to live off my painting, I needed to exhibit my work at the damn Salon.
The Salon favored classicism and historical paintings over realism and landscapes.
Being selected by the official jury would be no small feat, but I didn't have any choice: nobody bought a painting unless it had been shown at the Salon.
I studied the competition for a way to stand out from the crowd.
It wasn't going to be easy.
Palais de l'Industrie - Paris.
Standing out would be virtually impossible.
What's worse, a bad review could destroy my career.
Plus, a noted academic had to vouch for your work: always the same old song: shenanigans, nepotism and hidden agendas.
What a nuisance!
But there was no other way.
If I wanted to live off my work, I had to get accepted at the Salon.
But something unusual came to pass, that year of 1863.

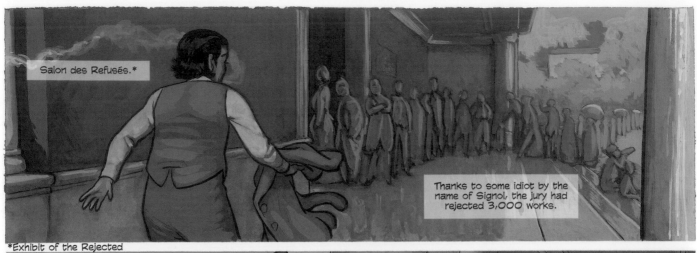

Salon des Refusés.*

Thanks to some idiot by the name of Signol, the jury had rejected 3,000 works.

*Exhibit of the Rejected

It caused such a stir that Napoleon III himself had to intervene and bring the president of the jury, another idiot by the name of Nieuwerkerke, to task.

And so the rejected works were shown to the public, who was to judge them itself. In truth, though, the public just wanted to have a little fun.

Every Sunday, 3,000 to 4,000 admission tickets were sold, mainly to morons come to mock what they didn't understand.

A few of my "rejected" friends, such as Pissarro, Fantin, Guillaumin, Jongkind and Cézanne, were thus able to exhibit their work. They figured it was as good a way as any to get exposure.

That year, one painting in particular got all the attention.

The most controversial one in the show.

A work I just had to see with my own eyes.

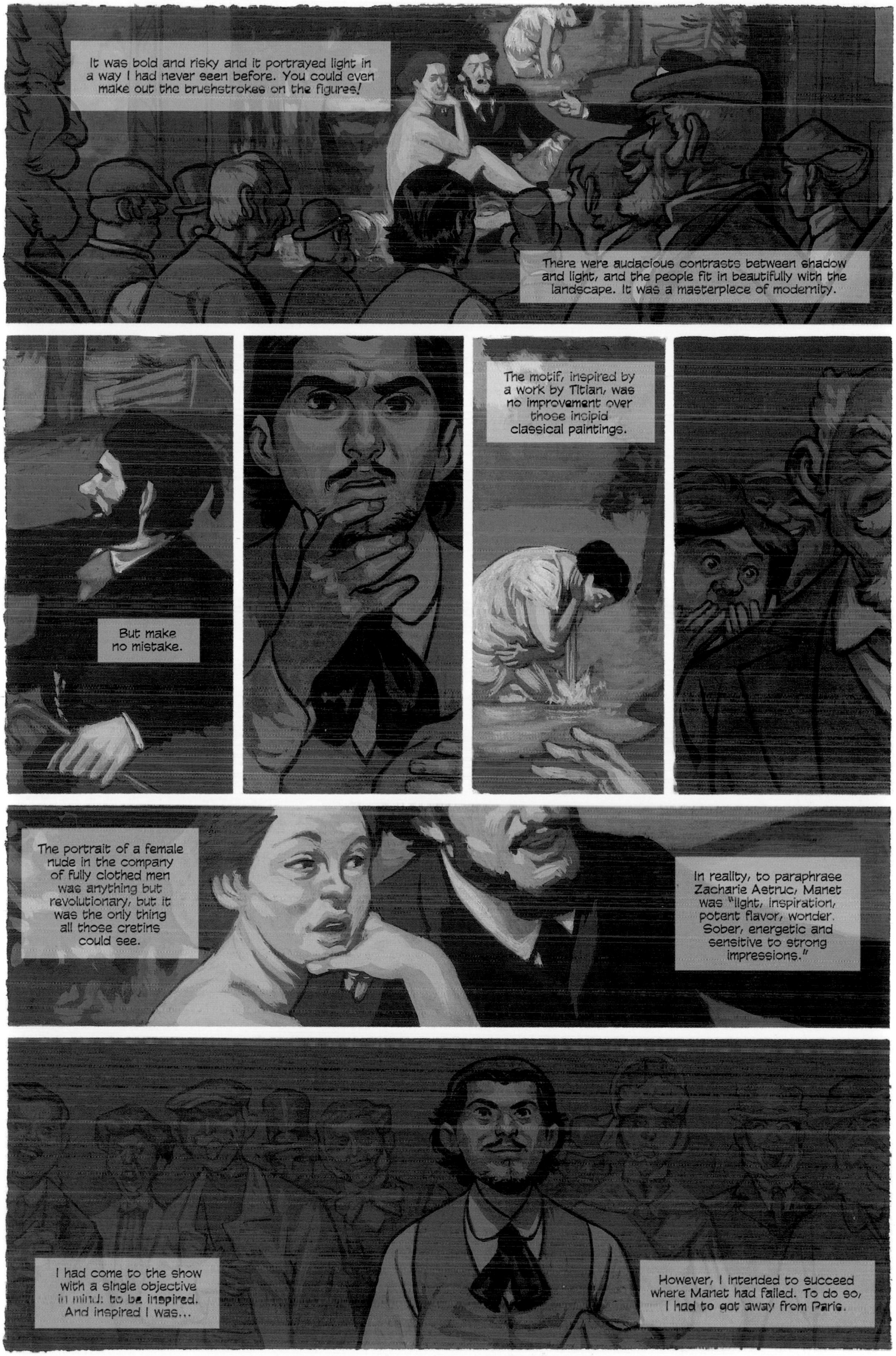
It was bold and risky and it portrayed light in a way I had never seen before. You could even make out the brushstrokes on the figures!
There were audacious contrasts between shadow and light, and the people fit in beautifully with the landscape. It was a masterpiece of modernity.
But make no mistake.
The motif, inspired by a work by Titian, was no improvement over those insipid classical paintings.
The portrait of a female nude in the company of fully clothed men was anything but revolutionary, but it was the only thing all those cretins could see.
In reality, to paraphrase Zacharie Astruc, Manet was "light, inspiration, potent flavor, wonder. Sober, energetic and sensitive to strong impressions."
I had come to the show with a single objective in mind: to be inspired. And inspired I was...
However, I intended to succeed where Manet had failed. To do so, I had to get away from Paris.

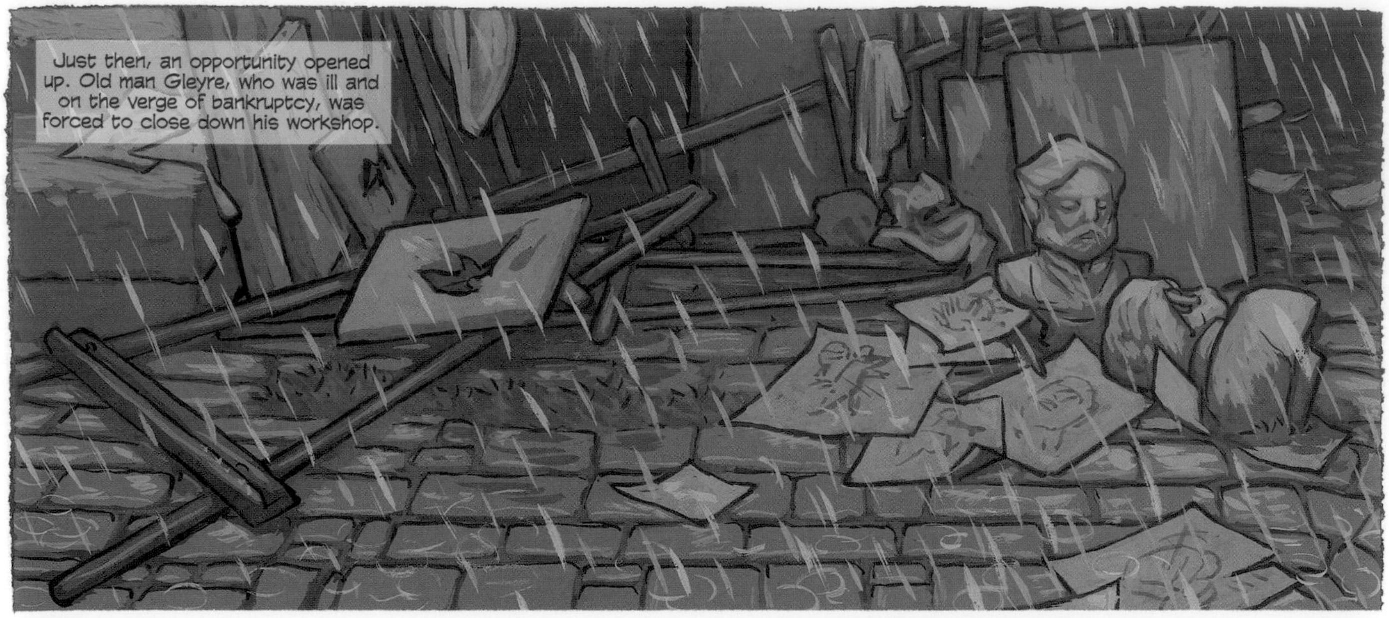
Just then, an opportunity opened up. Old man Gleyre, who was ill and on the verge of bankruptcy, was forced to close down his workshop.

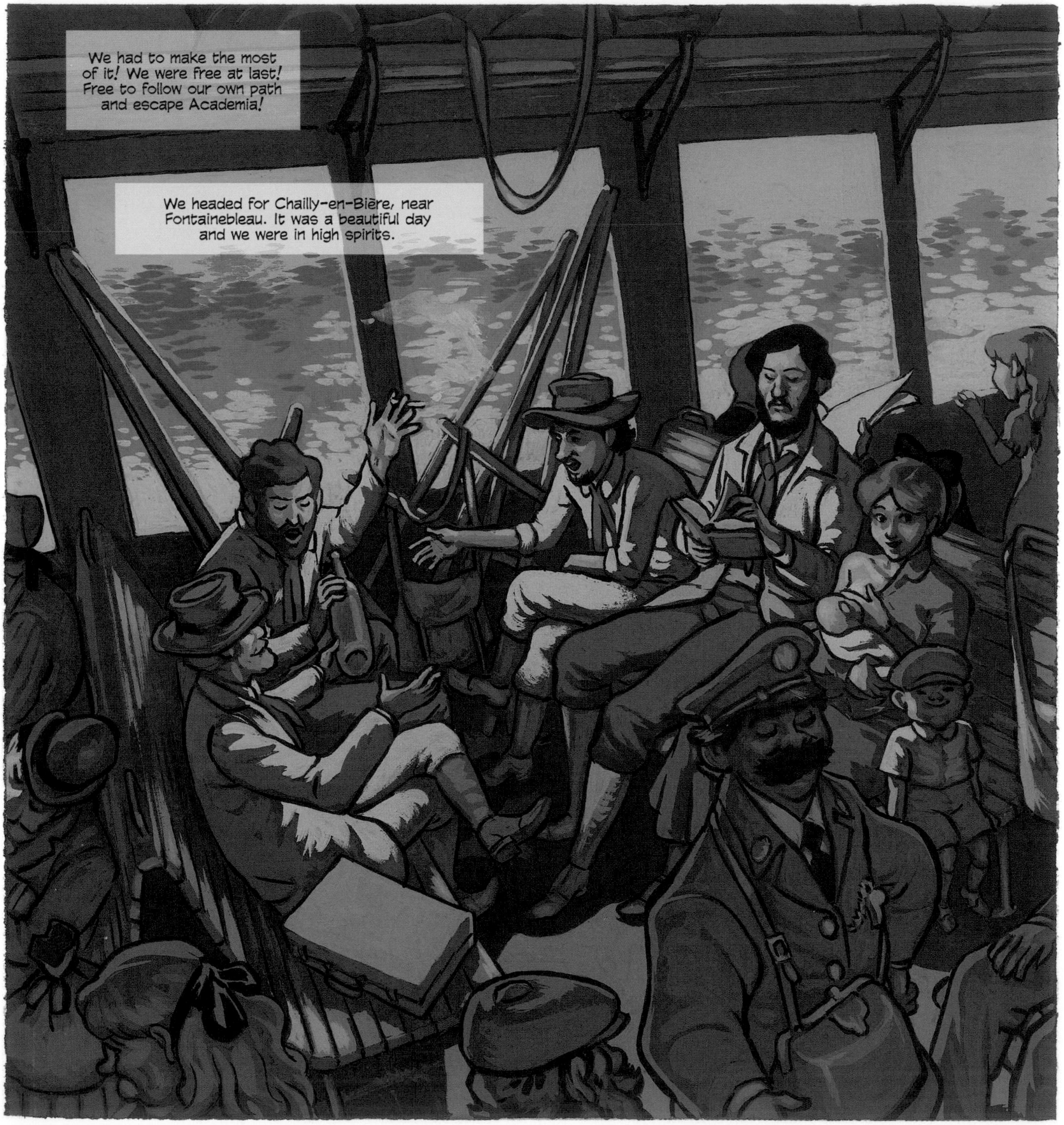
We had to make the most of it! We were free at last! Free to follow our own path and escape Academia!
We headed for Chailly-en-Bière, near Fontainebleau. It was a beautiful day and we were in high spirits.

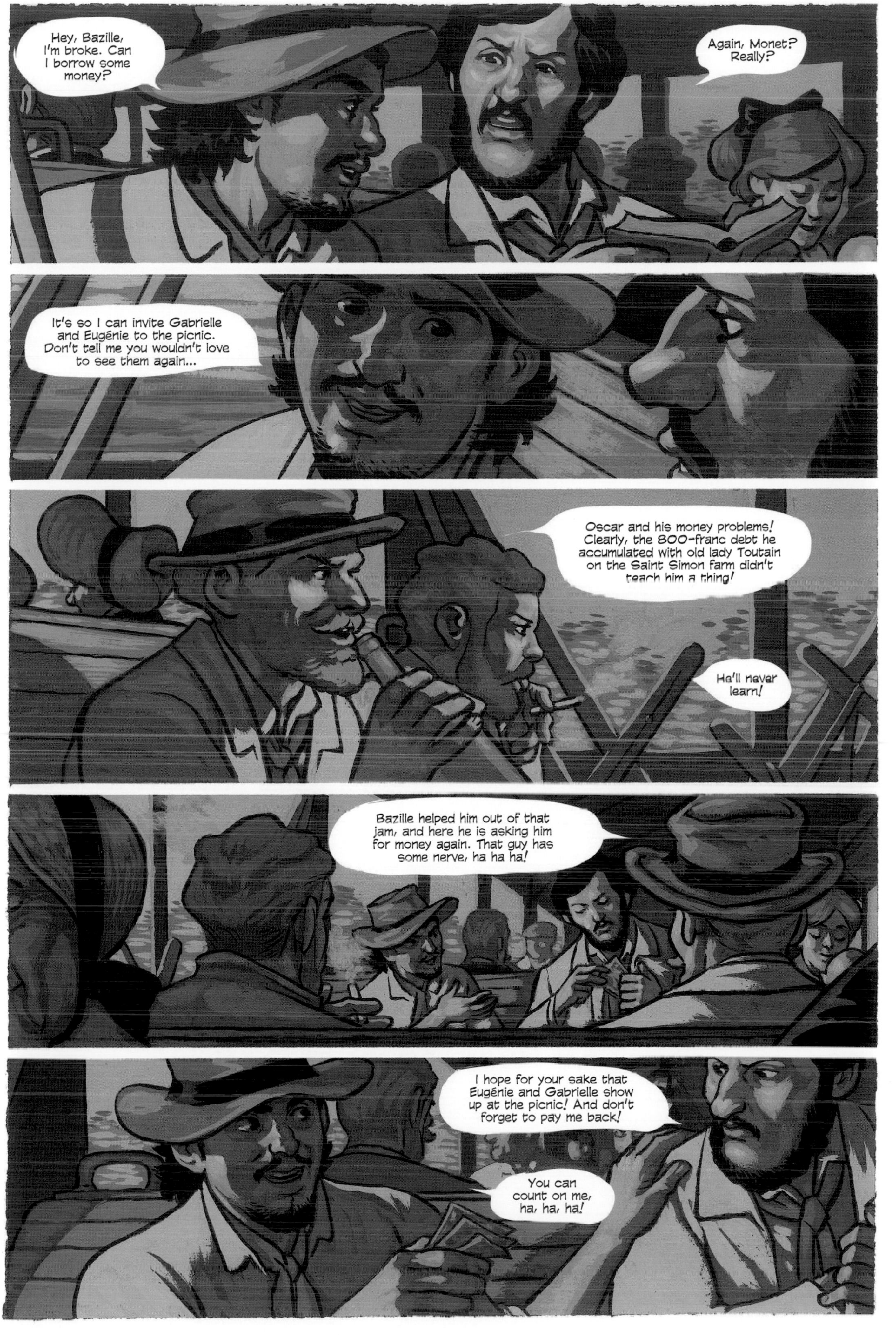
Hey, Bazille, I'm broke. Can I borrow some money?
Again, Monet? Really?
It's so I can invite Gabrielle and Eugénie to the picnic. Don't tell me you wouldn't love to see them again...
Oscar and his money problems! Clearly, the 800-franc debt he accumulated with old lady Toutain on the Saint Simon farm didn't teach him a thing!
He'll never learn!
Bazille helped him out of that jam, and here he is asking him for money again. That guy has some nerve, ha ha ha!
I hope for your sake that Eugénie and Gabrielle show up at the picnic! And don't forget to pay me back!
You can count on me, ha, ha, ha!

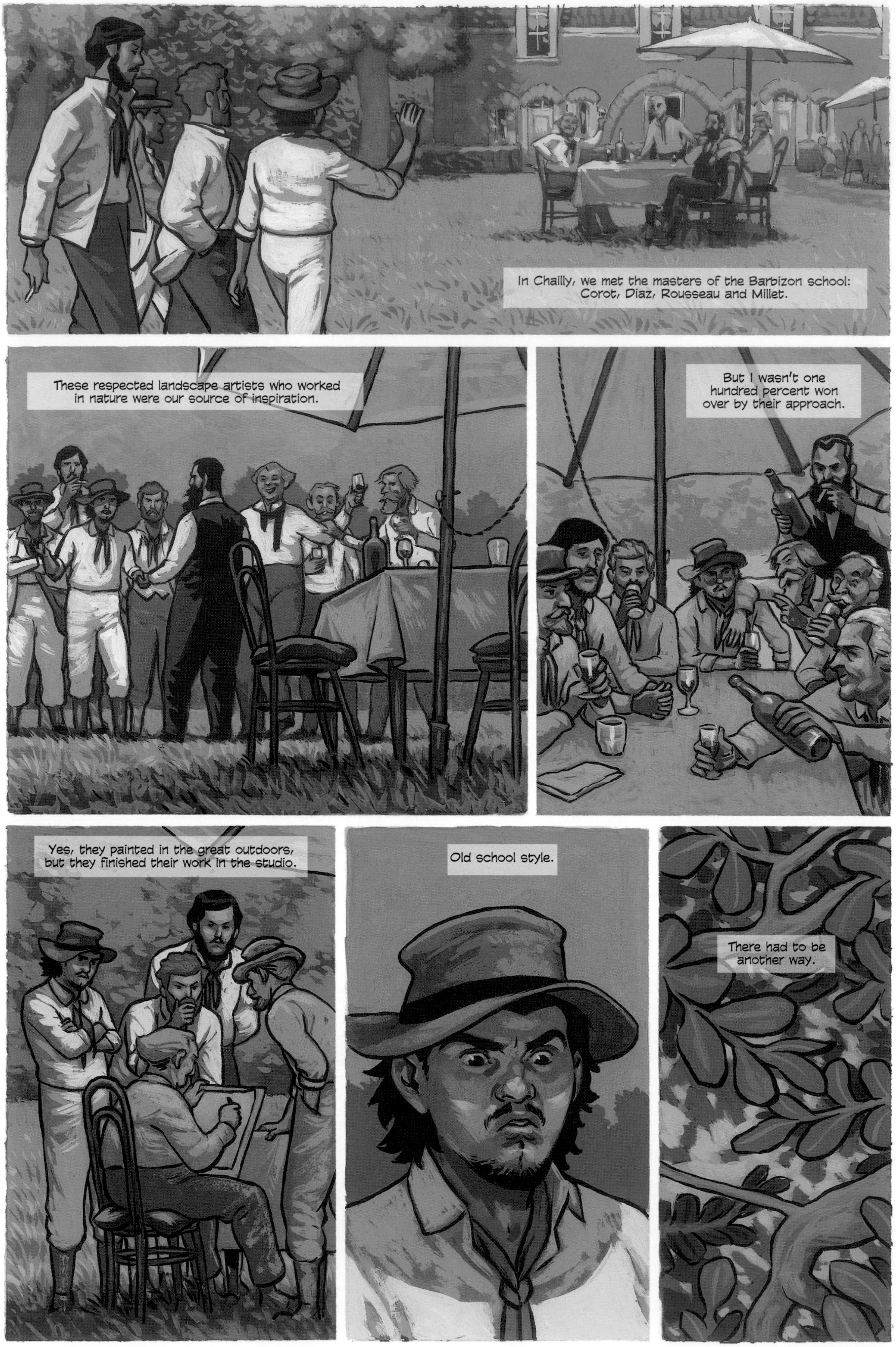
In Chailly, we met the masters of the Barbizon school: Corot, Diaz, Rousseau and Millet.
These respected landscape artists who worked in nature were our source of inspiration.
But I wasn't one hundred percent won over by their approach.
Yes, they painted in the great outdoors, but they finished their work in the studio.
Old school style.
There had to be another way.

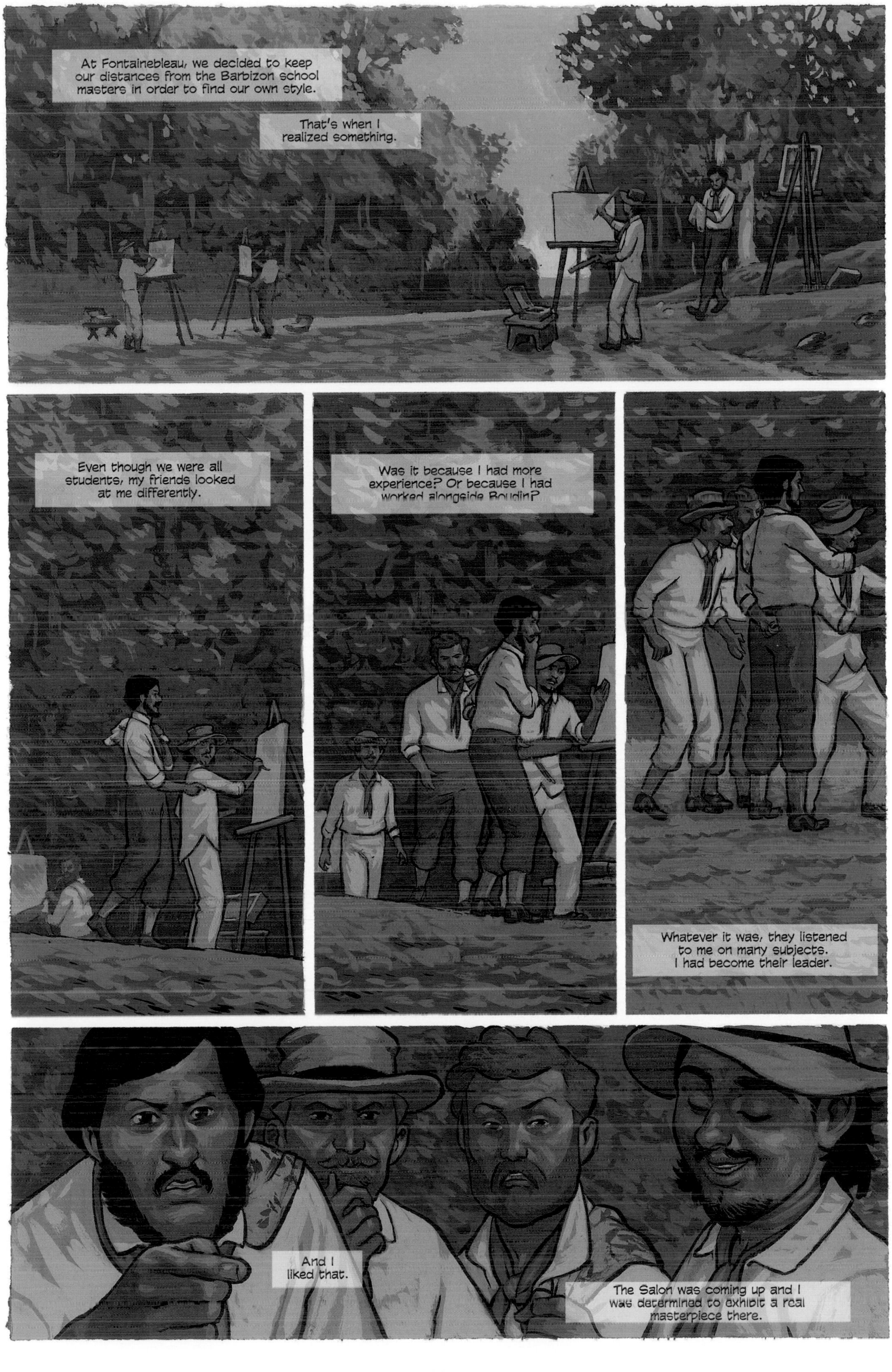
At Fontainebleau, we decided to keep our distances from the Barbizon school masters in order to find our own style.
That's when I realized something.
Even though we were all students, my friends looked at me differently.
Was it because I had more experience? Or because I had worked alongside Boudin?
Whatever it was, they listened to me on many subjects. I had become their leader.
And I liked that.
The Salon was coming up and I was determined to exhibit a real masterpiece there.

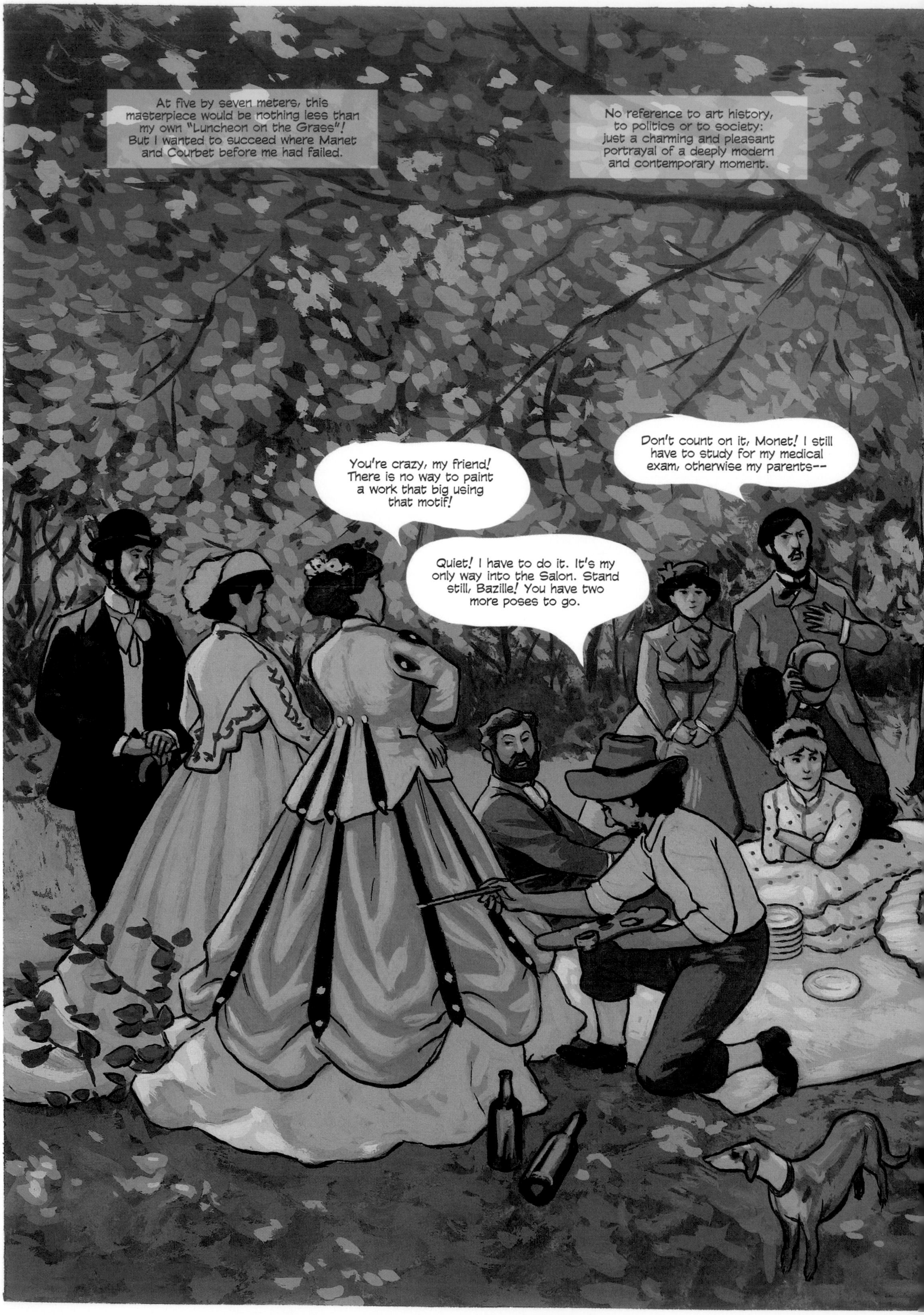
At five by seven meters, this masterpiece would be nothing less than my own "Luncheon on the Grass"! But I wanted to succeed where Manet and Courbet before me had failed.
No reference to art history, to politics or to society: just a charming and pleasant portrayal of a deeply modern and contemporary moment.
You're crazy, my friend! There is no way to paint a work that big using that motif!
Don't count on it, Monet! I still have to study for my medical exam, otherwise my parents--
Quiet! I have to do it. It's my only way into the Salon. Stand still, Bazille! You have two more poses to go.

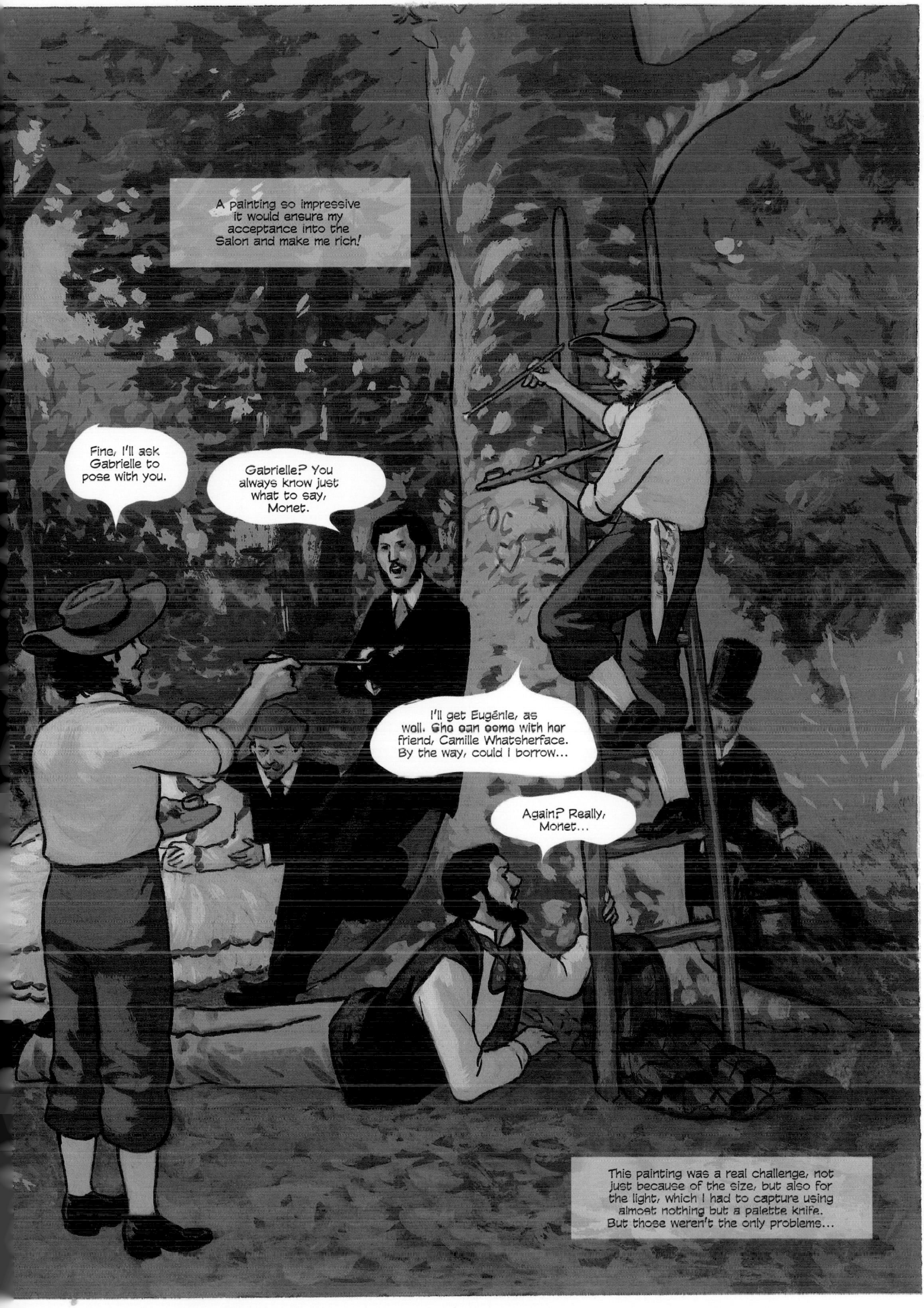
A painting so impressive it would ensure my acceptance into the Salon and make me rich!
Fine, I'll ask Gabrielle to pose with you.
Gabrielle? You always know just what to say, Monet.
I'll get Eugénie, as well. She can come with her friend, Camille Whatsherface. By the way, could I borrow...
Again? Really, Monet...
This painting was a real challenge, not just because of the size, but also for the light, which I had to capture using almost nothing but a palette knife. But those weren't the only problems...

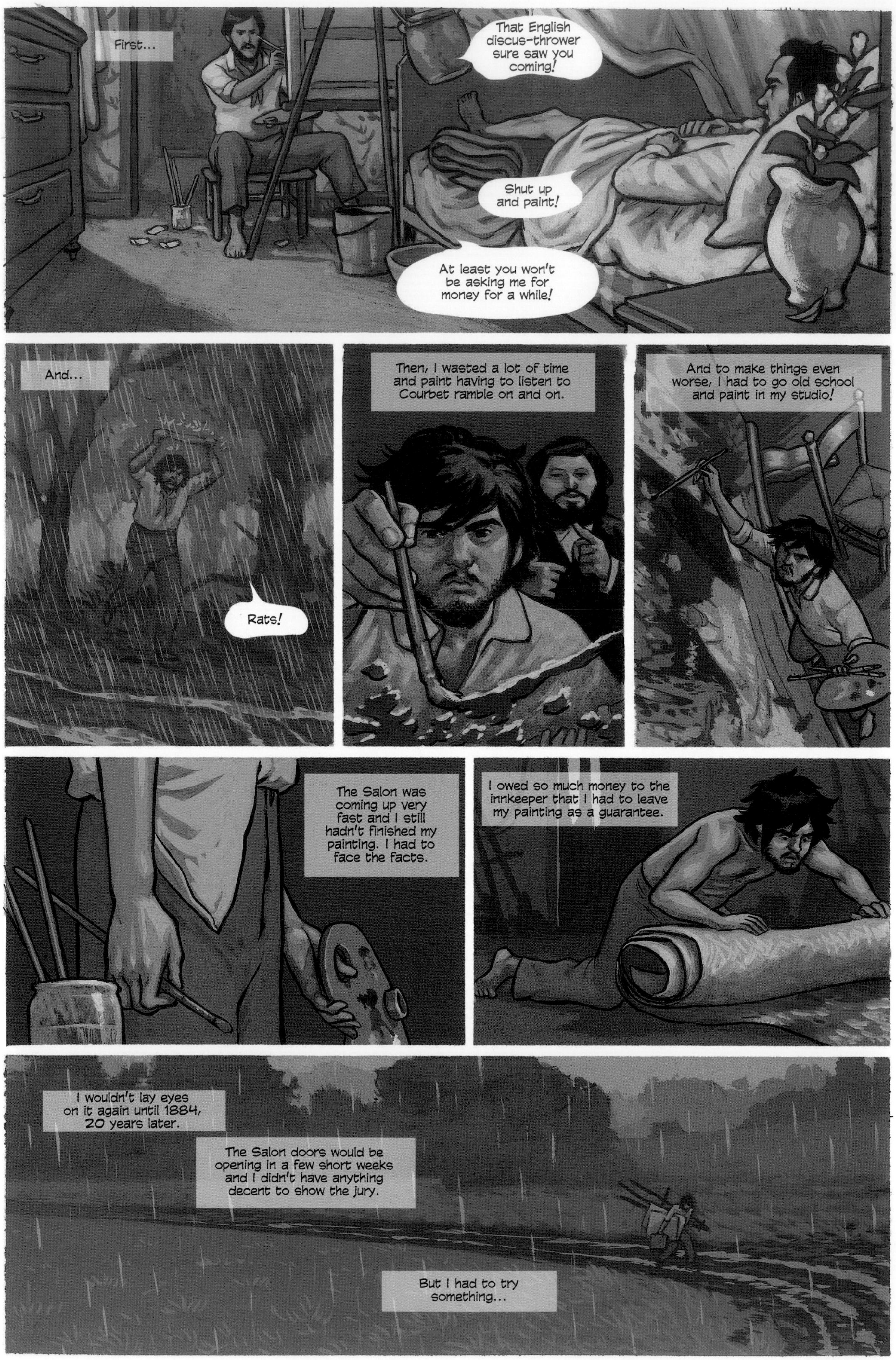

First...
That English discus-thrower sure saw you coming!
Shut up and paint!
At least you won't be asking me for money for a while!
And...
Rats!
Then, I wasted a lot of time and paint having to listen to Courbet ramble on and on.
And to make things even worse, I had to go old school and paint in my studio!
The Salon was coming up very fast and I still hadn't finished my painting. I had to face the facts.
I owed so much money to the innkeeper that I had to leave my painting as a guarantee.
I wouldn't lay eyes on it again until 1884, 20 years later.
The Salon doors would be opening in a few short weeks and I didn't have anything decent to show the jury.
But I had to try something...

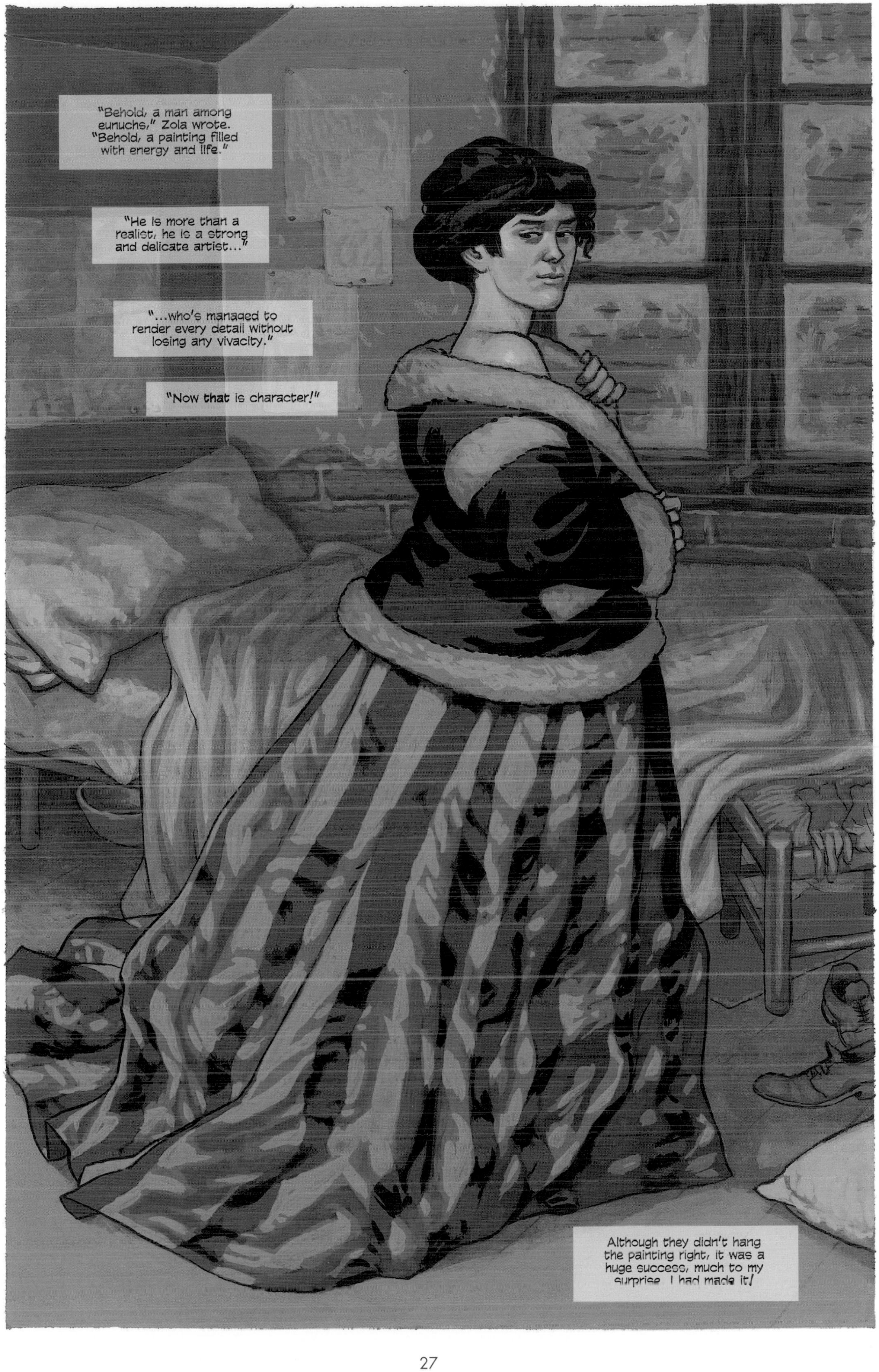
"Behold, a man among eunuchs," Zola wrote. "Behold, a painting filled with energy and life."
"He is more than a realist, he is a strong and delicate artist..."
"...who's managed to render every detail without losing any vivacity."
"Now that is character!"
Although they didn't hang the painting right, it was a huge success, much to my surprise. I had made it!

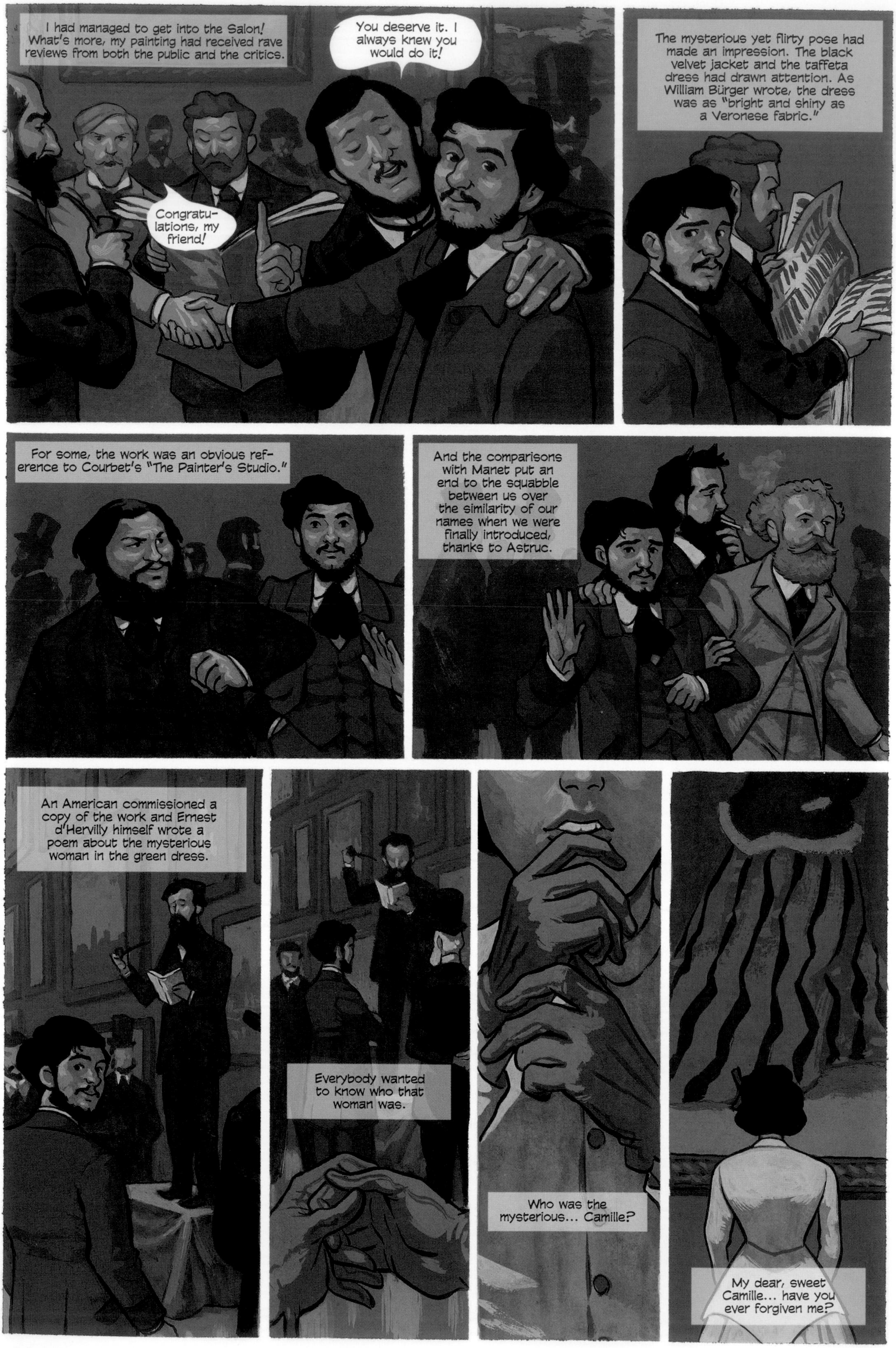
I had managed to get into the Salon! What's more, my painting had received rave reviews from both the public and the critics.
You deserve it. I always knew you would do it!
Congratulations, my friend!
The mysterious yet flirty pose had made an impression. The black velvet jacket and the taffeta dress had drawn attention. As William Bürger wrote, the dress was as "bright and shiny as a Veronese fabric."
For some, the work was an obvious reference to Courbet's "The Painter's Studio."
And the comparisons with Manet put an end to the squabble between us over the similarity of our names when we were finally introduced, thanks to Astruc.
An American commissioned a copy of the work and Ernest d'Hervilly himself wrote a poem about the mysterious woman in the green dress.
Everybody wanted to know who that woman was.
Who was the mysterious... Camille?
My dear, sweet Camille... have you ever forgiven me?

Her name was Camille Léonie Doncieux.
She was just 19 years old.

She had posed for "The Luncheon on the Grass" as well as for other paintings.

She was the daughter of a businessman and she loved the theater.

I tried so hard to forget you, Camille.

So hard that now, I can barely remember our love.

You were crazy about me.

I was Monet, the young bold painter with a promising future, according to the critics and the public.

You were my mistress and a popular topic of gossip in the art world.

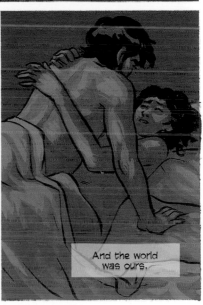

And the world was ours.

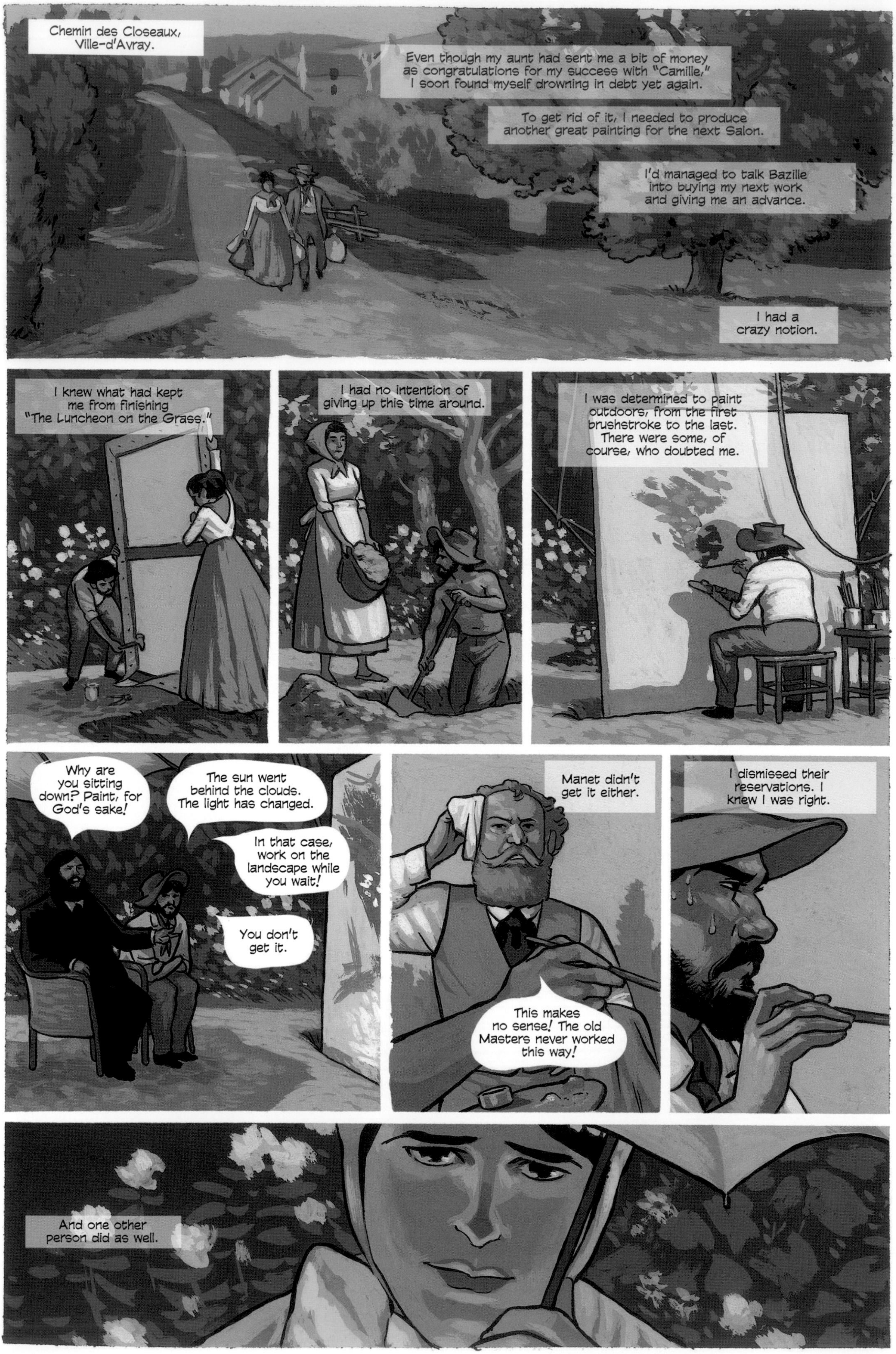
Chemin des Closeaux, Ville-d'Avray.
Even though my aunt had sent me a bit of money as congratulations for my success with "Camille," I soon found myself drowning in debt yet again.
To get rid of it, I needed to produce another great painting for the next Salon.
I'd managed to talk Bazille into buying my next work and giving me an advance.
I had a crazy notion.
I knew what had kept me from finishing "The Luncheon on the Grass."
I had no intention of giving up this time around.
I was determined to paint outdoors, from the first brushstroke to the last. There were some, of course, who doubted me.
Why are you sitting down? Paint, for God's sake!
The sun went behind the clouds. The light has changed.
In that case, work on the landscape while you wait!
You don't get it.
Manet didn't get it either.
This makes no sense! The old Masters never worked this way!
I dismissed their reservations. I knew I was right.
And one other person did as well.

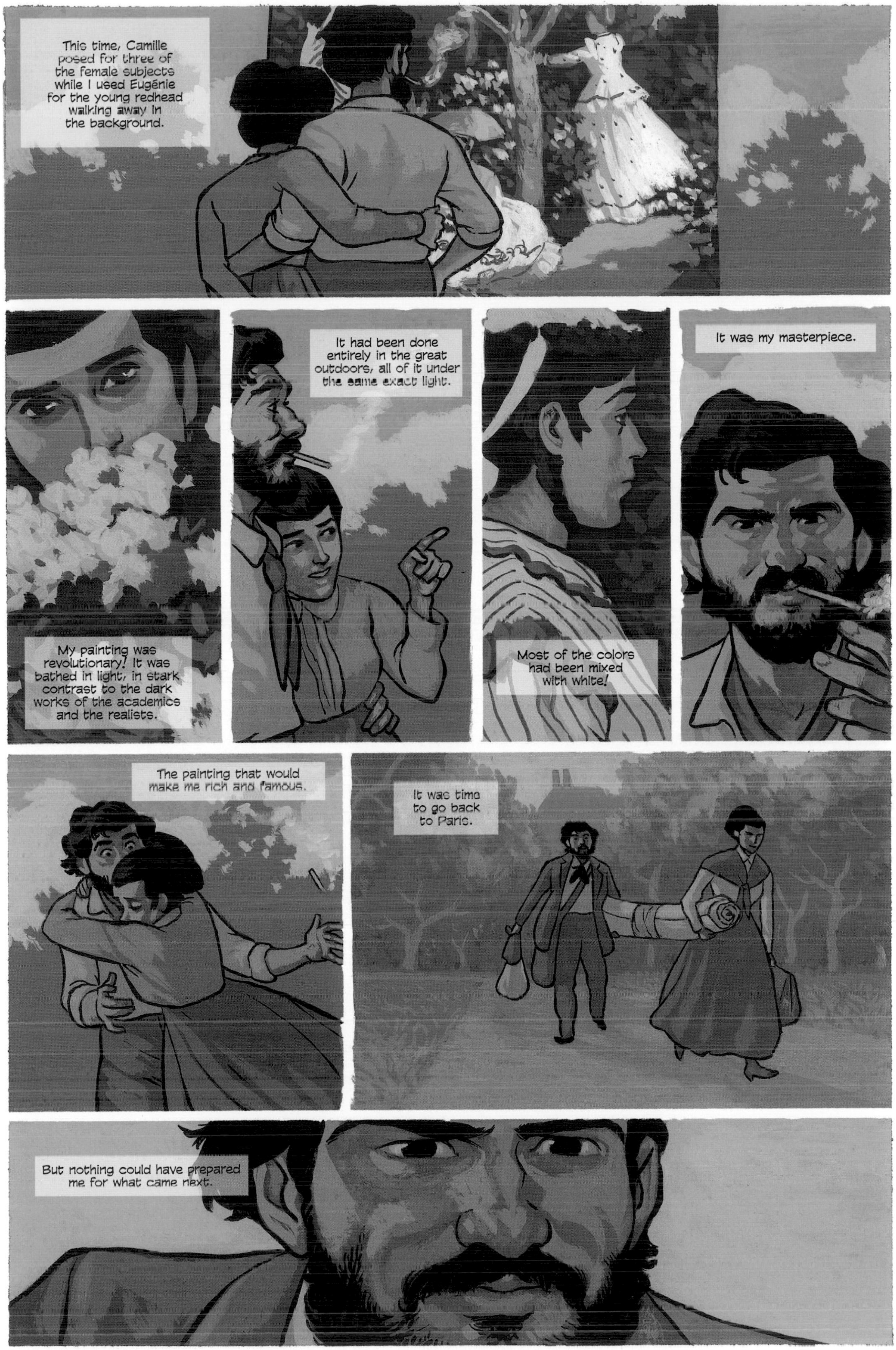
This time, Camille posed for three of the female subjects while I used Eugénie for the young redhead walking away in the background.
My painting was revolutionary! It was bathed in light, in stark contrast to the dark works of the academics and the realists.
It had been done entirely in the great outdoors, all of it under the same exact light.
Most of the colors had been mixed with white!
It was my masterpiece.
The painting that would make me rich and famous.
It was time to go back to Paris.
But nothing could have prepared me for what came next.

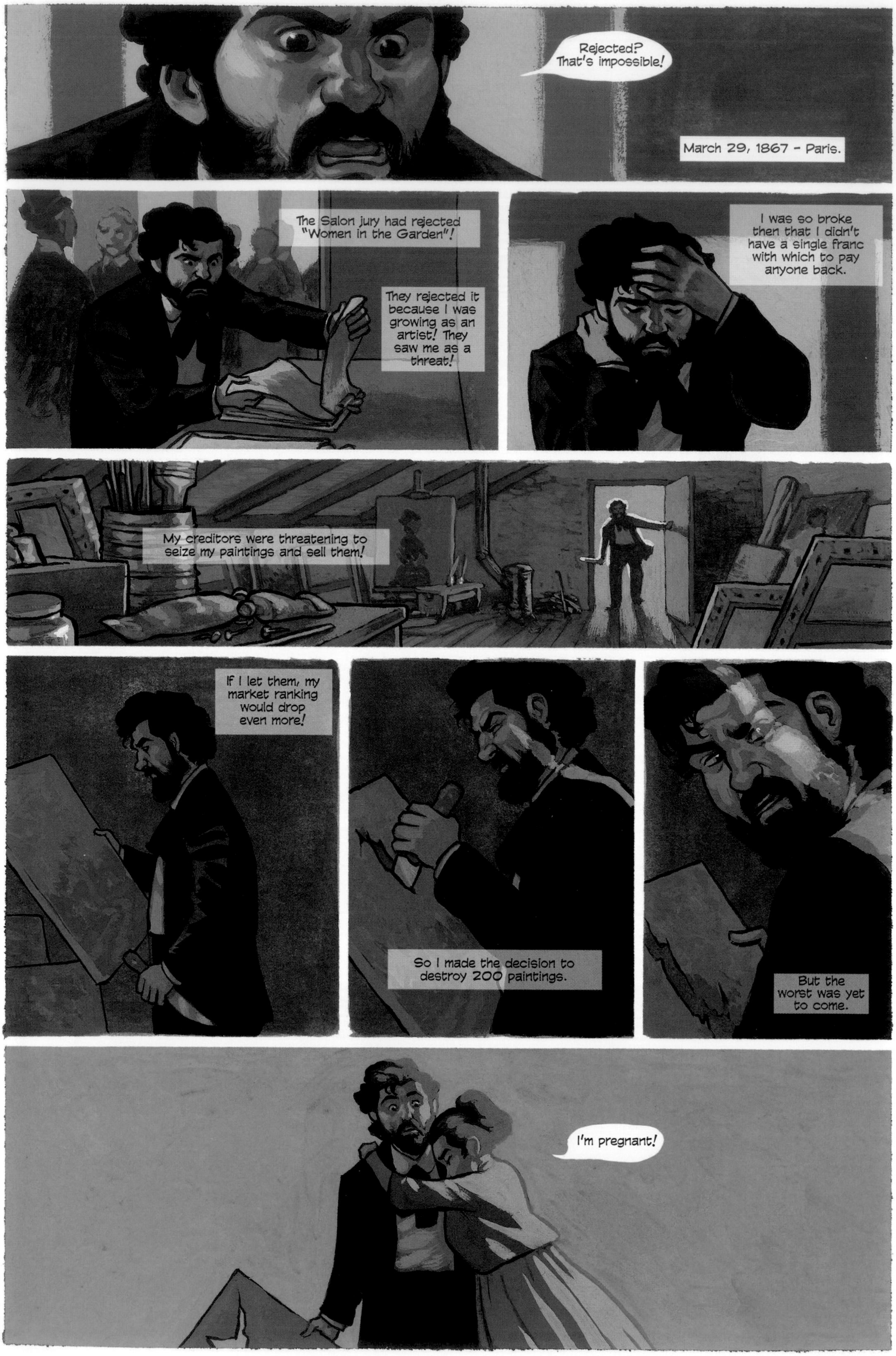
Rejected? That's impossible!
March 29, 1867 - Paris.
The Salon jury had rejected "Women in the Garden"!
They rejected it because I was growing as an artist! They saw me as a threat!
I was so broke then that I didn't have a single franc with which to pay anyone back.
My creditors were threatening to seize my paintings and sell them!
If I let them, my market ranking would drop even more!
So I made the decision to destroy 200 paintings.
But the worst was yet to come.
I'm pregnant!

It was an accident. I had no obligations towards Camille.

I wasn't even sure I loved her. I could leave her.

But...

...my aunt and my father had wasted no time finding out who the woman in the green silk dress was.

Since they didn't approve of our relationship, they had decided to cut me off. My past success didn't matter in the least to them!

They were nothing but provincial hypocrites!

My own father had had an illegitimate daughter with a servant, for heaven's sake!

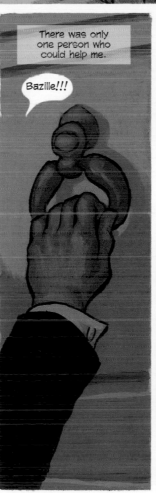

There was only one person who could help me.

Bazille!!!

You again!

33

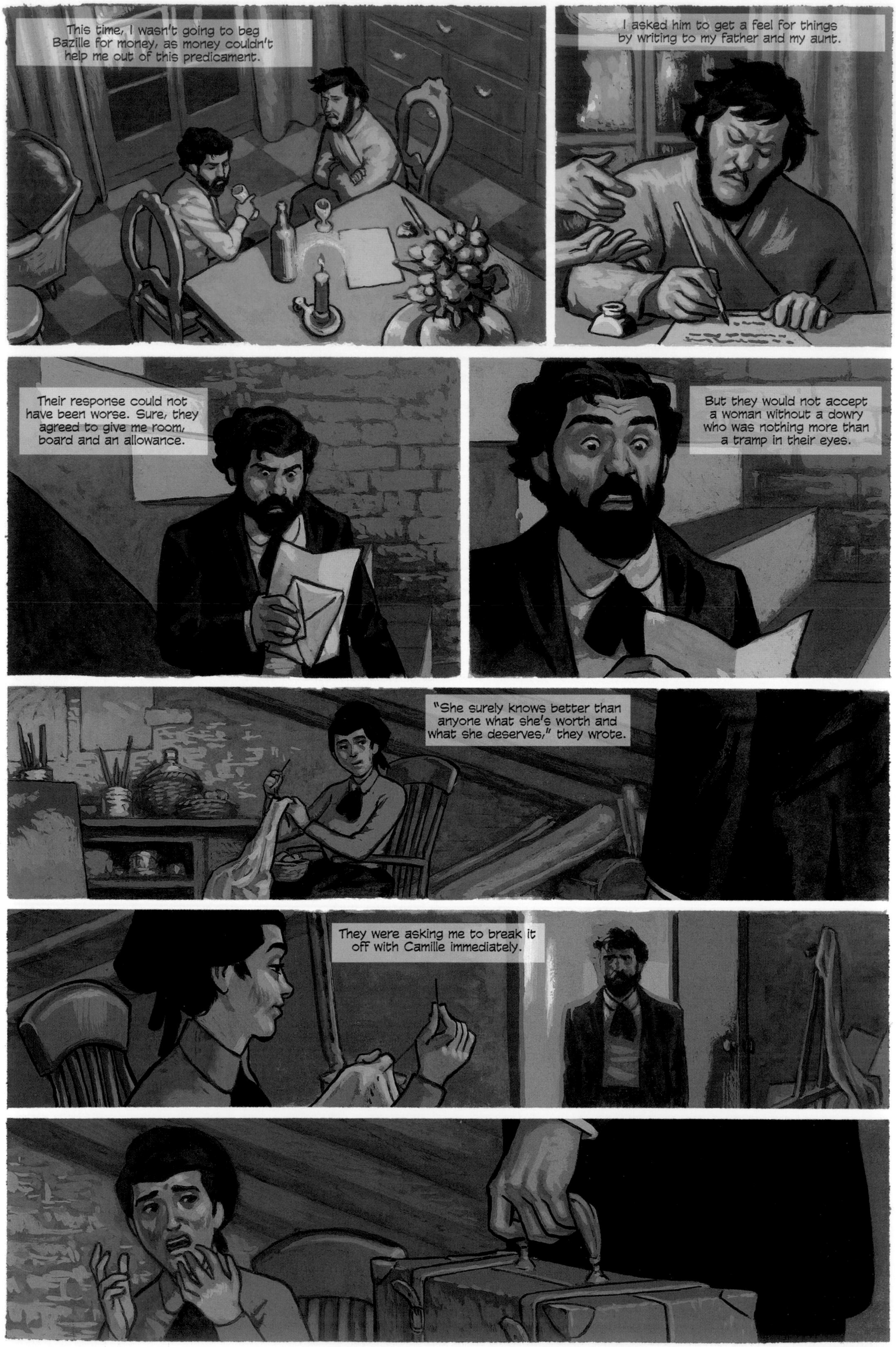

This time, I wasn't going to beg Bazille for money, as money couldn't help me out of this predicament.
I asked him to get a feel for things by writing to my father and my aunt.
Their response could not have been worse. Sure, they agreed to give me room, board and an allowance.
But they would not accept a woman without a dowry who was nothing more than a tramp in their eyes.
"She surely knows better than anyone what she's worth and what she deserves," they wrote.
They were asking me to break it off with Camille immediately.

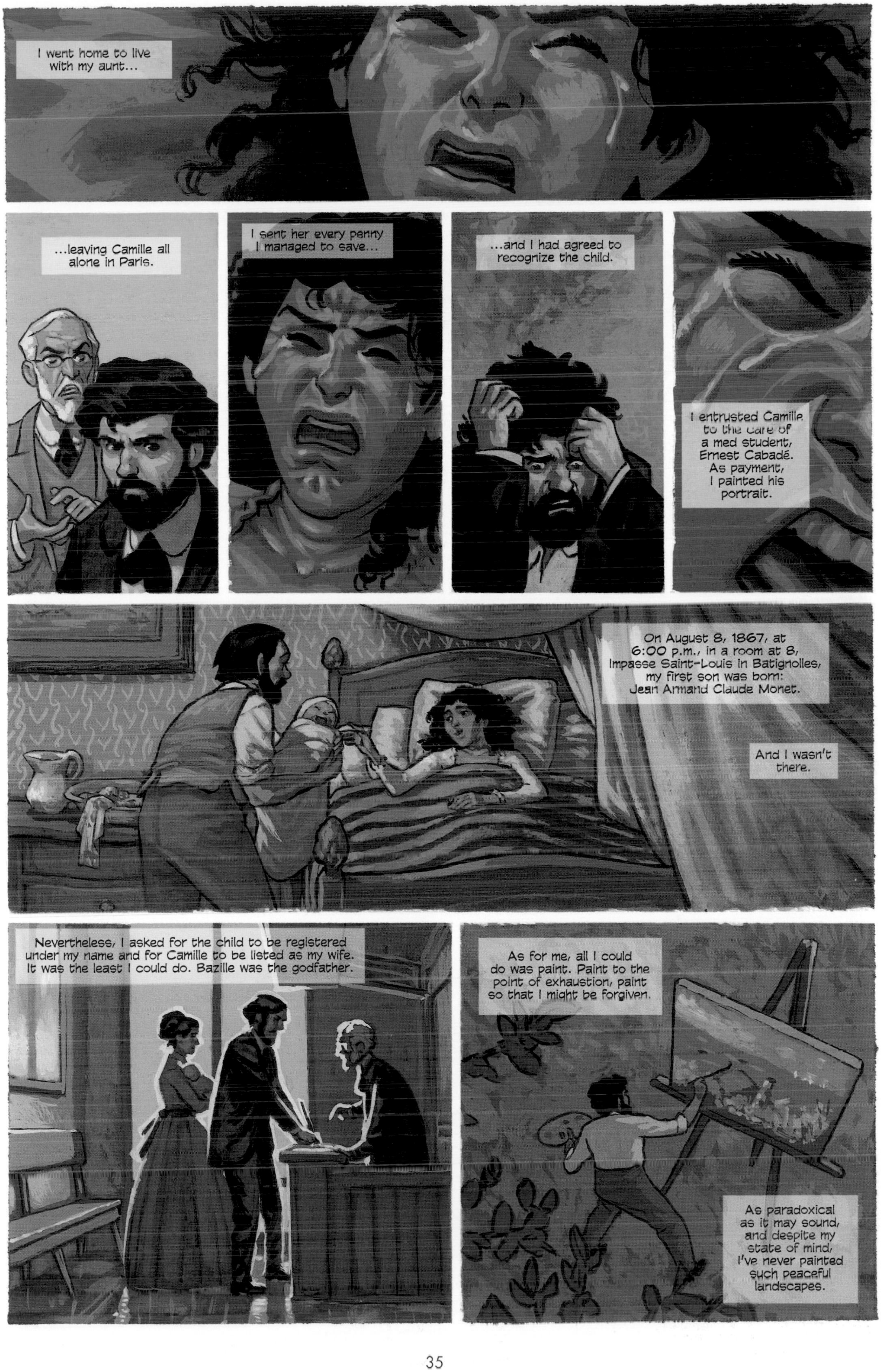
I went home to live with my aunt...
...leaving Camille all alone in Paris.
I sent her every penny I managed to save...
...and I had agreed to recognize the child.
I entrusted Camille to the care of a med student, Ernest Cabadé. As payment, I painted his portrait.
On August 8, 1867, at 6:00 p.m., in a room at 8, Impasse Saint-Louis in Batignolles, my first son was born: Jean Armand Claude Monet.
And I wasn't there.
Nevertheless, I asked for the child to be registered under my name and for Camille to be listed as my wife. It was the least I could do. Bazille was the godfather.
As for me, all I could do was paint. Paint to the point of exhaustion, paint so that I might be forgiven.
As paradoxical as it may sound, and despite my state of mind, I've never painted such peaceful landscapes.

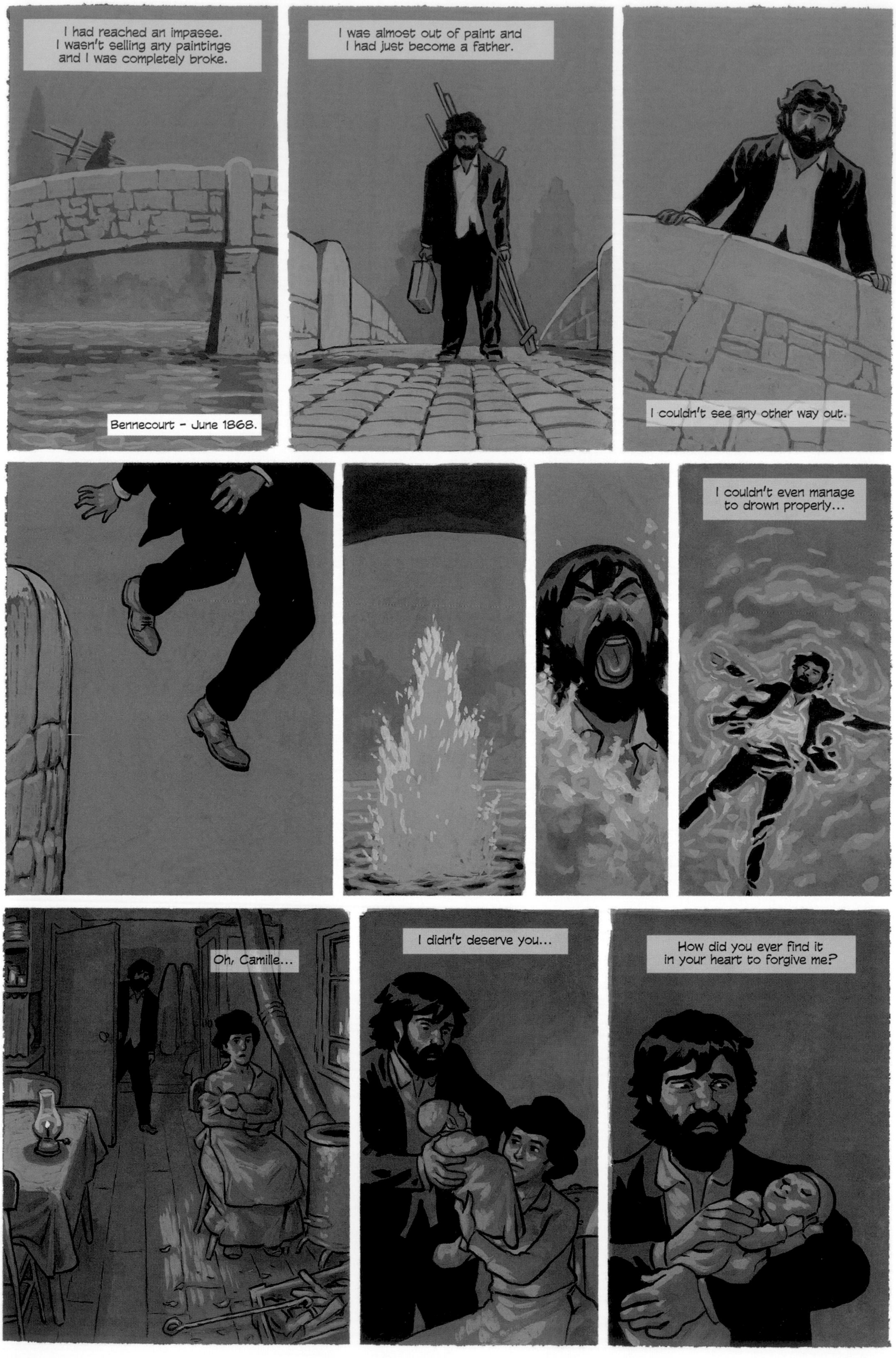
I had reached an impasse.
I wasn't selling any paintings
and I was completely broke.
Bennecourt - June 1868.
I was almost out of paint and
I had just become a father.
I couldn't see any other way out.
I couldn't even manage
to drown properly...
Oh, Camille...
I didn't deserve you...
How did you ever find it
in your heart to forgive me?

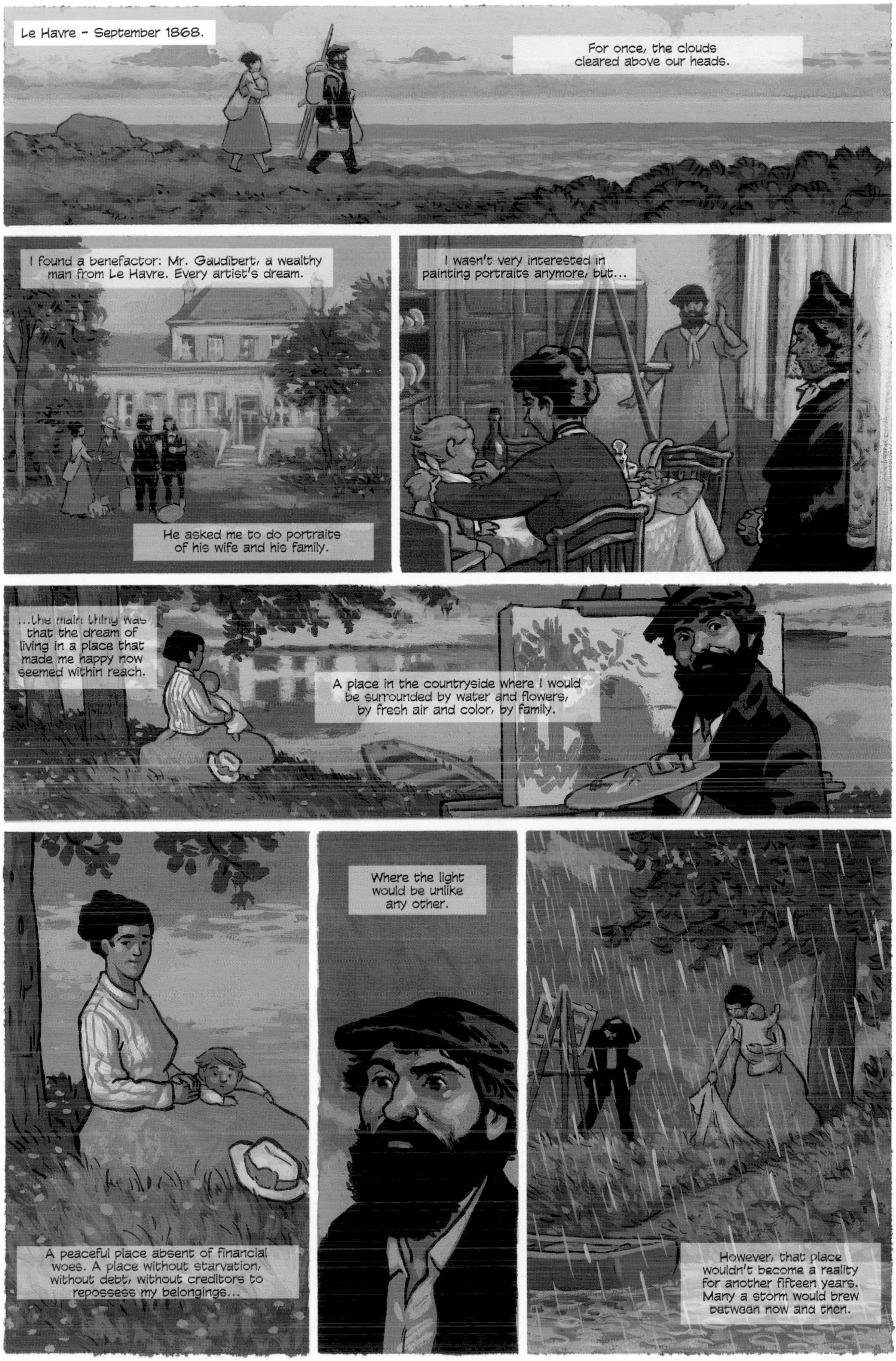
Le Havre - September 1868.
For once, the clouds cleared above our heads.
I found a benefactor: Mr. Gaudibert, a wealthy man from Le Havre. Every artist's dream.
He asked me to do portraits of his wife and his family.
I wasn't very interested in painting portraits anymore, but...
...the main thing was that the dream of living in a place that made me happy now seemed within reach.
A place in the countryside where I would be surrounded by water and flowers, by fresh air and color, by family.
A peaceful place absent of financial woes. A place without starvation, without debt, without creditors to repossess my belongings...
Where the light would be unlike any other.
However, that place wouldn't become a reality for another fifteen years. Many a storm would brew between now and then.

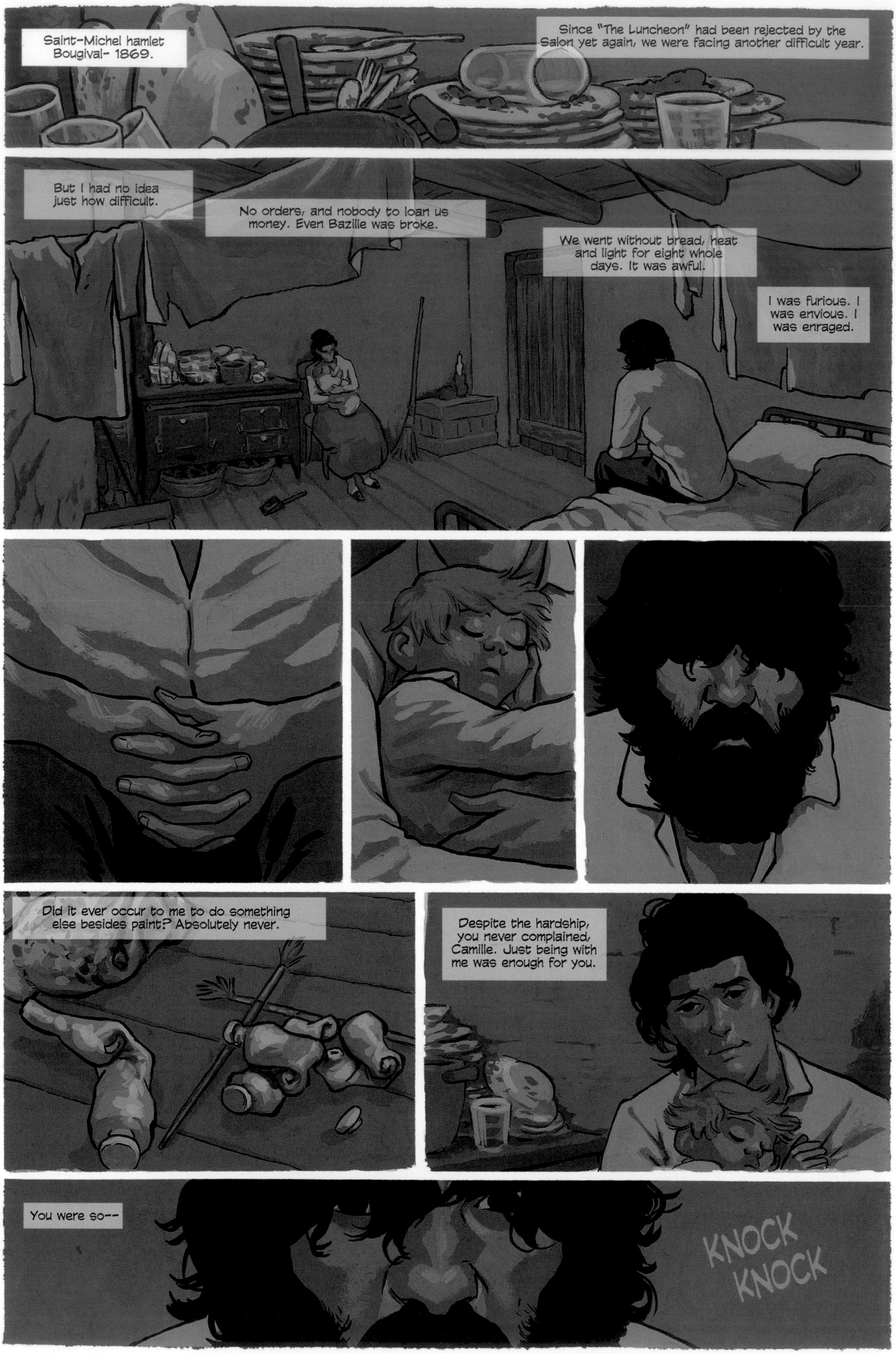

Saint-Michel hamlet Bougival- 1869.
Since "The Luncheon" had been rejected by the Salon yet again, we were facing another difficult year.
But I had no idea just how difficult.
No orders, and nobody to loan us money. Even Bazille was broke.
We went without bread, heat and light for eight whole days. It was awful.
I was furious. I was envious. I was enraged.
Did it ever occur to me to do something else besides paint? Absolutely never.
Despite the hardship, you never complained, Camille. Just being with me was enough for you.
You were so--
KNOCK KNOCK

It was thanks to him that I made it out of that impasse.

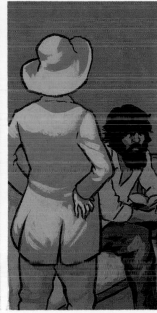

My old buddy Renoir.

Those days working side by side are among my favorite memories. We had completely different personalities, yes...

...but we learned so much from each other.

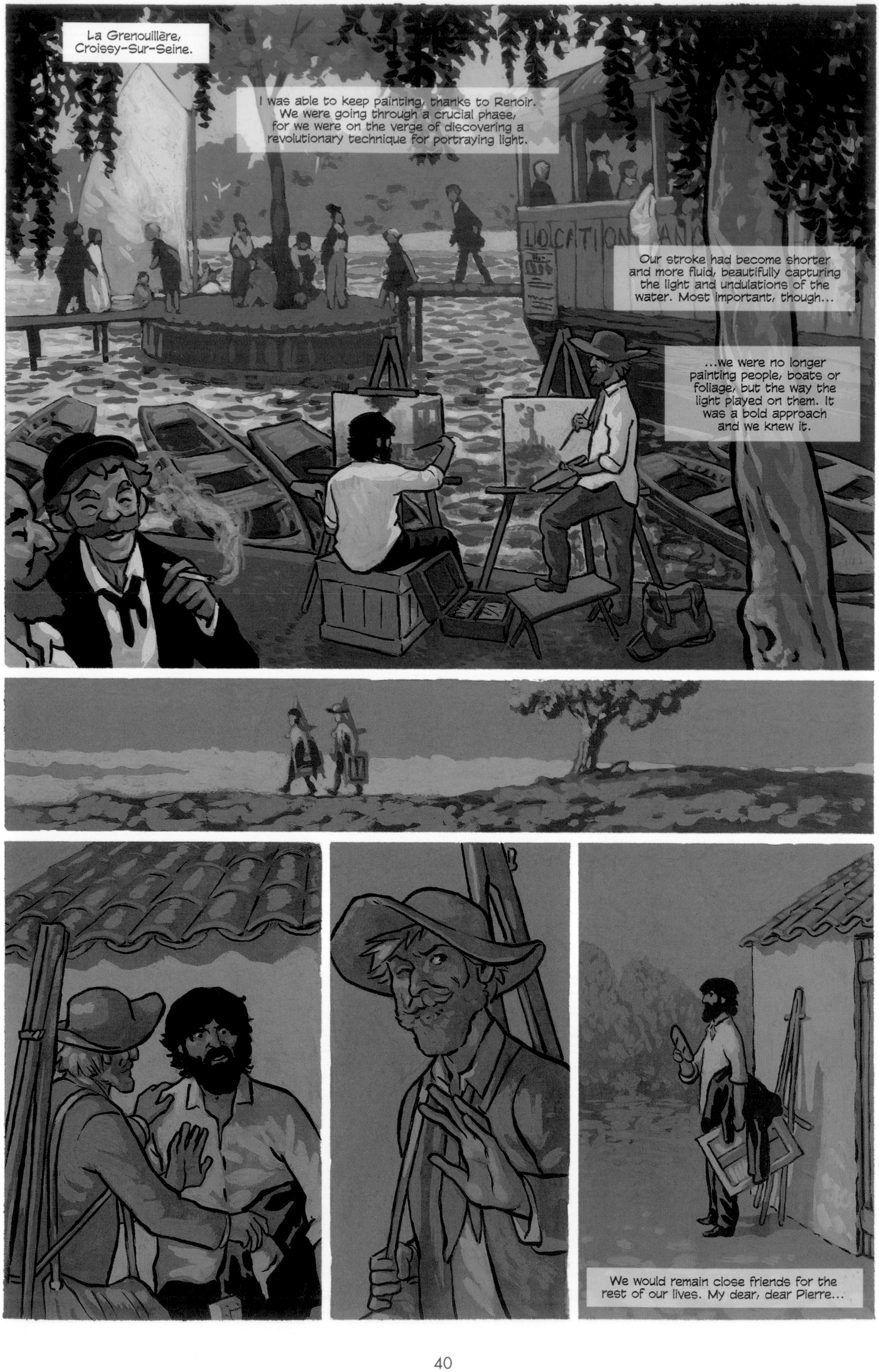
La Grenouillère, Croissy-Sur-Seine.
I was able to keep painting, thanks to Renoir. We were going through a crucial phase, for we were on the verge of discovering a revolutionary technique for portraying light.
LOCATION
Our stroke had become shorter and more fluid, beautifully capturing the light and undulations of the water. Most important, though...
...we were no longer painting people, boats or foliage, but the way the light played on them. It was a bold approach and we knew it.
We would remain close friends for the rest of our lives. My dear, dear Pierre...

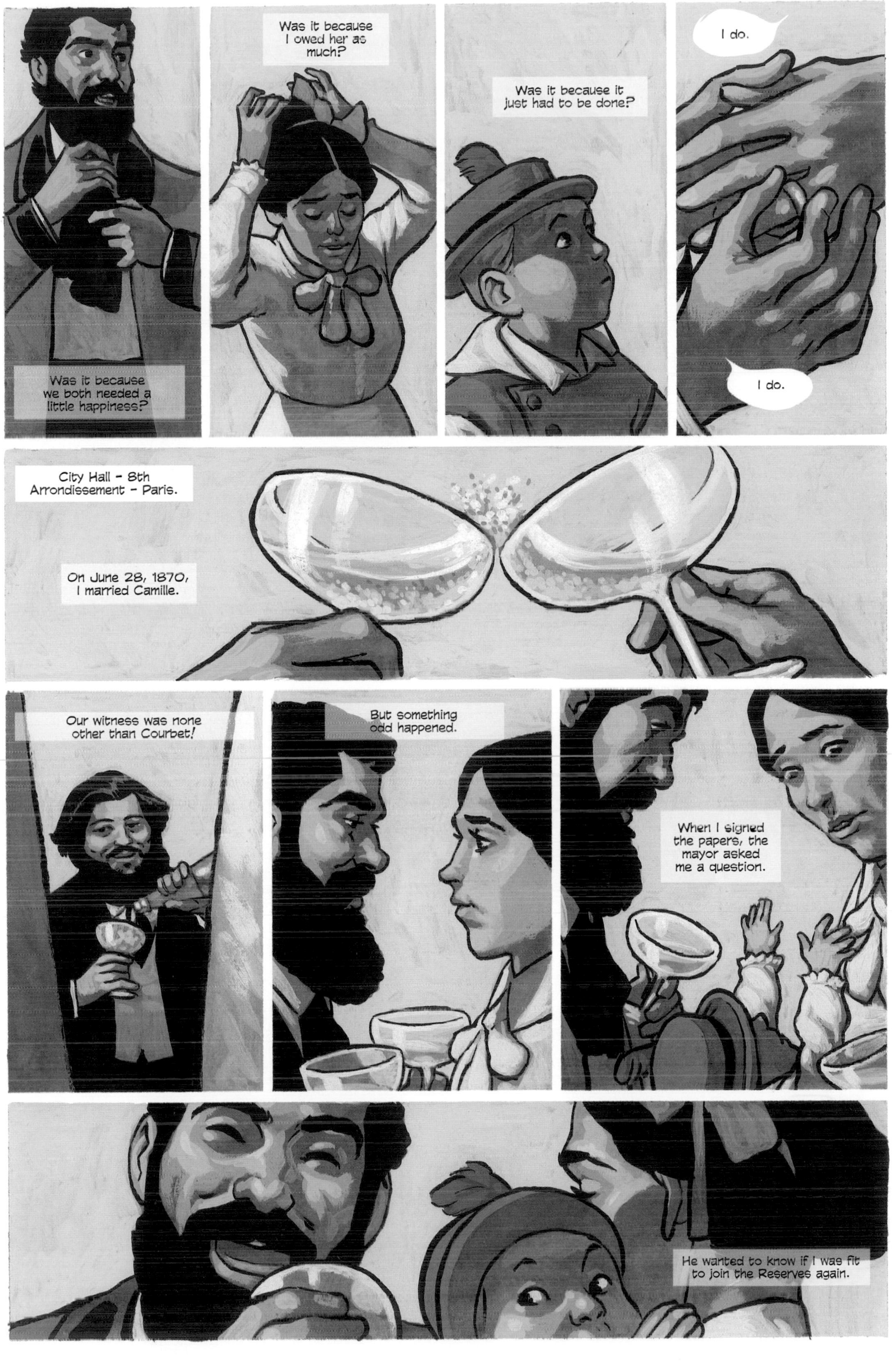
Was it because
we both needed a
little happiness?
Was it because
I owed her as
much?
Was it because it
just had to be done?
I do.
I do.
City Hall - 8th
Arrondissement - Paris.
On June 28, 1870,
I married Camille.
Our witness was none
other than Courbet!
But something
odd happened.
When I signed
the papers, the
mayor asked
me a question.
He wanted to know if I was fit
to join the Reserves again.

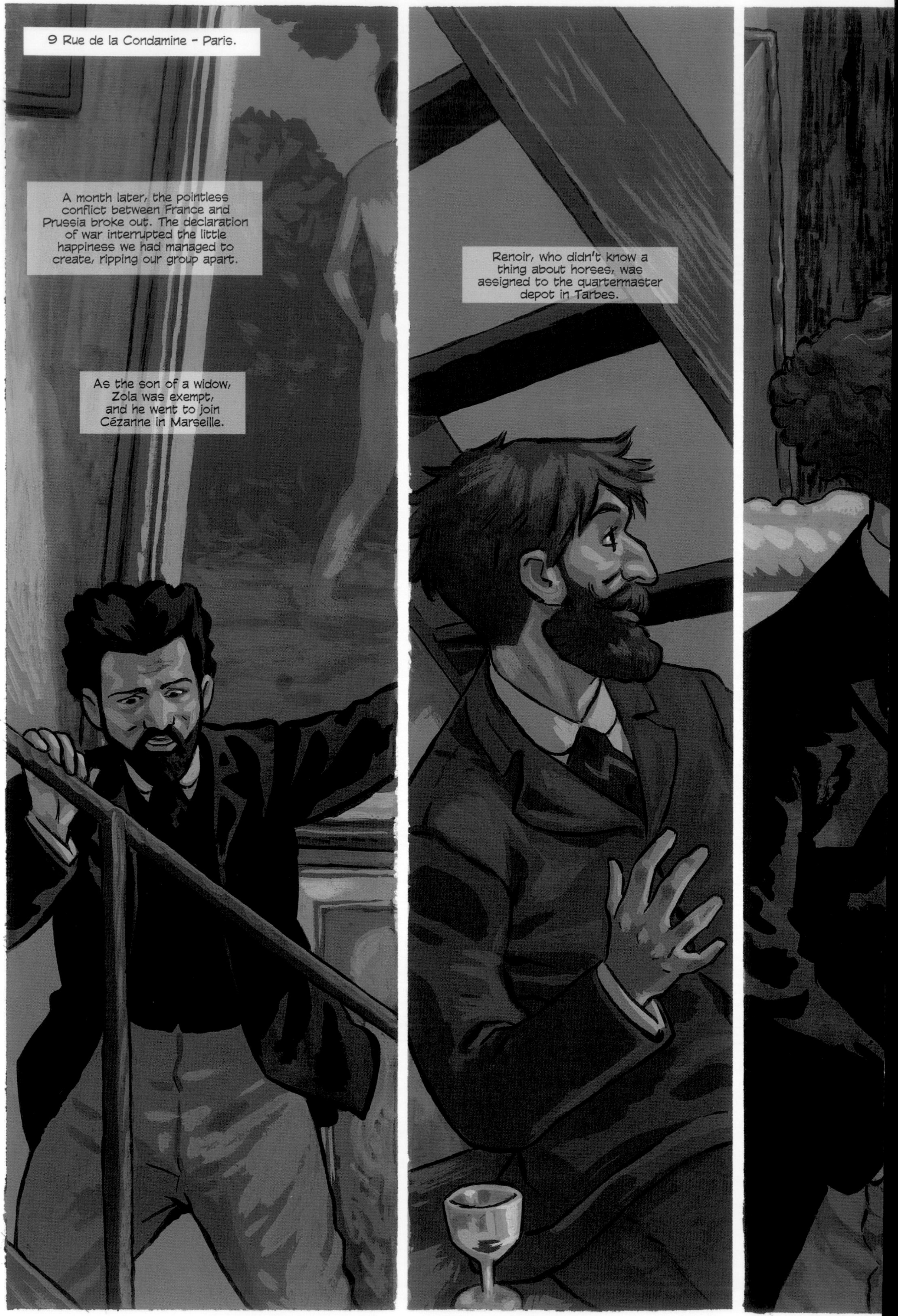
9 Rue de la Condamine - Paris.
A month later, the pointless conflict between France and Prussia broke out. The declaration of war interrupted the little happiness we had managed to create, ripping our group apart.
As the son of a widow, Zola was exempt, and he went to join Cézanne in Marseille.
Renoir, who didn't know a thing about horses, was assigned to the quartermaster depot in Tarbes.

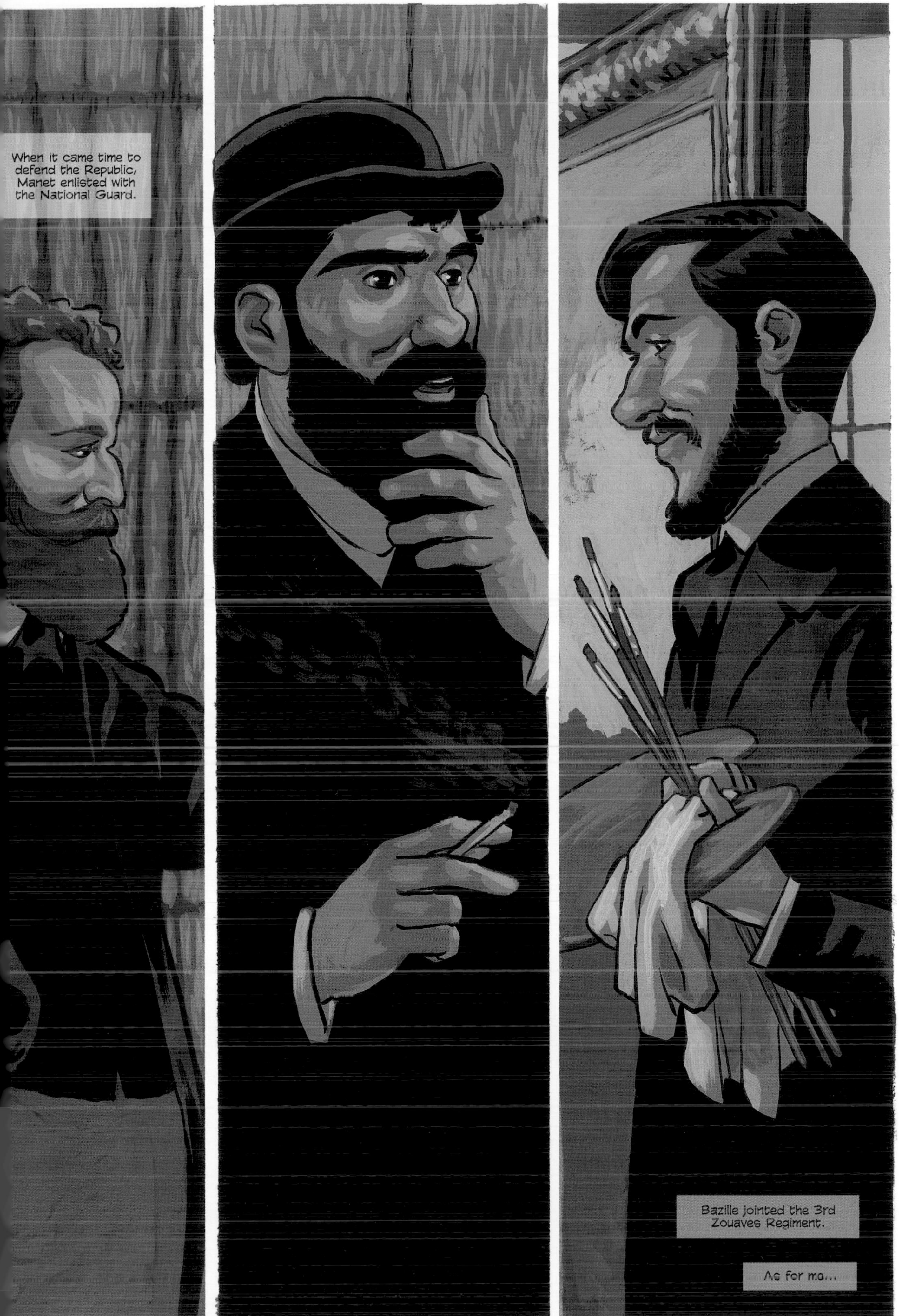
When it came time to defend the Republic, Manet enlisted with the National Guard.
Bazille jointed the 3rd Zouaves Regiment.
As for me...

Trouville – Fall 1870.

...I had no interest in their war.

I refused to die for Napoleon III, Gambetta, Thiers, or anyone else.

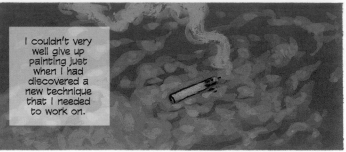

I couldn't very well give up painting just when I had discovered a new technique that I needed to work on.

London.

The ever-changing London light was going to be a considerable challenge, mainly because of the fog, which I would end up loathing.

I brought Camille along. First we moved to a flat in Piccadilly before settling into No. 1, Bath Place in Kensington.

Thank goodness there were some familiar faces there! Pissarro was one of them.

As well as Daubigny and my dear old friend Boudin. Together, we formed a sort of small society of exiled French painters, which would later prove to be key.

Most notably when I was introduced to Paul Durand-Ruel.

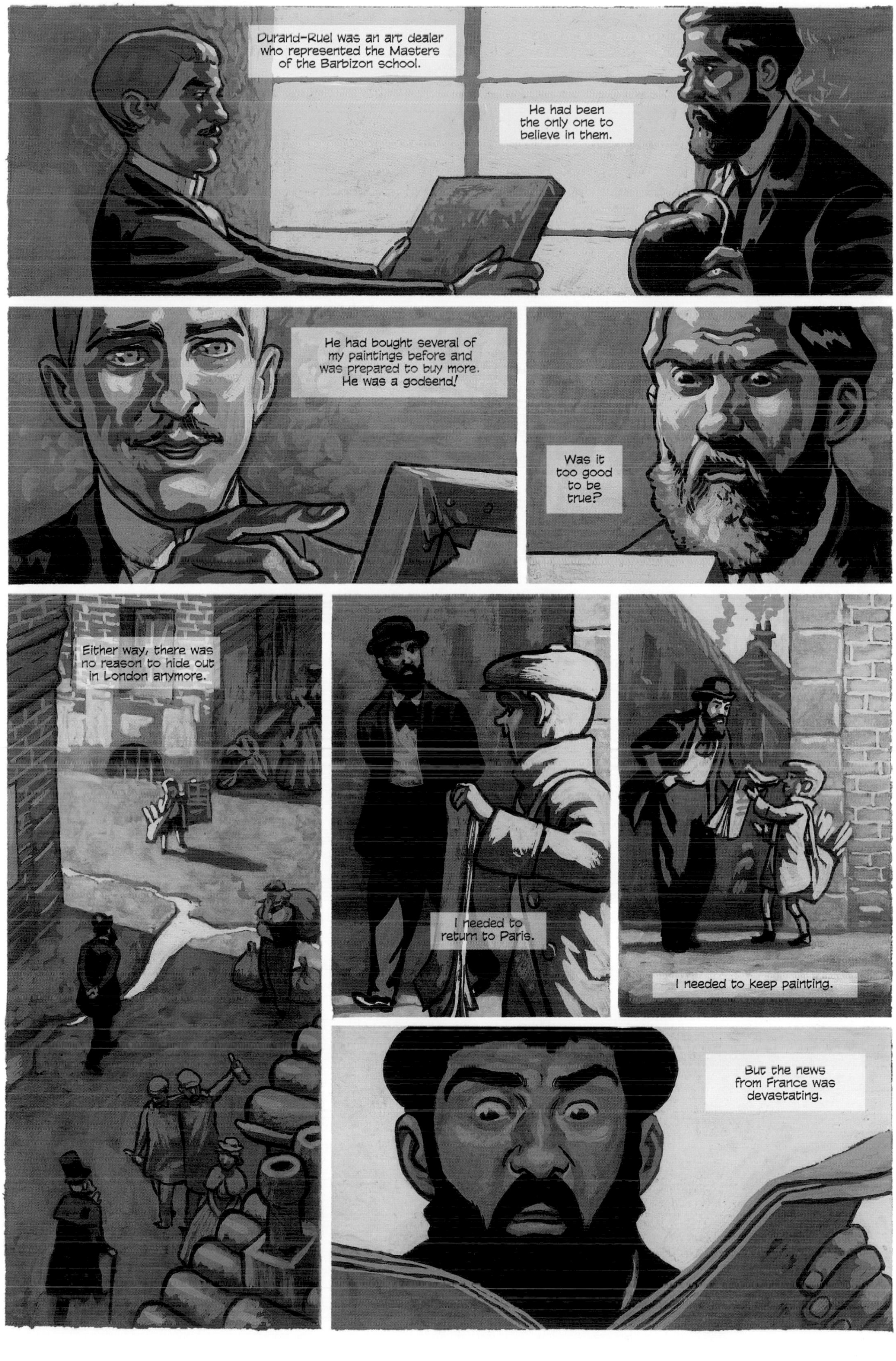
Durand-Ruel was an art dealer who represented the Masters of the Barbizon school.
He had been the only one to believe in them.
He had bought several of my paintings before and was prepared to buy more. He was a godsend!
Was it too good to be true?
Either way, there was no reason to hide out in London anymore.
I needed to return to Paris.
I needed to keep painting.
But the news from France was devastating.

After the deadly war and the German siege, the Commune had suffered a bloody repression.

Famine, pillaging, massacres... What was happening to my beloved Paris?

Courbet and several of our friends were in prison and potentially facing the death penalty.

But it got worse...

Bazille was dead.

Killed on the battlefield. At the age of twenty-nine.

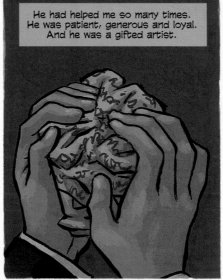

He had helped me so many times. He was patient, generous and loyal. And he was a gifted artist.

Who would I turn to now, in my times of need?

Argenteuil - 1871.

We went back to France and settled into a place that bore a strong resemblance to my dream house.

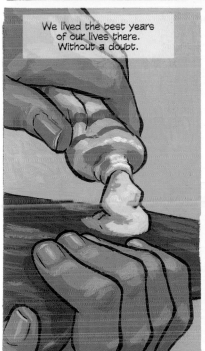

We lived the best years of our lives there. Without a doubt.

My father had died and left me a little money. Not as much as I had hoped for, but thanks to Durand-Ruel's acquisitions, I was earning 14,000 francs a year.

We even had two servants and a gardener on our payroll. It was a great life, which I took to very well.

I painted more works in Argenteuil than in the thirteen previous years combined. Happiness was making me prolific.

I even set up a workshop in a row-boat so I could be closer to the water! And guess who came to do my portrait?

Stubborn old Manet had recovered his senses and was learning to paint the light...

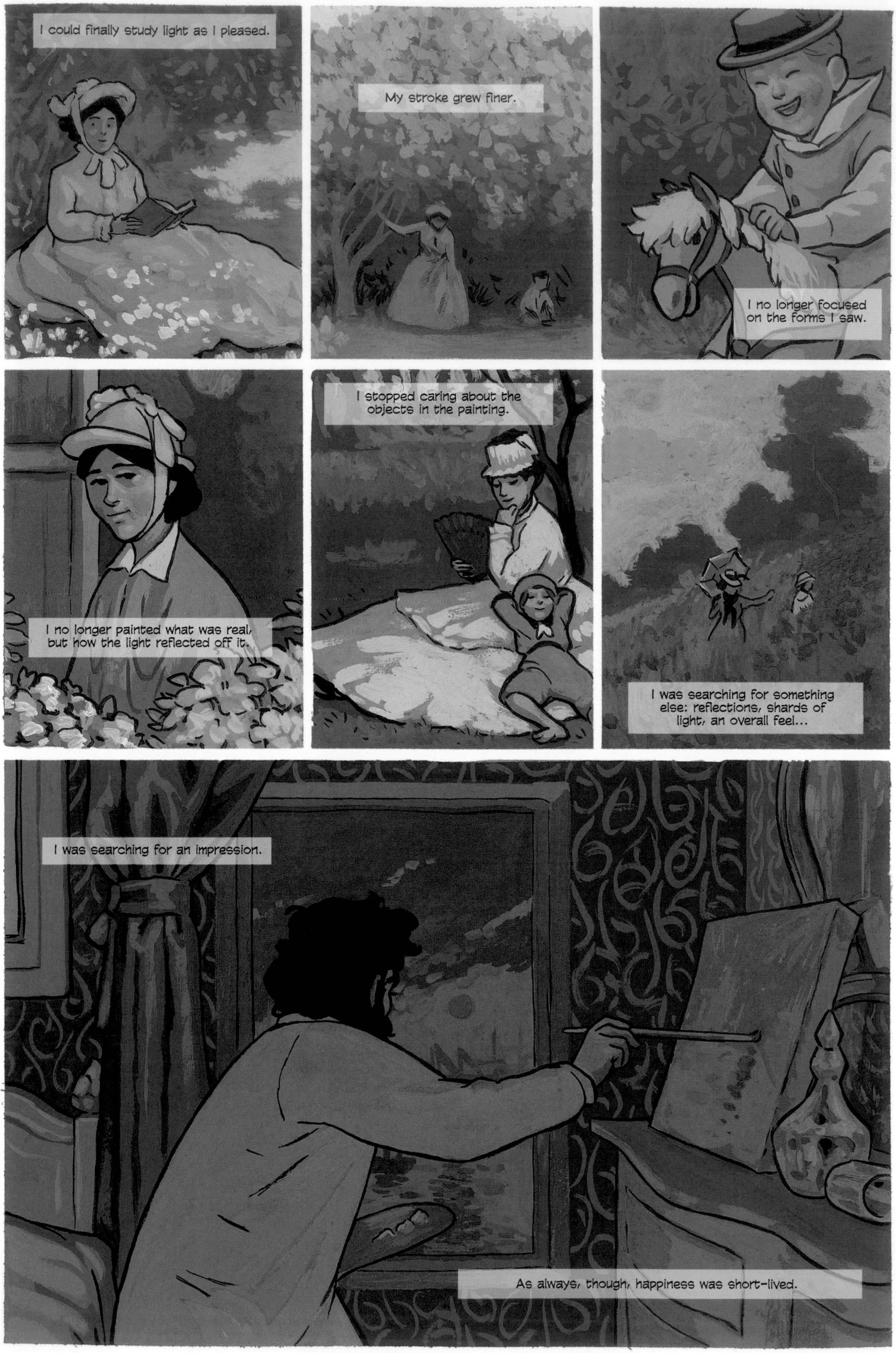
I could finally study light as I pleased.
My stroke grew finer.
I no longer focused on the forms I saw.
I no longer painted what was real, but how the light reflected off it.
I stopped caring about the objects in the painting.
I was searching for something else: reflections, shards of light, an overall feel...
I was searching for an impression.
As always, though, happiness was short-lived.

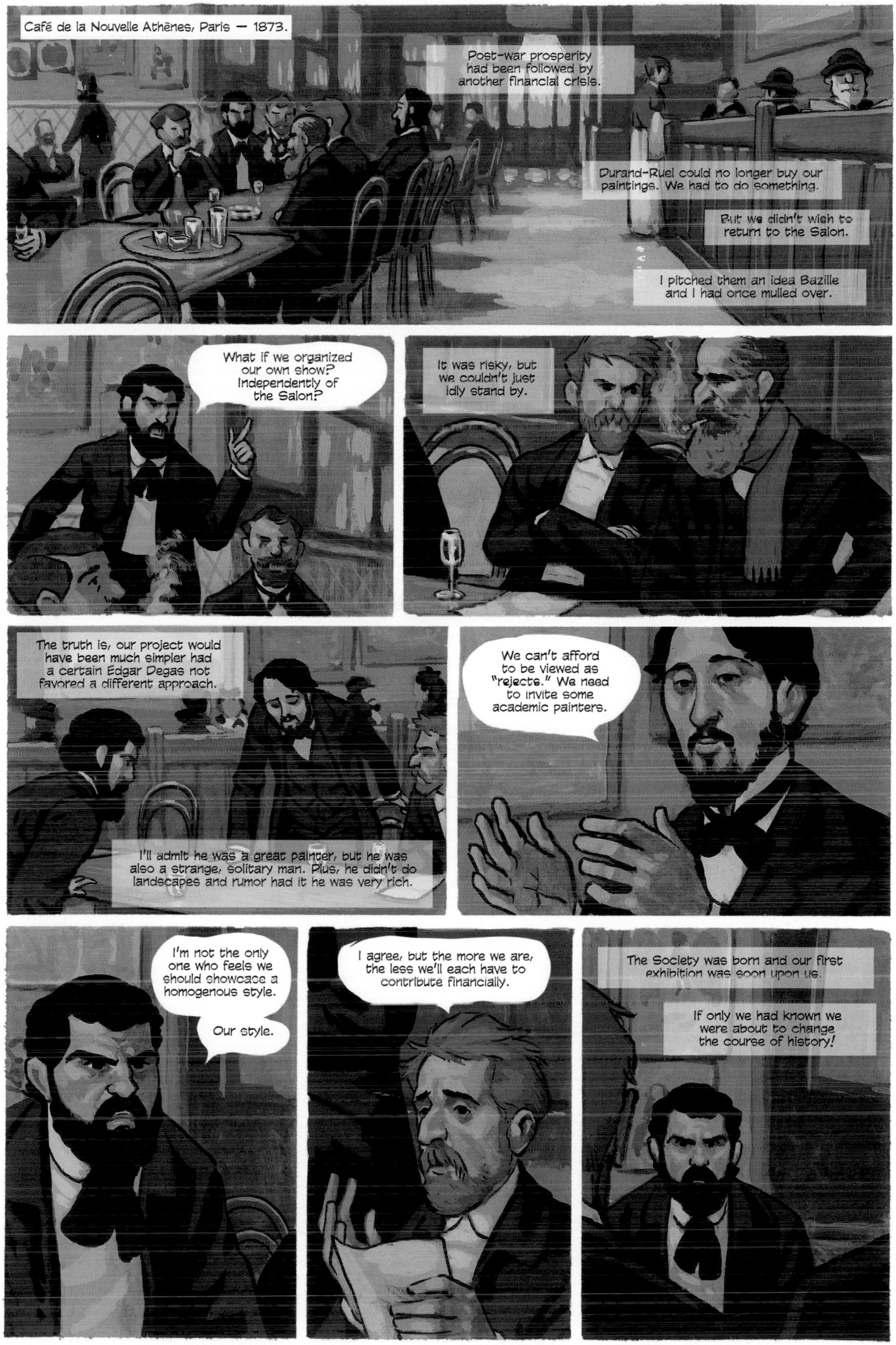

Café de la Nouvelle Athènes, Paris — 1873.
Post-war prosperity had been followed by another financial crisis.
Durand-Ruel could no longer buy our paintings. We had to do something.
But we didn't wish to return to the Salon.
I pitched them an idea Bazille and I had once mulled over.
What if we organized our own show? Independently of the Salon?
It was risky, but we couldn't just idly stand by.
The truth is, our project would have been much simpler had a certain Edgar Degas not favored a different approach.
I'll admit he was a great painter, but he was also a strange, solitary man. Plus, he didn't do landscapes and rumor had it he was very rich.
We can't afford to be viewed as "rejects." We need to invite some academic painters.
I'm not the only one who feels we should showcase a homogenous style.
Our style.
I agree, but the more we are, the less we'll each have to contribute financially.
The Society was born and our first exhibition was soon upon us.
If only we had known we were about to change the course of history!

The exhibit was to be held in the former studio of a photographer named Nadar, on boulevard des Capucines.

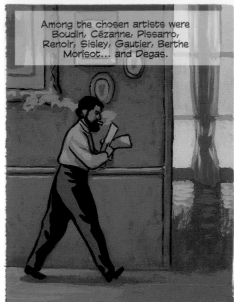

Among the chosen artists were Boudin, Cézanne, Pissarro, Renoir, Sisley, Gautier, Berthe Morisot... and Degas.

While Pierre hung the works, his brother Edmond produced the exhibition catalogue.

Hey! Monet!

Have you seen your titles? "Village Street," "Morning in the Village," "Village in the Snow," etc.

What's wrong with that?

It lacks originality.

This one, for instance, is titled "View of Le Havre." Can't you think of a better name?

"Impression"?

Sold! We'll call it "Impression, Sunrise." Pierre, your friend is a great painter but his titles leave much to be desired.

If only I had known...

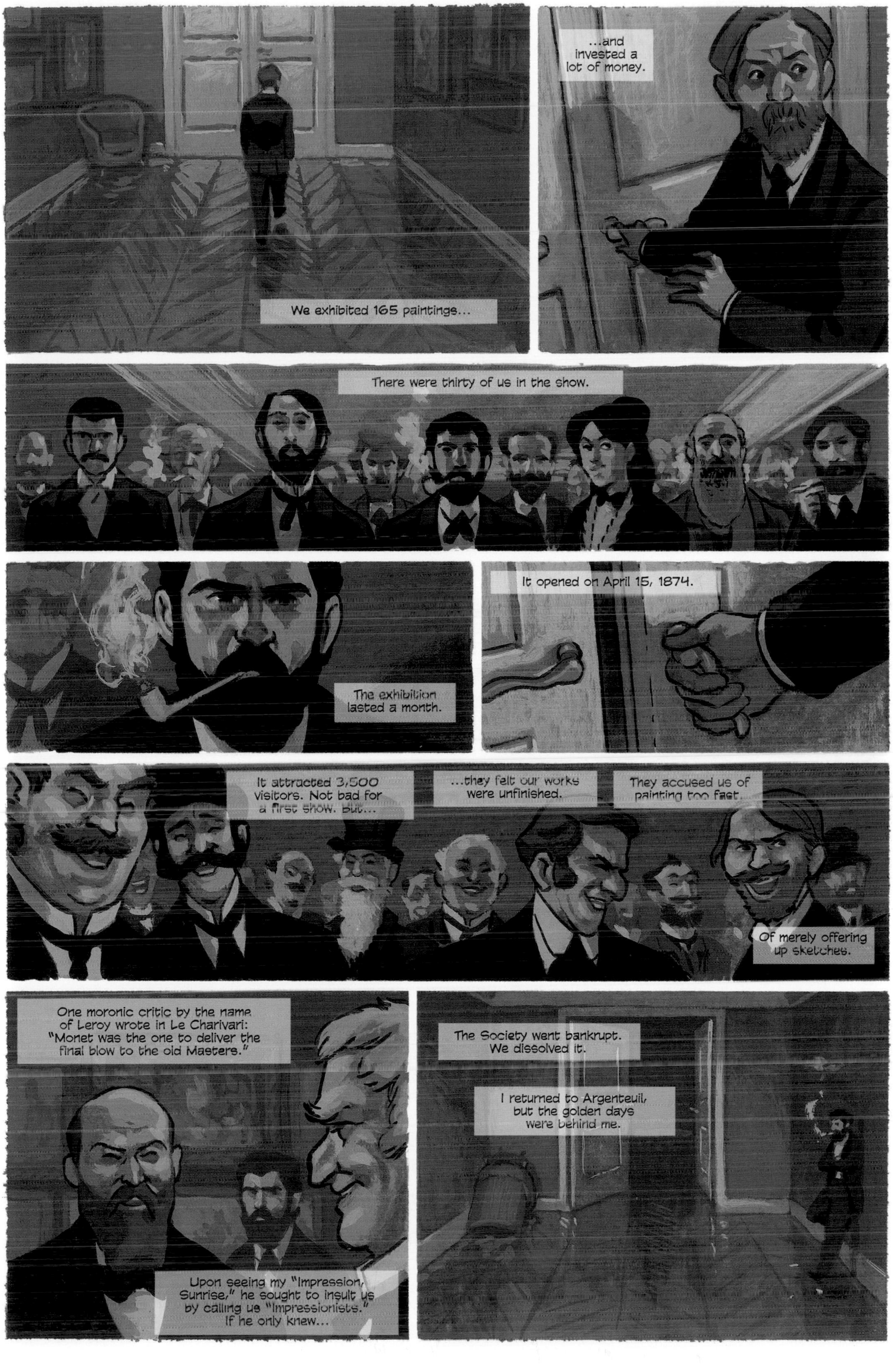
We exhibited 165 paintings...
...and invested a lot of money.
There were thirty of us in the show.
The exhibition lasted a month.
It opened on April 15, 1874.
It attracted 3,500 visitors. Not bad for a first show. But...
...they felt our works were unfinished.
They accused us of painting too fast.
Of merely offering up sketches.
One moronic critic by the name of Leroy wrote in Le Charivari: "Monet was the one to deliver the final blow to the old Masters."
Upon seeing my "Impression, Sunrise," he sought to insult us by calling us "Impressionists." If he only knew...
The Society went bankrupt. We dissolved it.
I returned to Argenteuil, but the golden days were behind me.

A failure of that scope was damaging.

Our aim in founding the Society had been to support each other.

To promote our work, to help one another and to protect ourselves.

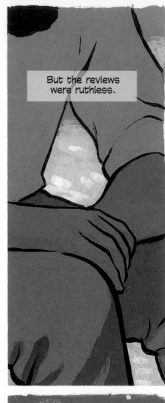
But the reviews were ruthless.

We had such a terrible reputation now that nobody commissioned our work anymore.

What where we to do?

There was only one thing to do...

The only thing we could do...

Keep painting.

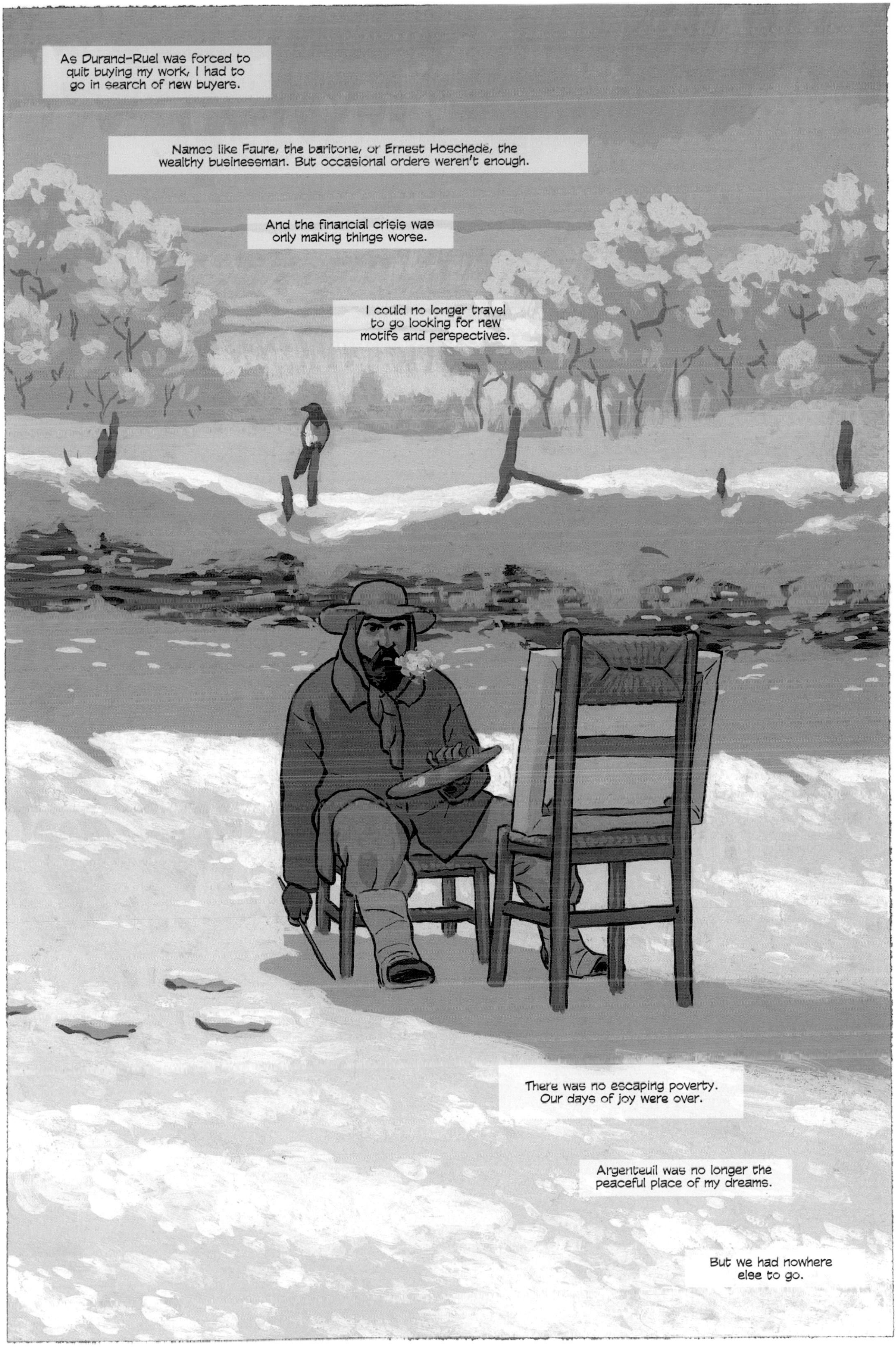
As Durand-Ruel was forced to quit buying my work, I had to go in search of new buyers.
Names like Faure, the baritone, or Ernest Hoschede, the wealthy businessman. But occasional orders weren't enough.
And the financial crisis was only making things worse.
I could no longer travel to go looking for new motifs and perspectives.
There was no escaping poverty. Our days of joy were over.
Argenteuil was no longer the peaceful place of my dreams.
But we had nowhere else to go.

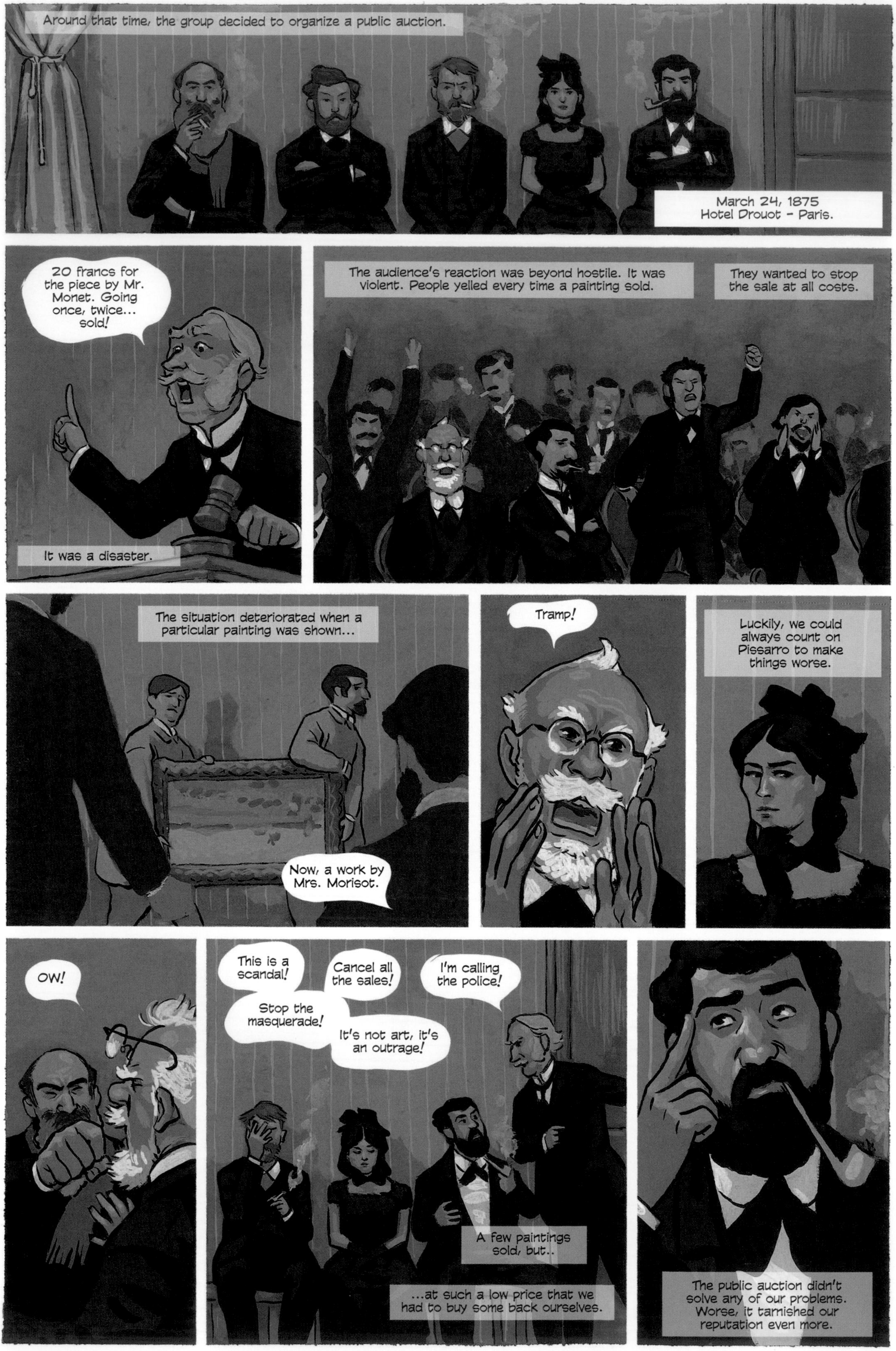

Around that time, the group decided to organize a public auction.
March 24, 1875
Hotel Drouot - Paris.
20 francs for the piece by Mr. Monet. Going once, twice... sold!
It was a disaster.
The audience's reaction was beyond hostile. It was violent. People yelled every time a painting sold.
They wanted to stop the sale at all costs.
The situation deteriorated when a particular painting was shown...
Now, a work by Mrs. Morisot.
Tramp!
Luckily, we could always count on Pissarro to make things worse.
OW!
This is a scandal!
Cancel all the sales!
I'm calling the police!
Stop the masquerade!
It's not art, it's an outrage!
A few paintings sold, but..
...at such a low price that we had to buy some back ourselves.
The public auction didn't solve any of our problems. Worse, it tarnished our reputation even more.

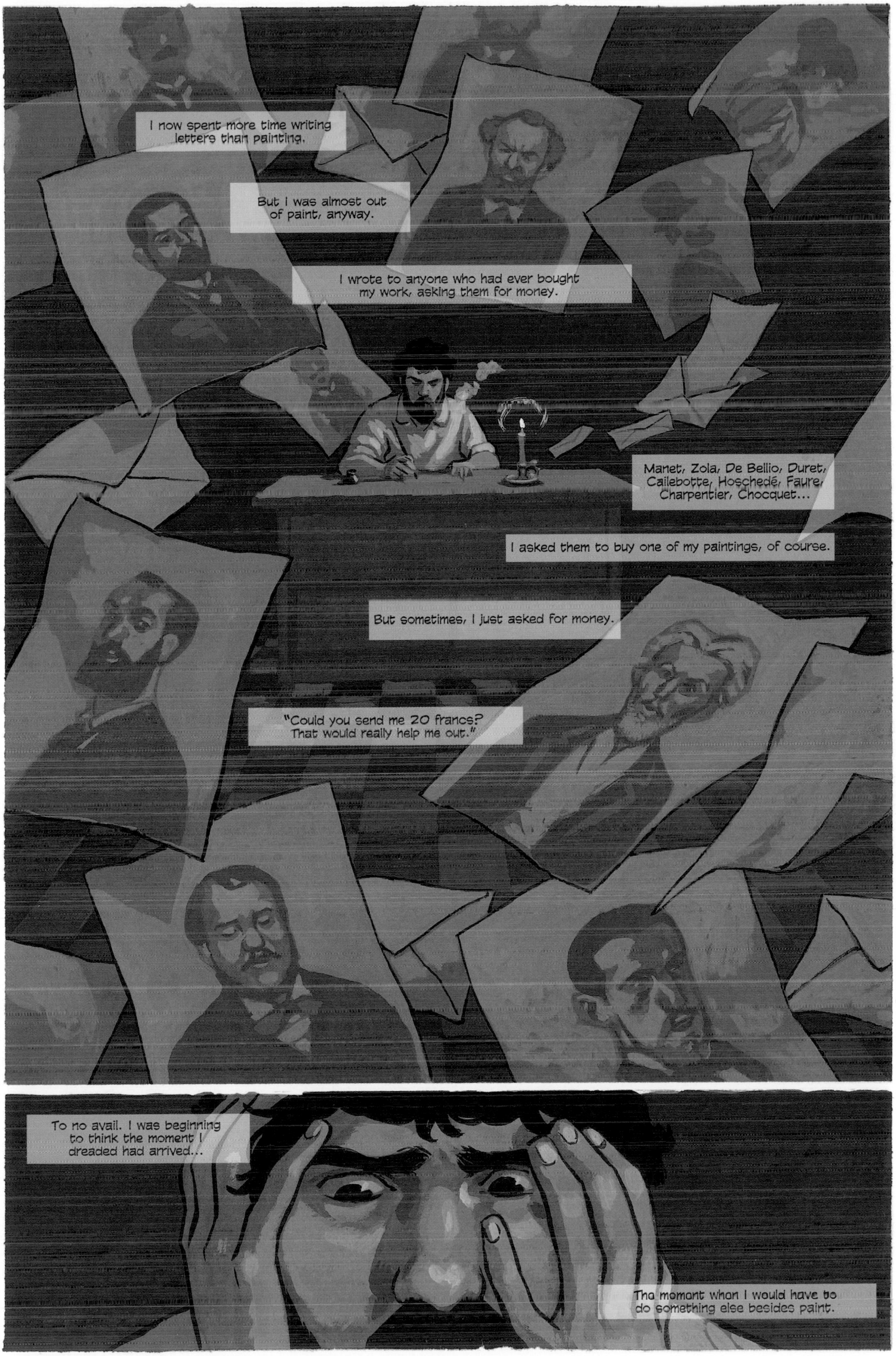

I now spent more time writing letters than painting.
But I was almost out of paint, anyway.
I wrote to anyone who had ever bought my work, asking them for money.
Manet, Zola, De Bellio, Duret, Caillebotte, Hoschedé, Faure, Charpentier, Chocquet...
I asked them to buy one of my paintings, of course.
But sometimes, I just asked for money.
"Could you send me 20 francs? That would really help me out."
To no avail. I was beginning to think the moment I dreaded had arrived...
The moment when I would have to do something else besides paint.

In 1876, we put up another Impressionist show, this time at Durand-Ruel's gallery.

Once again, it attracted nothing but laughter and scorn. But we were convinced it was better to endure the jeers than to not have our work seen at all.

11 Rue le Peletier, Paris.

Again, I was viewed as the leader of the group. That was something, at least..

Perhaps that's why Manet introduced me to Ernest Hoschedé.

A wealthy fabric merchant.

He wanted to be a patron of the arts and had already bought one or two of my works in the past.

Against all odds, he asked me to spend the summer working at his chateau in Montgeron!

As it had in the past, fate smiled on us just when we needed it the most.

But I was preoccupied.

Camille was ill.

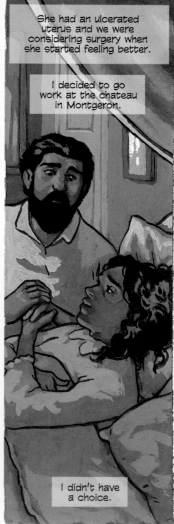

She had an ulcerated uterus and we were considering surgery when she started feeling better.

I decided to go work at the chateau in Montgeron.

I didn't have a choice.

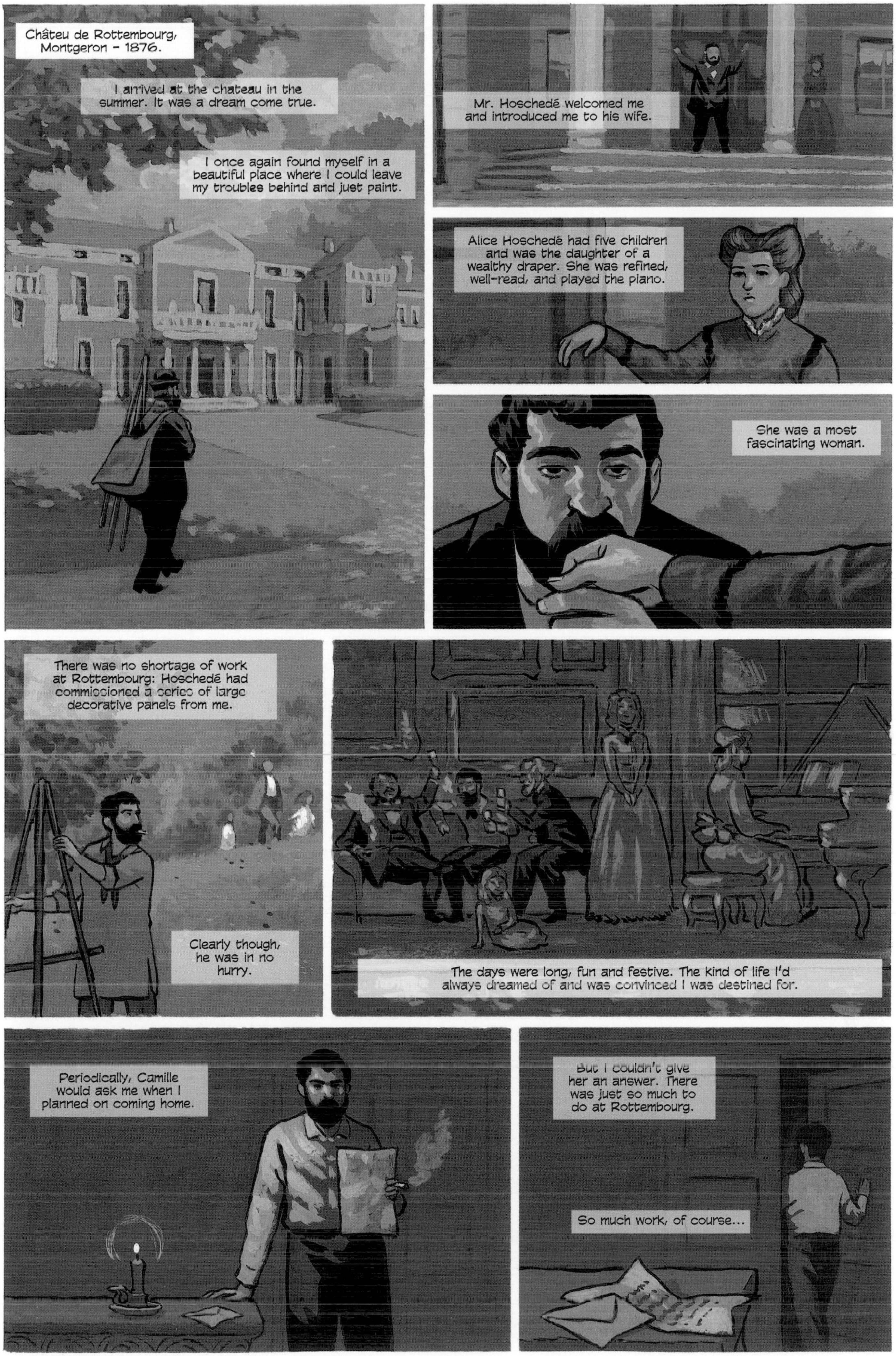

Châteu de Rottembourg, Montgeron – 1876.
I arrived at the chateau in the summer. It was a dream come true.
I once again found myself in a beautiful place where I could leave my troubles behind and just paint.
Mr. Hoschedé welcomed me and introduced me to his wife.
Alice Hoschedé had five children and was the daughter of a wealthy draper. She was refined, well-read, and played the piano.
She was a most fascinating woman.
There was no shortage of work at Rottembourg: Hoschedé had commissioned a series of large decorative panels from me.
Clearly though, he was in no hurry.
The days were long, fun and festive. The kind of life I'd always dreamed of and was convinced I was destined for.
Periodically, Camille would ask me when I planned on coming home.
But I couldn't give her an answer. There was just so much to do at Rottembourg.
So much work, of course...

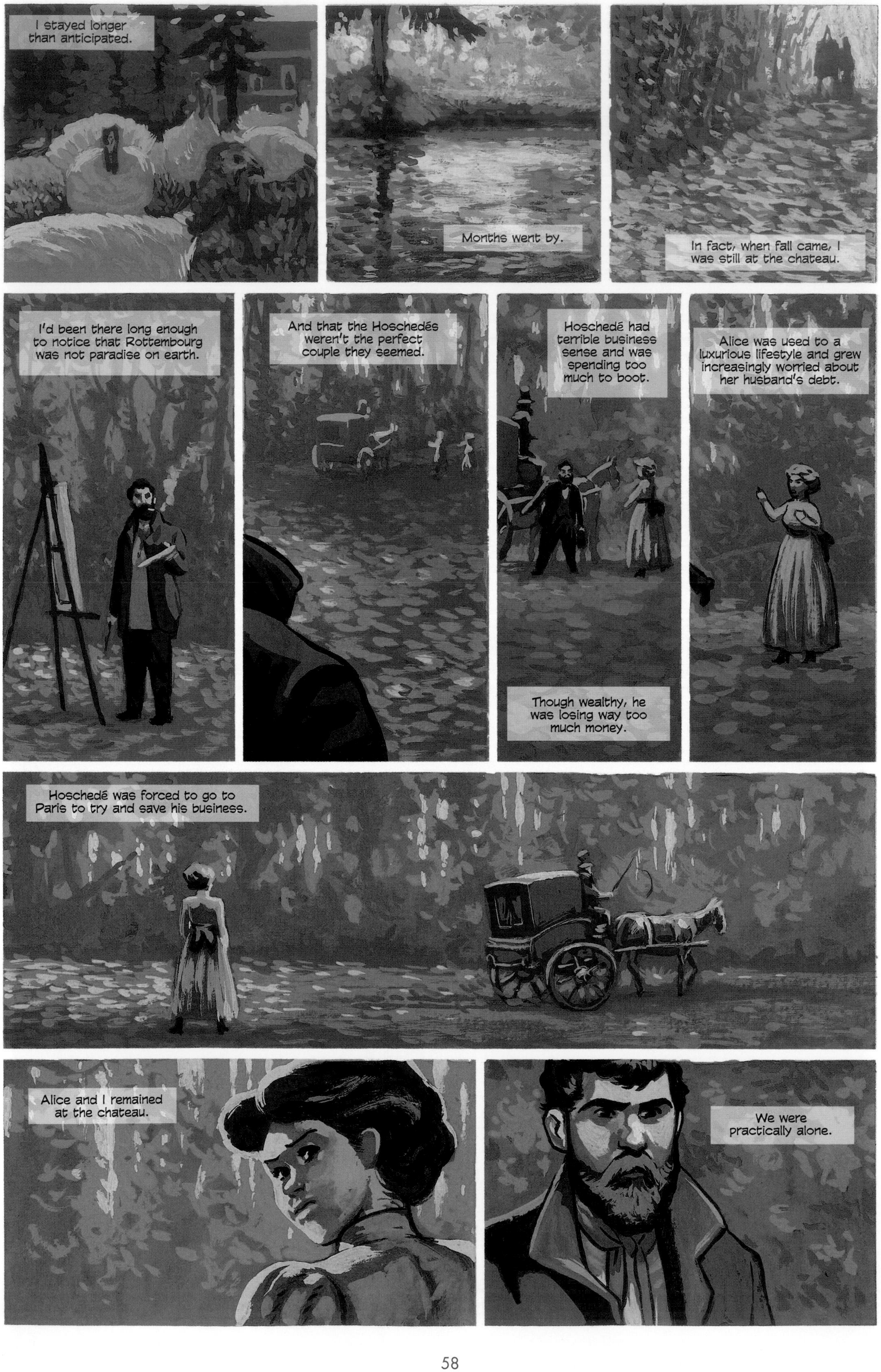
I stayed longer than anticipated.
Months went by.
In fact, when fall came, I was still at the chateau.
I'd been there long enough to notice that Rottembourg was not paradise on earth.
And that the Hoschedés weren't the perfect couple they seemed.
Hoschedé had terrible business sense and was spending too much to boot.
Though wealthy, he was losing way too much money.
Alice was used to a luxurious lifestyle and grew increasingly worried about her husband's debt.
Hoschedé was forced to go to Paris to try and save his business.
Alice and I remained at the chateau.
We were practically alone.

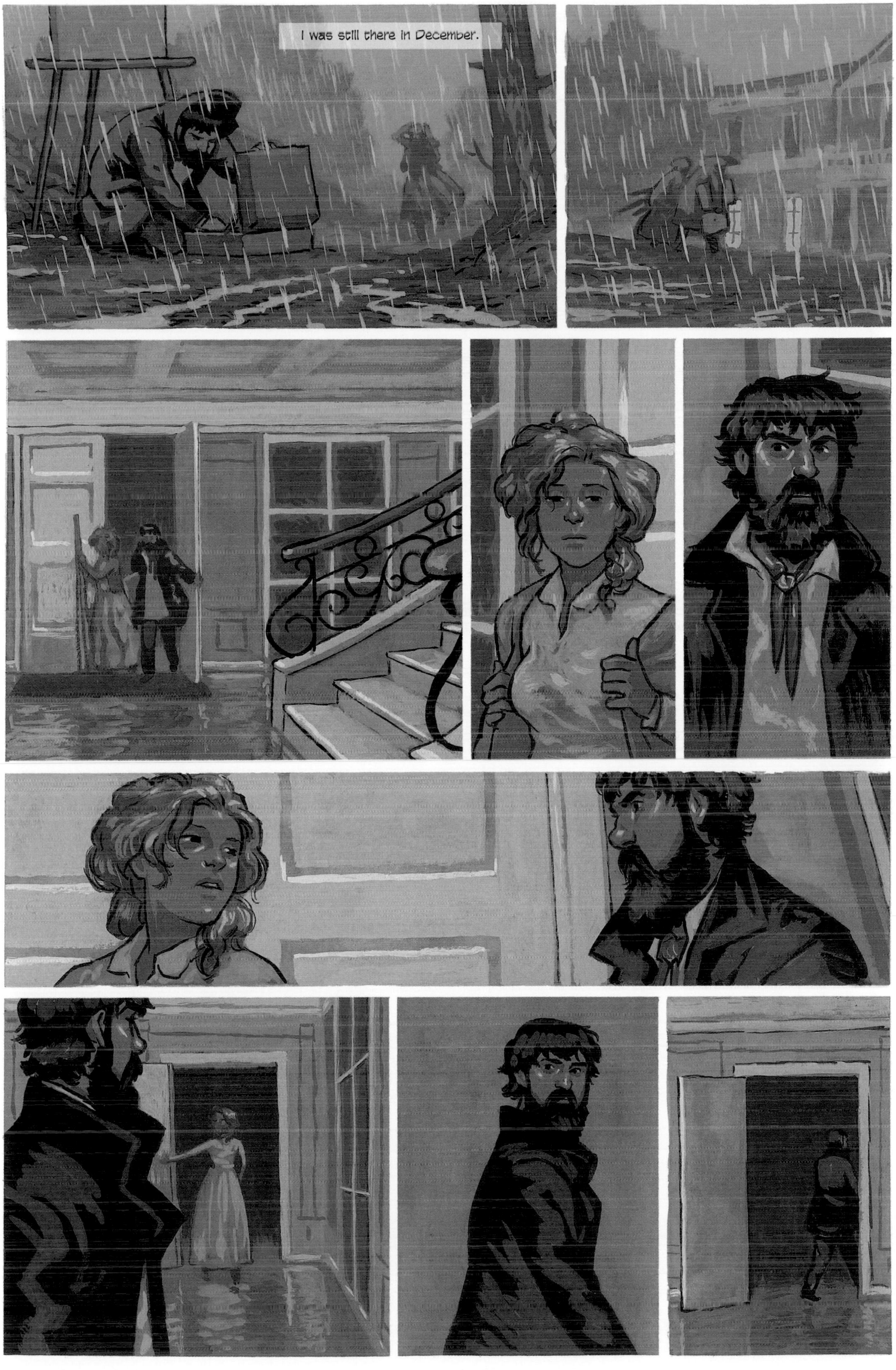
I was still there in December.

I eventually returned home.

Argenteuil - late 1876.

It was hard to come back to a world of misery.

So hard that I made some bad decisions.

I started spending without keeping track. I was aware of it, but I wanted to give my family everything they deserved.

I hired two servants, Marie and Sylvain, and a gardener, Lelièvre. I even leased a piano. And I treated myself to the best wine and tobacco.

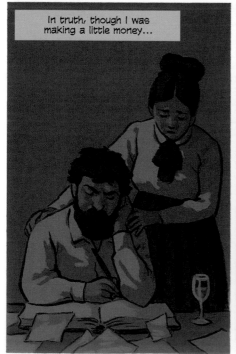

In truth, though I was making a little money...

...we were so much in debt we couldn't pay back our creditors.

It was just impossible.

So we decided to leave Argenteuil.

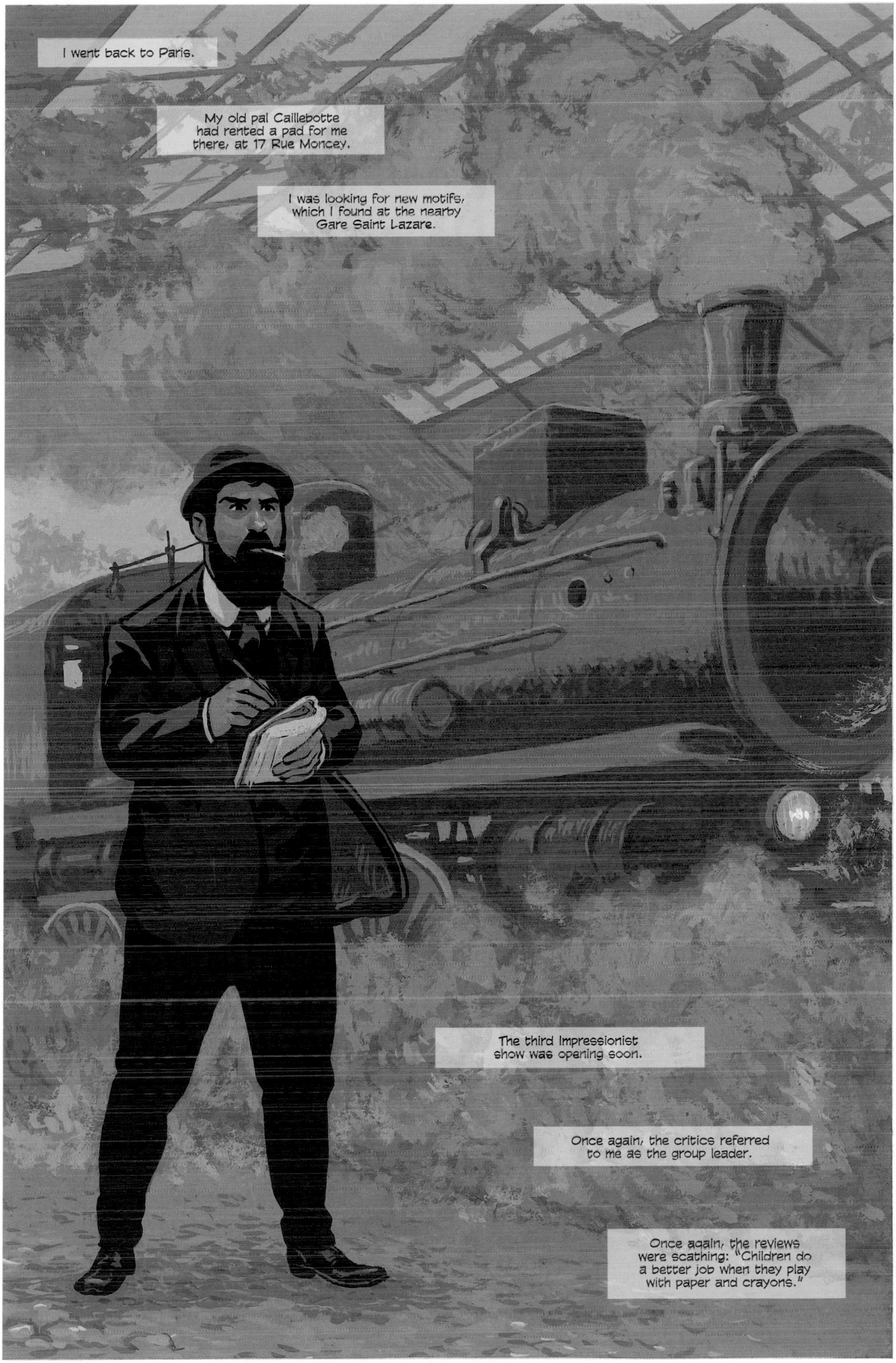
I went back to Paris.
My old pal Caillebotte had rented a pad for me there, at 17 Rue Moncey.
I was looking for new motifs, which I found at the nearby Gare Saint Lazare.
The third Impressionist show was opening soon.
Once again, the critics referred to me as the group leader.
Once again, the reviews were scathing: "Children do a better job when they play with paper and crayons."

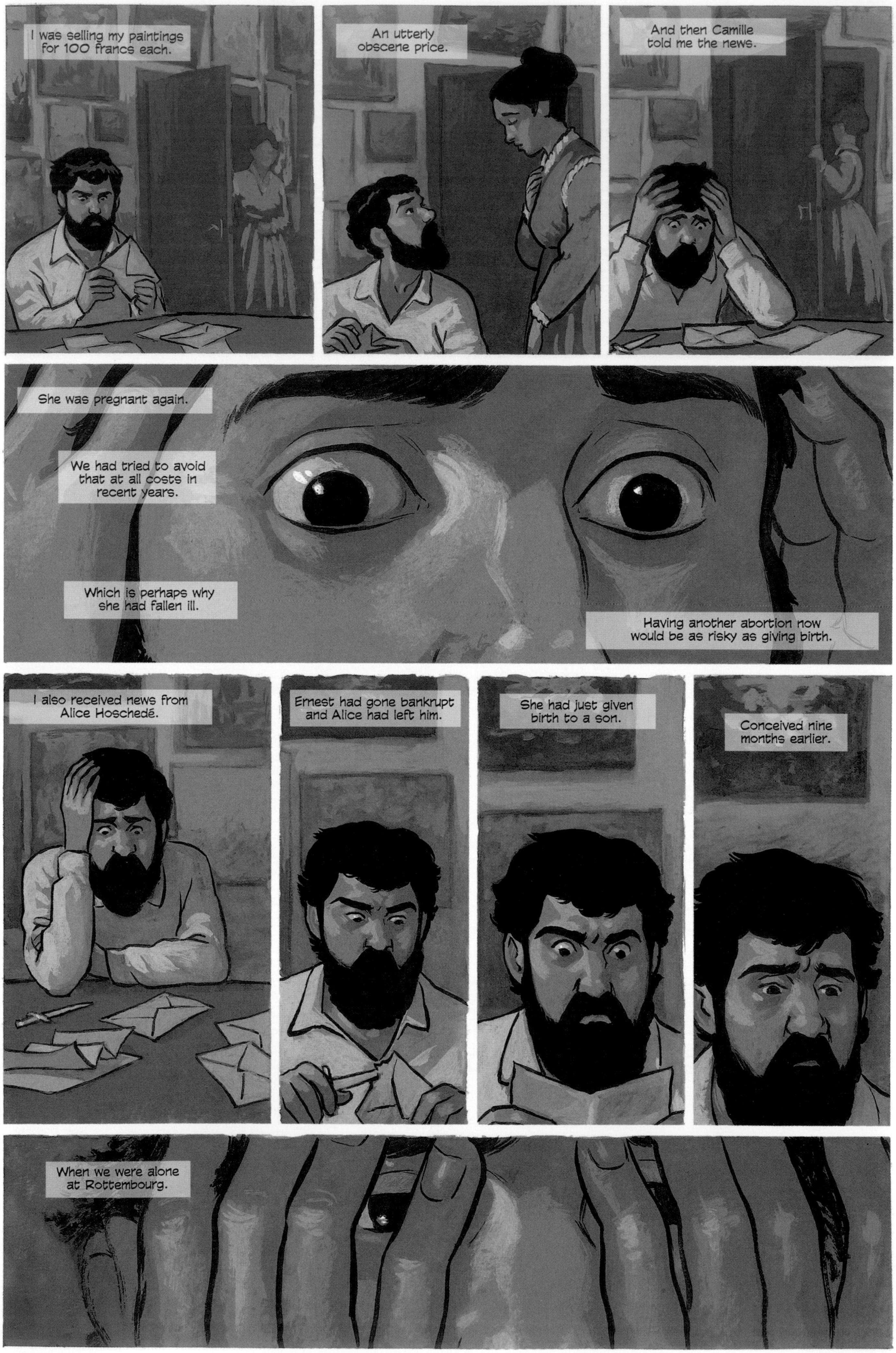
I was selling my paintings for 100 francs each.
An utterly obscene price.
And then Camille told me the news.
She was pregnant again.
We had tried to avoid that at all costs in recent years.
Which is perhaps why she had fallen ill.
Having another abortion now would be as risky as giving birth.
I also received news from Alice Hoschedé.
Ernest had gone bankrupt and Alice had left him.
She had just given birth to a son.
Conceived nine months earlier.
When we were alone at Rottembourg.

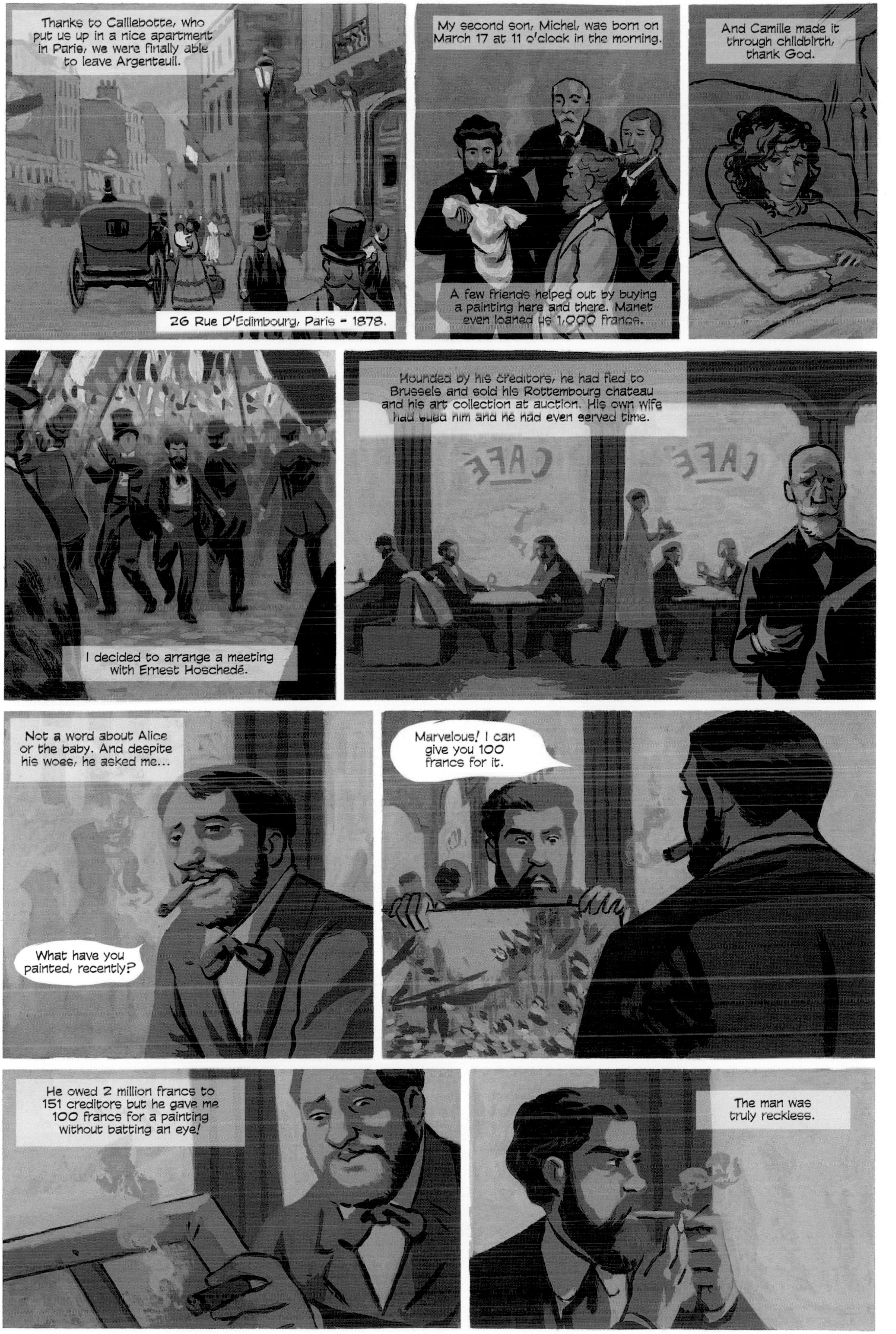
Thanks to Caillebotte, who put us up in a nice apartment in Paris, we were finally able to leave Argenteuil.
26 Rue D'Edimbourg, Paris - 1878.
My second son, Michel, was born on March 17 at 11 o'clock in the morning.
A few friends helped out by buying a painting here and there. Manet even loaned us 1,000 francs.
And Camille made it through childbirth, thank God.
I decided to arrange a meeting with Ernest Hoschedé.
Hounded by his creditors, he had fled to Brussels and sold his Rottembourg chateau and his art collection at auction. His own wife had sued him and he had even served time.
CAFÉ
CAFÉ
Not a word about Alice or the baby. And despite his woes, he asked me...
What have you painted, recently?
Marvelous! I can give you 100 francs for it.
He owed 2 million francs to 151 creditors but he gave me 100 francs for a painting without batting an eye!
The man was truly reckless.

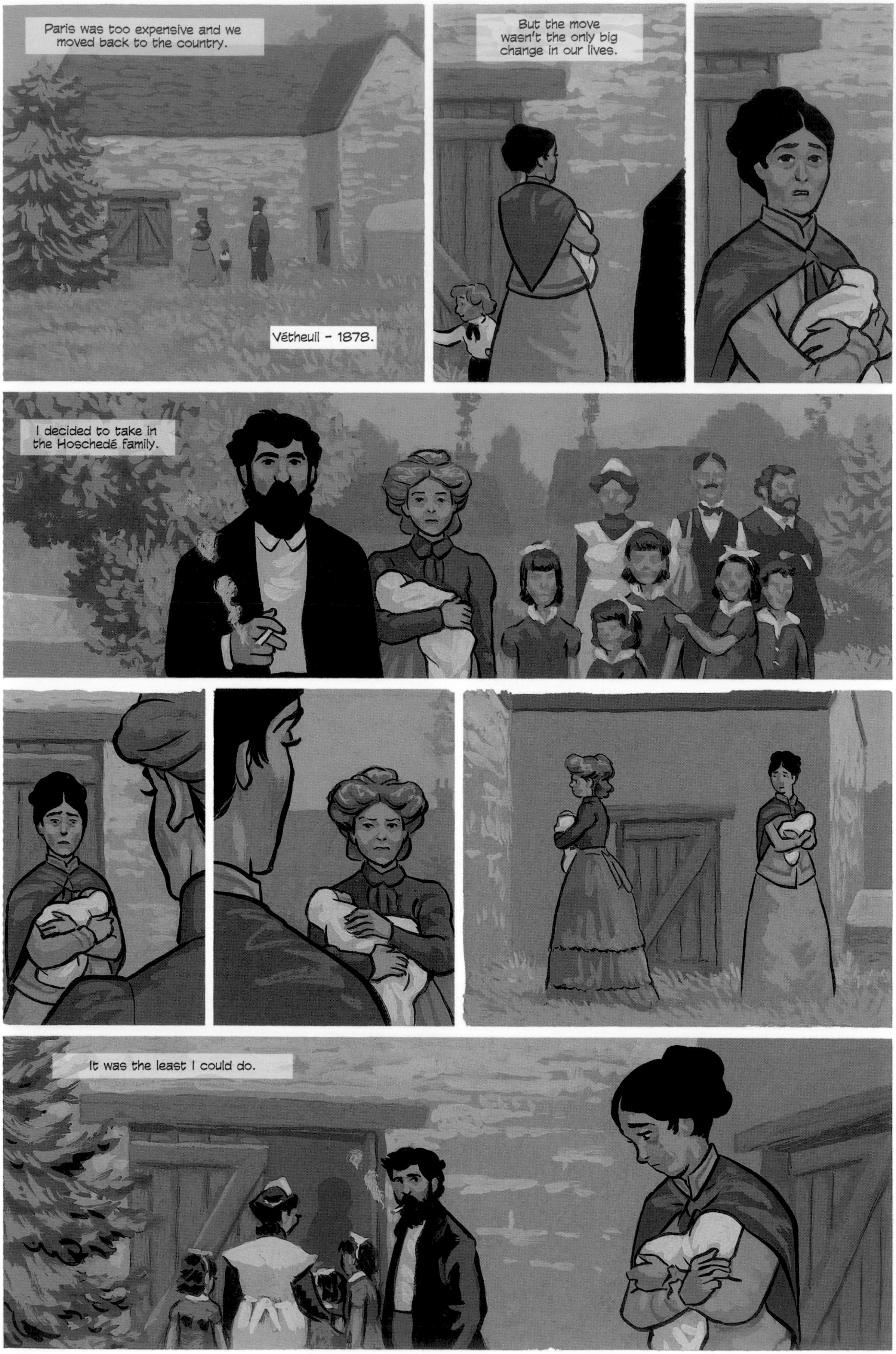
Paris was too expensive and we moved back to the country.
Vétheuil - 1878.
But the move wasn't the only big change in our lives.
I decided to take in the Hoschedé family.
It was the least I could do.

There were twelve of us, not counting Alice's servants, who eventually left us.

Ernest returned to Paris, leaving me in charge of both families.

This must have been an especially difficult time for Alice, who was used to a different lifestyle.

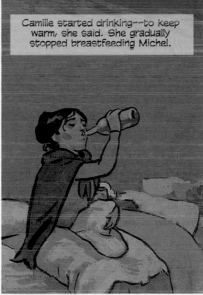

Camille started drinking--to keep warm, she said. She gradually stopped breastfeeding Michel.

Despite the hard times, we stayed in Vétheuil, as the landscapes there helped me produce work that sold easily. But it was barely enough to make ends meet.

We rented a different house in Vétheuil to better withstand the autumn chill. Then came winter.

I was depressed, fed up, and discouraged.

I nevertheless managed to paint Michel's baby portrait for Camille.

65

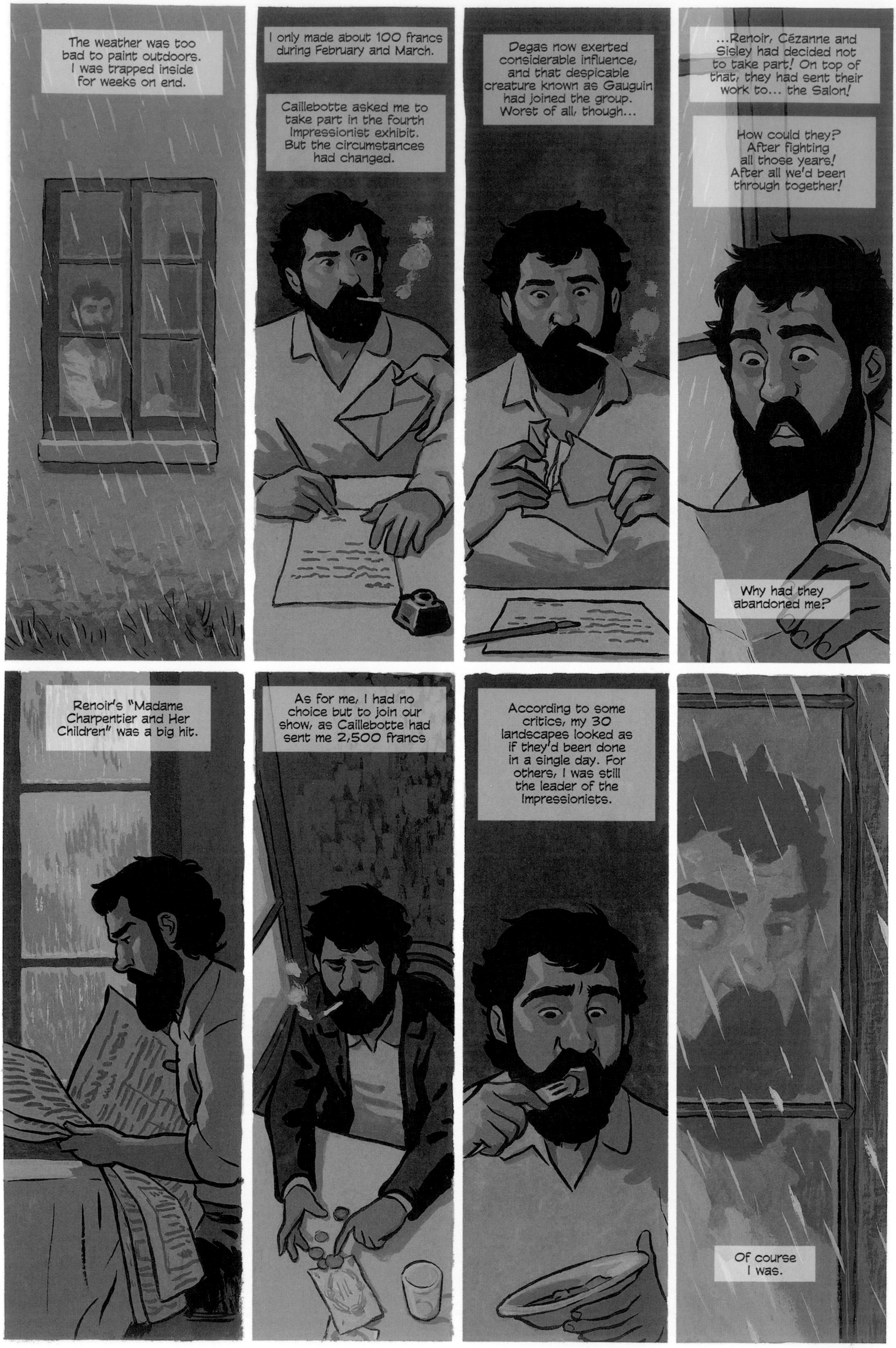
The weather was too bad to paint outdoors. I was trapped inside for weeks on end.
I only made about 100 francs during February and March.
Caillebotte asked me to take part in the fourth Impressionist exhibit. But the circumstances had changed.
Degas now exerted considerable influence, and that despicable creature known as Gauguin had joined the group. Worst of all, though...
...Renoir, Cézanne and Sisley had decided not to take part! On top of that, they had sent their work to... the Salon!
How could they? After fighting all those years! After all we'd been through together!
Why had they abandoned me?
Renoir's "Madame Charpentier and Her Children" was a big hit.
As for me, I had no choice but to join our show, as Caillebotte had sent me 2,500 francs
According to some critics, my 30 landscapes looked as if they'd been done in a single day. For others, I was still the leader of the Impressionists.
Of course I was.

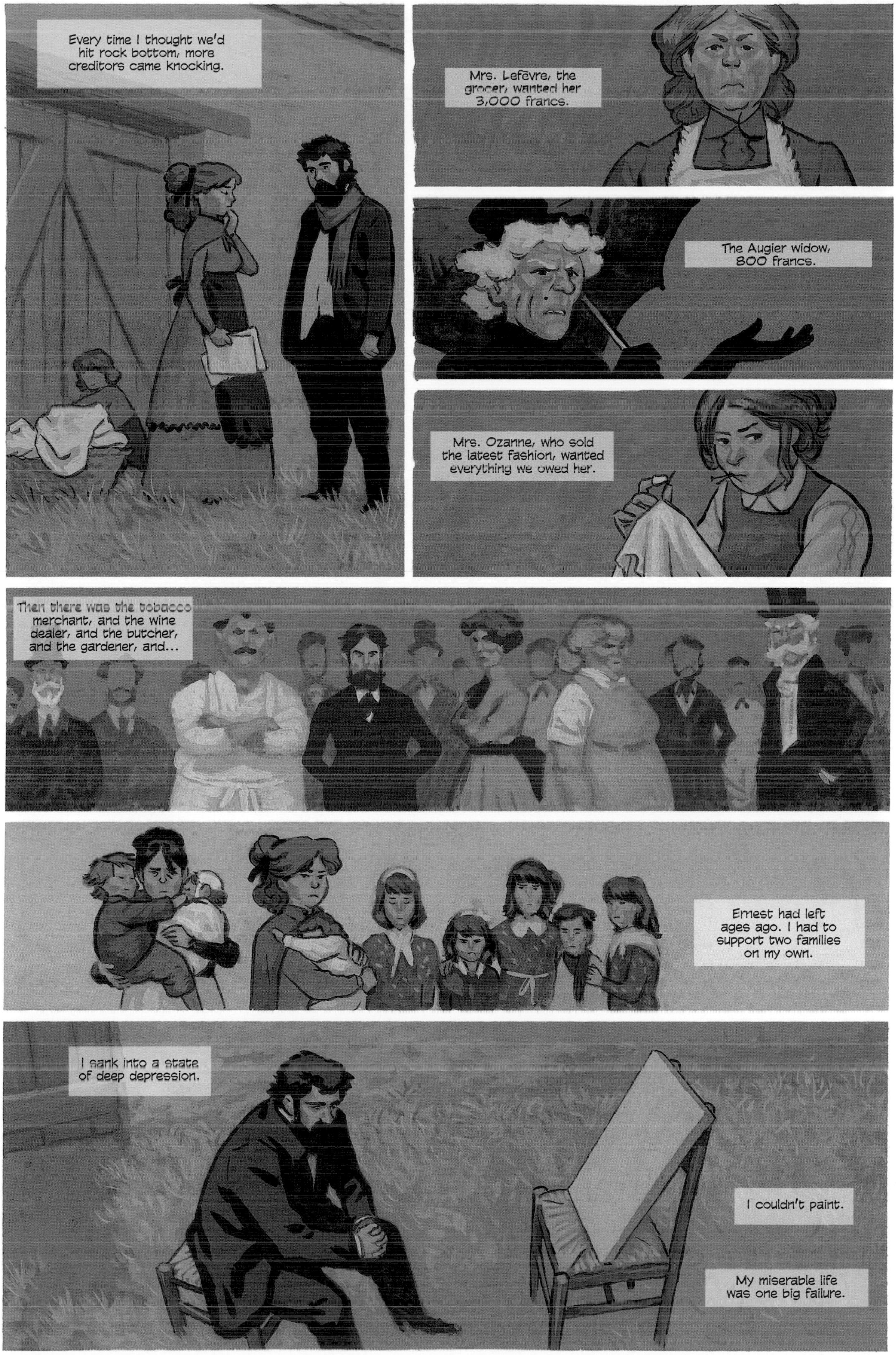
Every time I thought we'd hit rock bottom, more creditors came knocking.
Mrs. Lefèvre, the grocer, wanted her 3,000 francs.
The Augier widow, 800 francs.
Mrs. Ozanne, who sold the latest fashion, wanted everything we owed her.
Then there was the tobacco merchant, and the wine dealer, and the butcher, and the gardener, and...
Ernest had left ages ago. I had to support two families on my own.
I sank into a state of deep depression.
I couldn't paint.
My miserable life was one big failure.

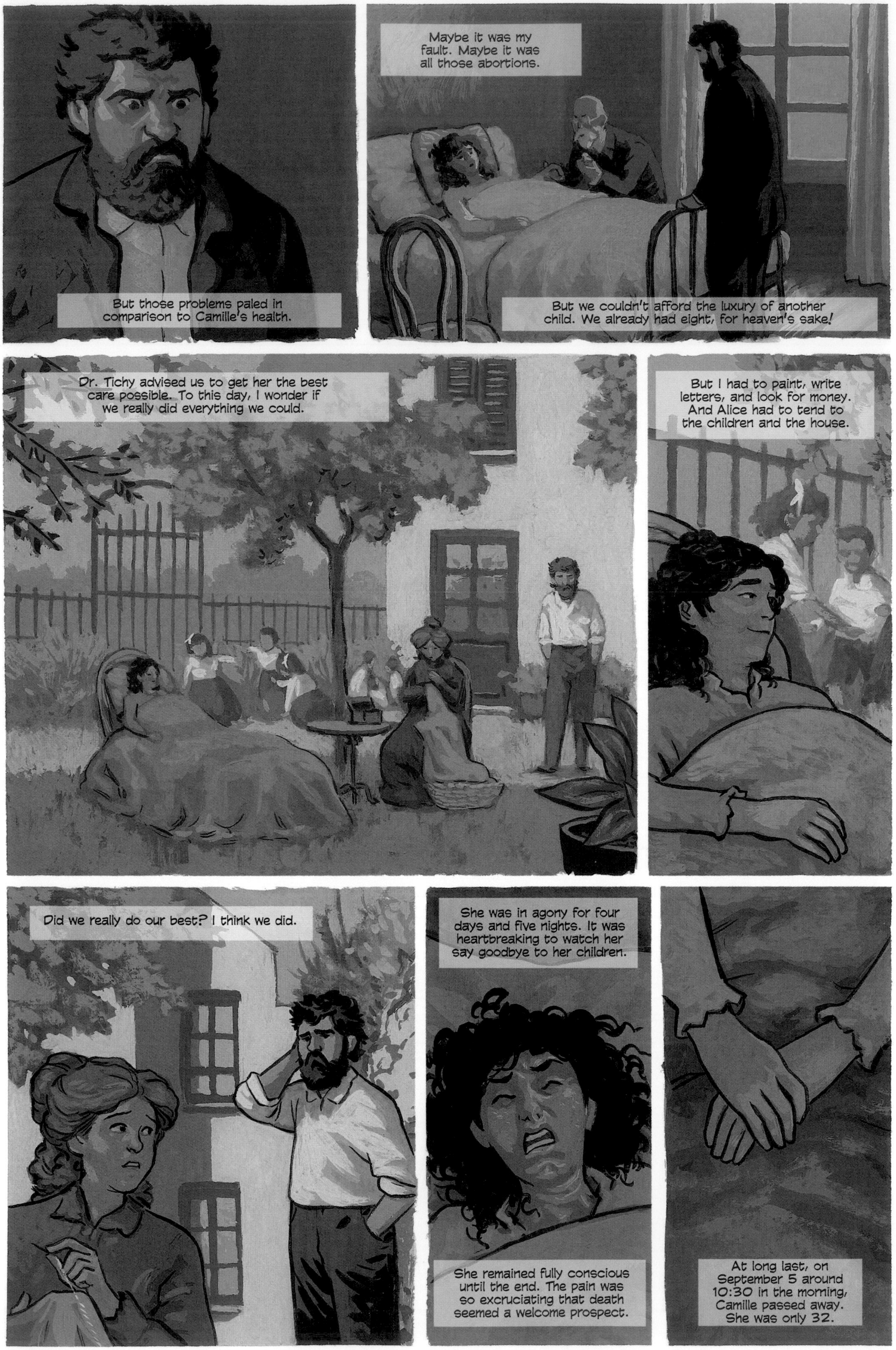
But those problems paled in comparison to Camille's health.
Maybe it was my fault. Maybe it was all those abortions.
But we couldn't afford the luxury of another child. We already had eight, for heaven's sake!
Dr. Tichy advised us to get her the best care possible. To this day, I wonder if we really did everything we could.
But I had to paint, write letters, and look for money. And Alice had to tend to the children and the house.
Did we really do our best? I think we did.
She was in agony for four days and five nights. It was heartbreaking to watch her say goodbye to her children.
She remained fully conscious until the end. The pain was so excruciating that death seemed a welcome prospect.
At long last, on September 5 around 10:30 in the morning, Camille passed away. She was only 32.

I was so broke I had to ask de Bellio to retrieve Camille's medallion at the pawnshop.

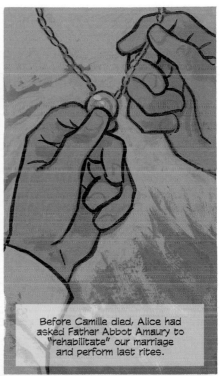

Before Camille died, Alice had asked Father Abbot Amaury to "rehabilitate" our marriage and perform last rites.

While I was at her bedside, a few hours before the funeral, a strange feeling came over me.

I caught myself...

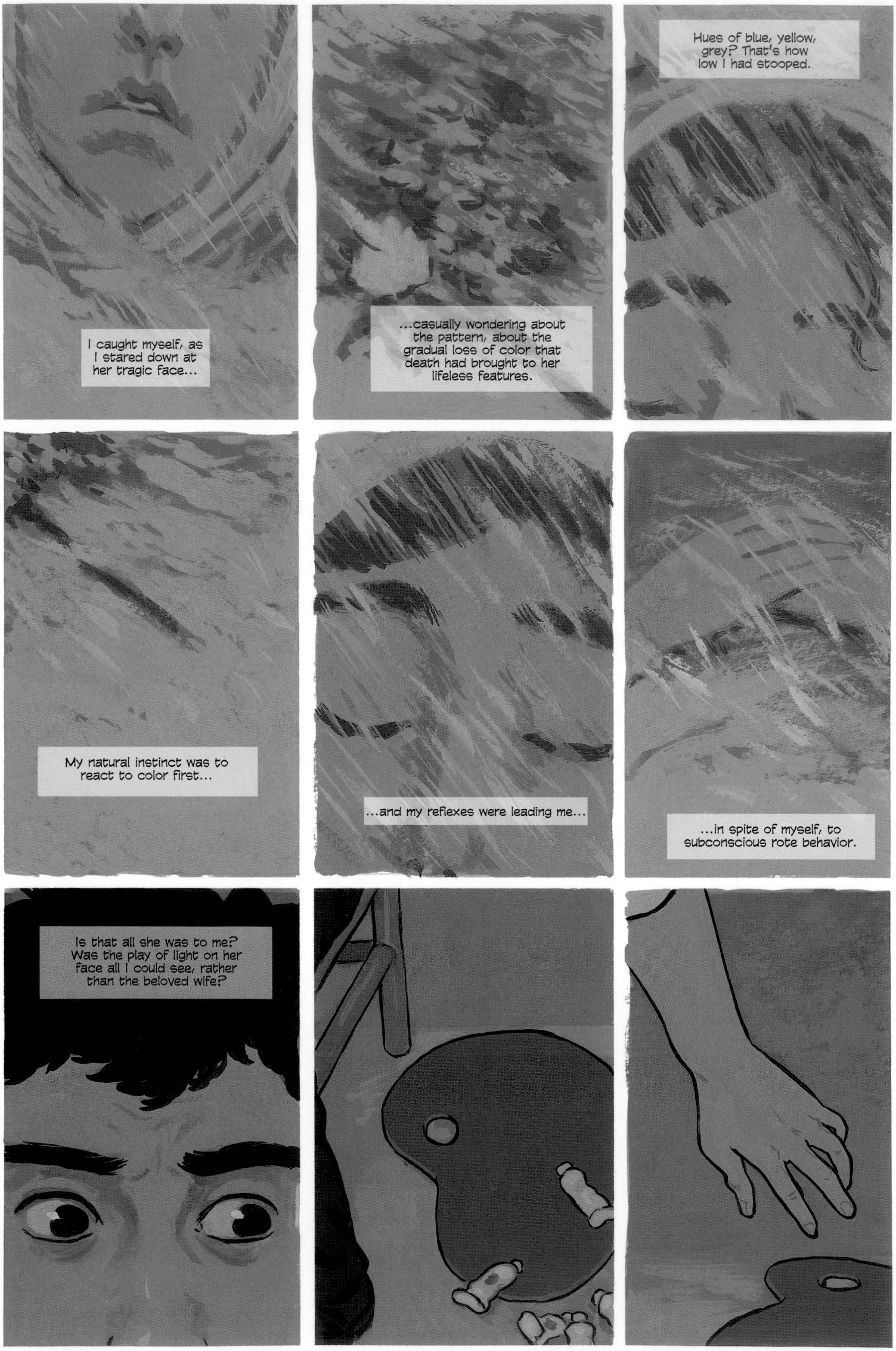

I caught myself, as I stared down at her tragic face...
...casually wondering about the pattern, about the gradual loss of color that death had brought to her lifeless features.
Hues of blue, yellow, grey? That's how low I had stooped.
My natural instinct was to react to color first...
...and my reflexes were leading me...
...in spite of myself, to subconscious rote behavior.
Is that all she was to me? Was the play of light on her face all I could see, rather than the beloved wife?

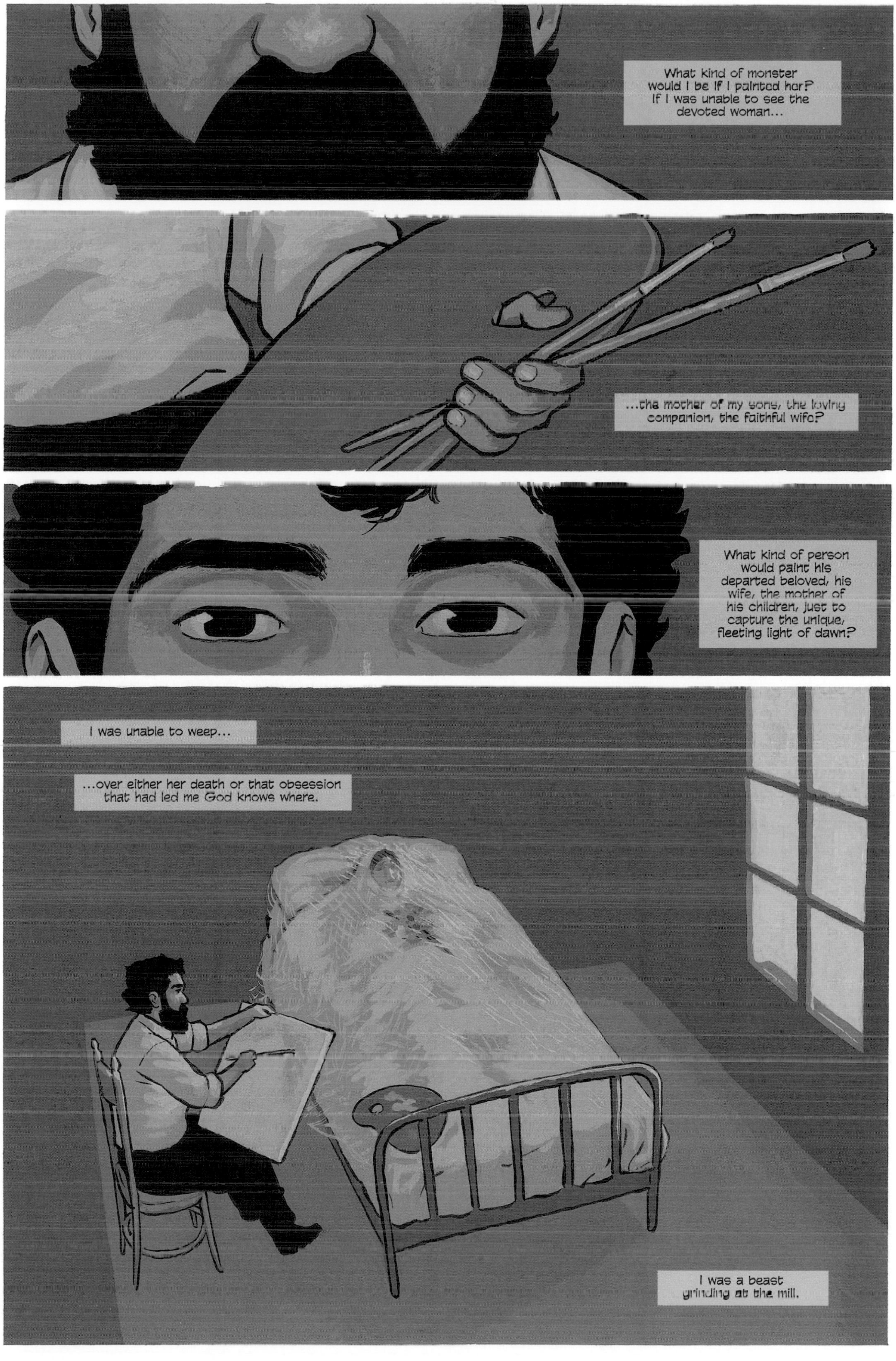
What kind of monster would I be if I painted her? If I was unable to see the devoted woman...
...the mother of my sons, the loving companion, the faithful wife?
What kind of person would paint his departed beloved, his wife, the mother of his children, just to capture the unique, fleeting light of dawn?
I was unable to weep...
...over either her death or that obsession that had led me God knows where.
I was a beast grinding at the mill.

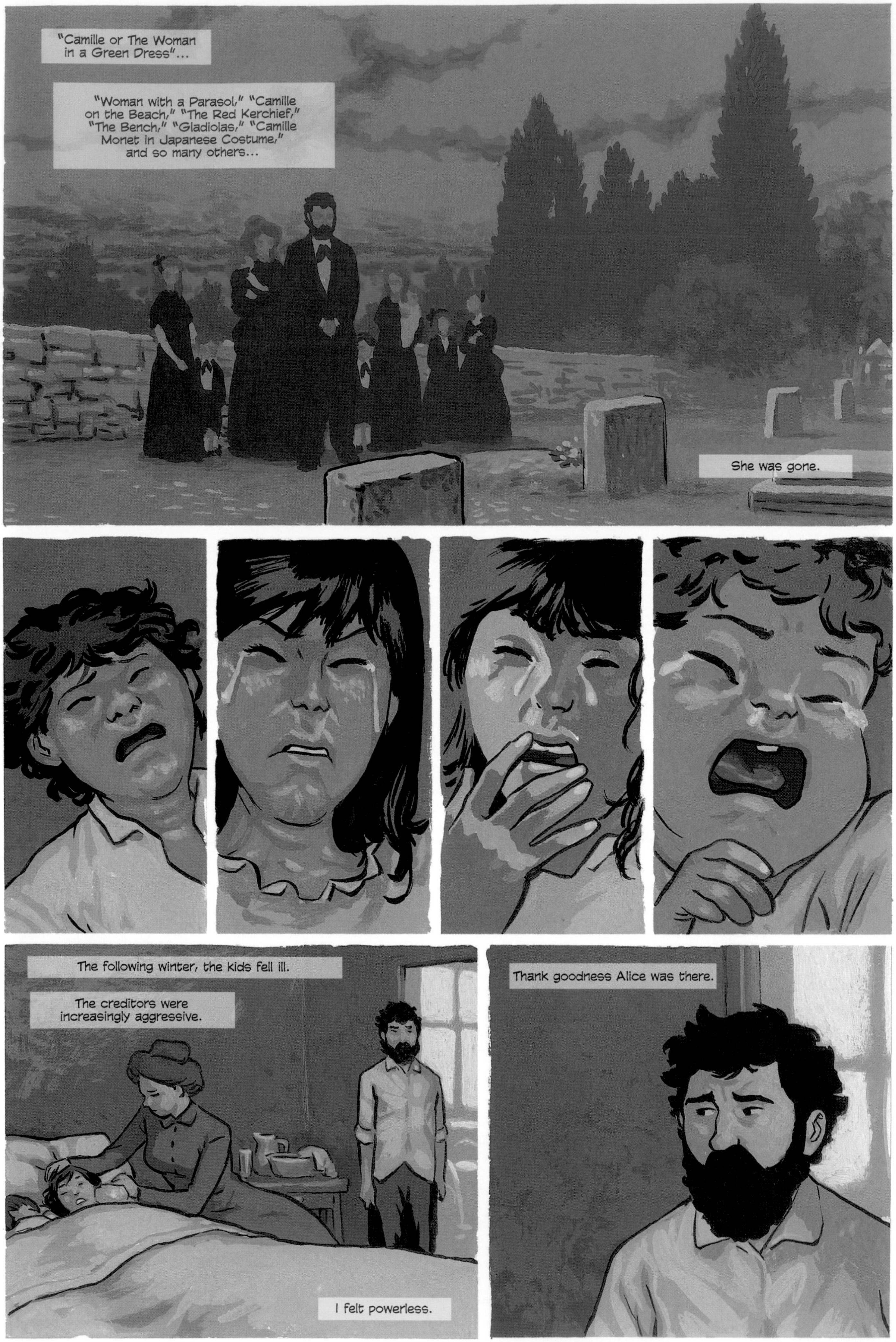
"Camille or The Woman in a Green Dress"...
"Woman with a Parasol," "Camille on the Beach," "The Red Kerchief," "The Bench," "Gladiolas," "Camille Monet in Japanese Costume," and so many others...
She was gone.
The following winter, the kids fell ill.
The creditors were increasingly aggressive.
I felt powerless.
Thank goodness Alice was there.

She dealt with Madeleine, the cook, who threatened to leave.

Madame Origet, who wanted to evict us.

The launderers in Follainville.

And even the butter lady, to whom we only owed 30 francs.

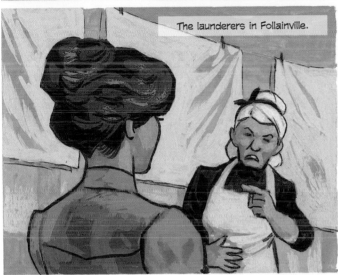

Imagine what it must have been...

...for a woman like Alice...

...accustomed to a life of luxury...

...to live in abject poverty.

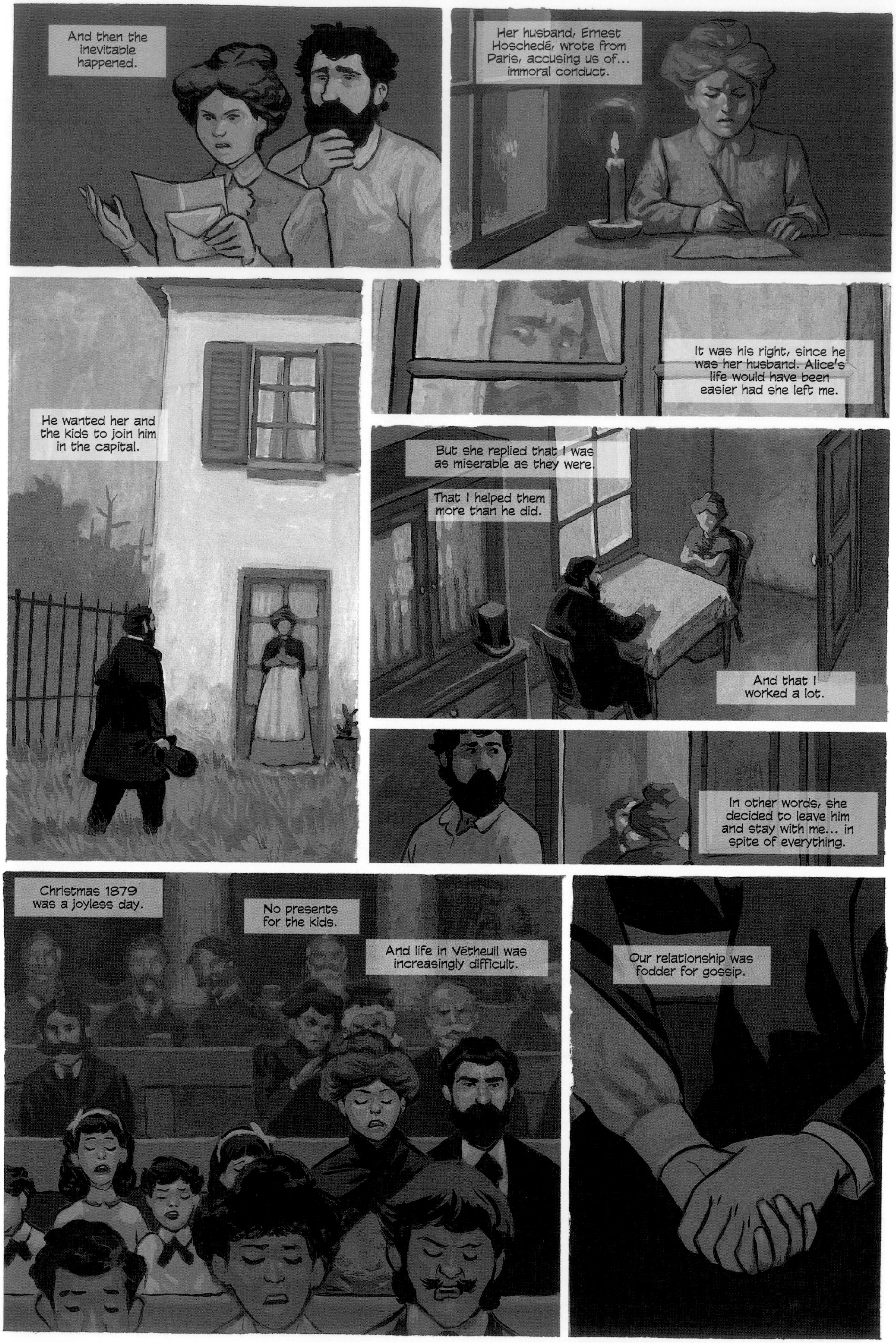
And then the inevitable happened.
Her husband, Ernest Hoschedé, wrote from Paris, accusing us of... immoral conduct.
He wanted her and the kids to join him in the capital.
It was his right, since he was her husband. Alice's life would have been easier had she left me.
But she replied that I was as miserable as they were.
That I helped them more than he did.
And that I worked a lot.
In other words, she decided to leave him and stay with me... in spite of everything.
Christmas 1879 was a joyless day.
No presents for the kids.
And life in Vétheuil was increasingly difficult.
Our relationship was fodder for gossip.

On December 28, all we had to our name was five francs.

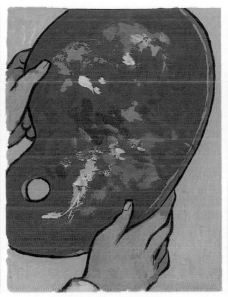

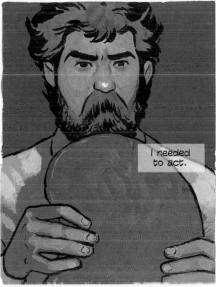

I needed to act.

I needed to regroup.

I needed to paint.

Alice was making a huge effort.

And I needed to measure up.

I had to have her at my side.

But that came at a price.

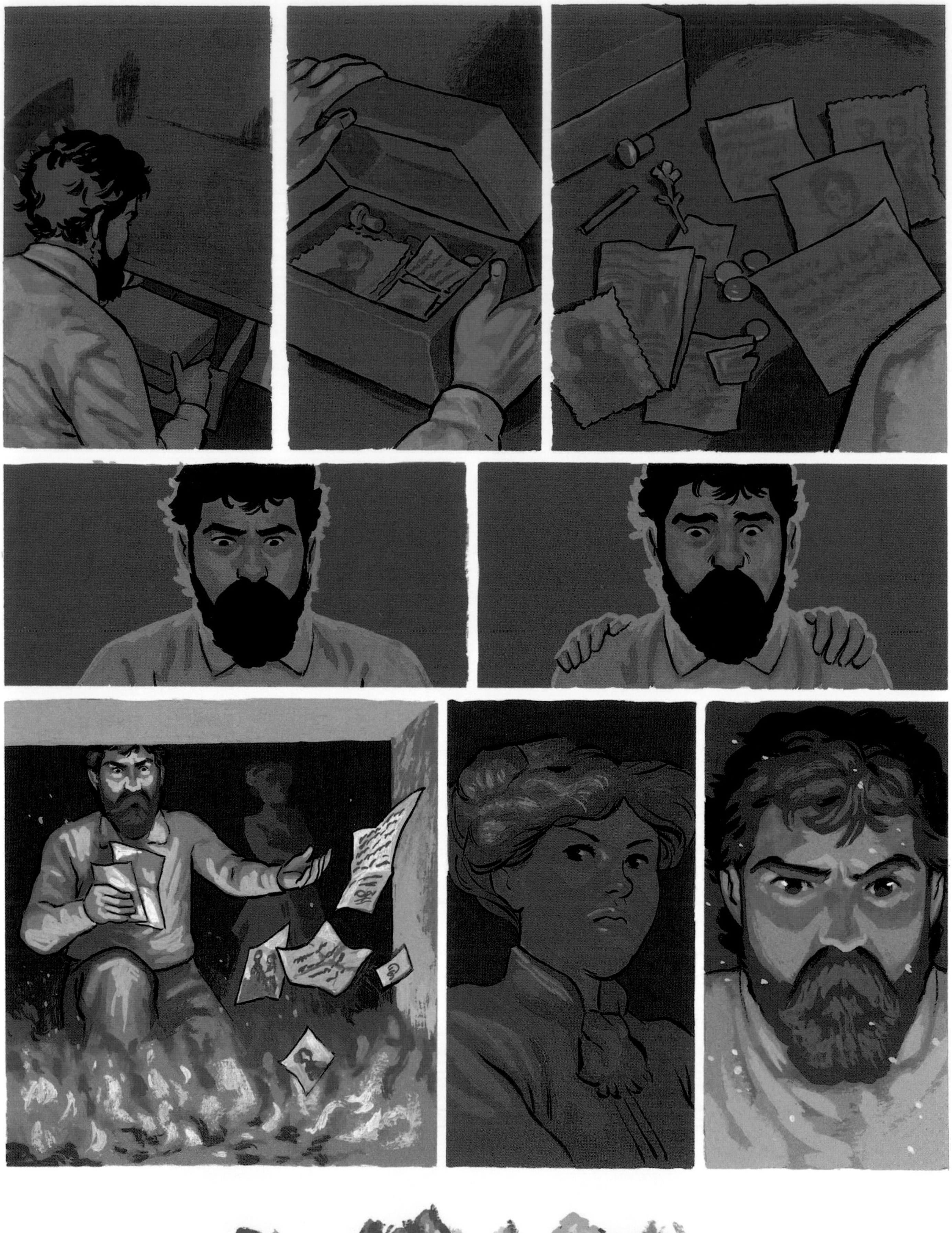

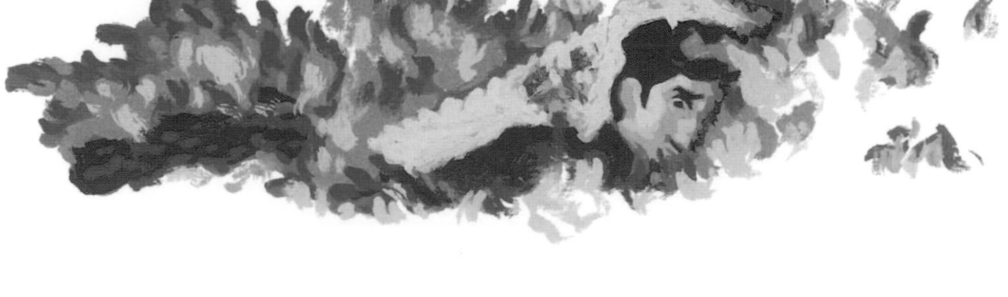

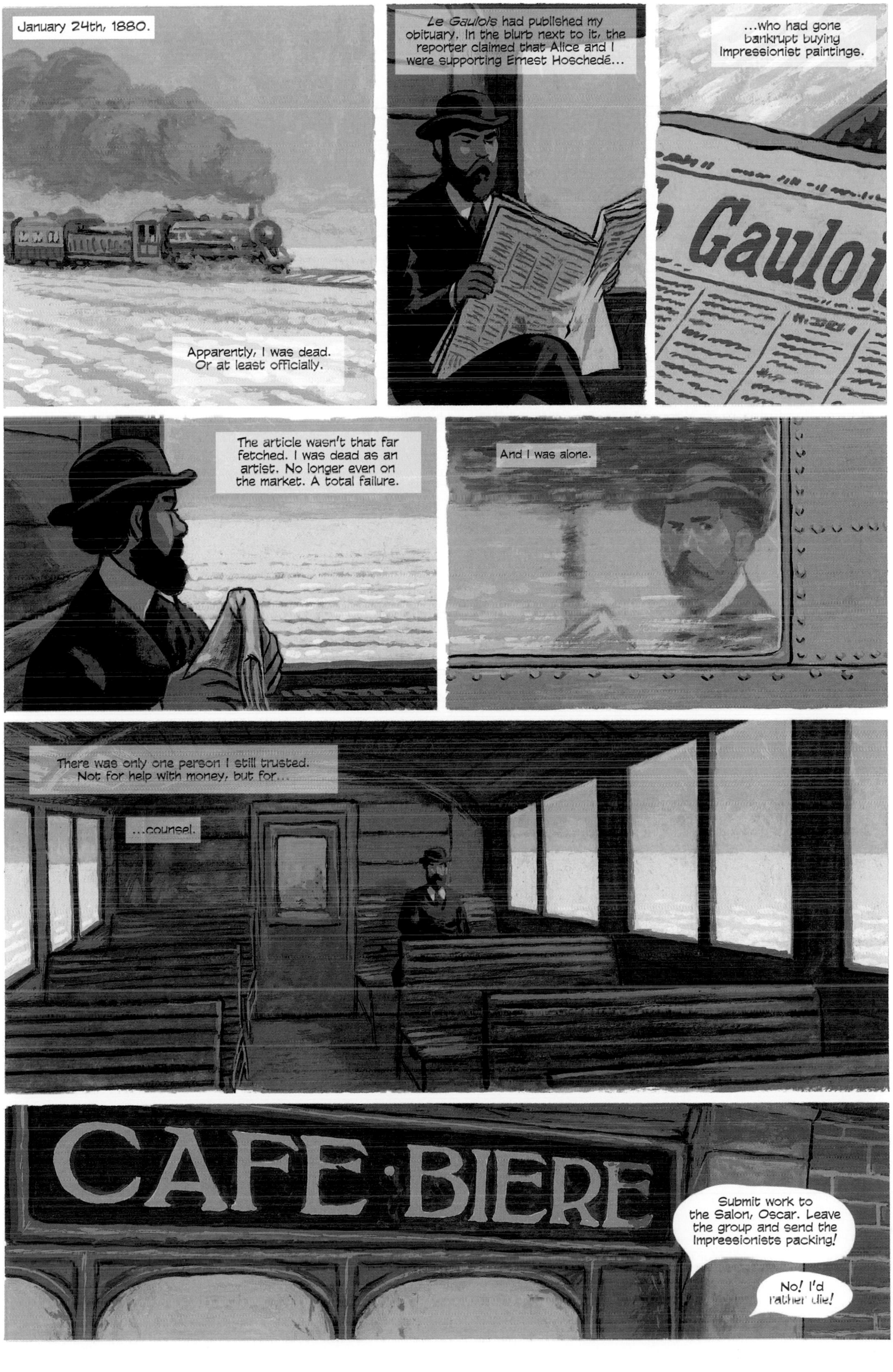
January 24th, 1880.
Apparently, I was dead. Or at least officially.
Le Gaulois had published my obituary. In the blurb next to it, the reporter claimed that Alice and I were supporting Ernest Hoschedé...
...who had gone bankrupt buying Impressionist paintings.
Gaulois
The article wasn't that far fetched. I was dead as an artist. No longer even on the market. A total failure.
And I was alone.
There was only one person I still trusted. Not for help with money, but for...
...counsel.
CAFE · BIERE
Submit work to the Salon, Oscar. Leave the group and send the Impressionists packing!
No! I'd rather die!

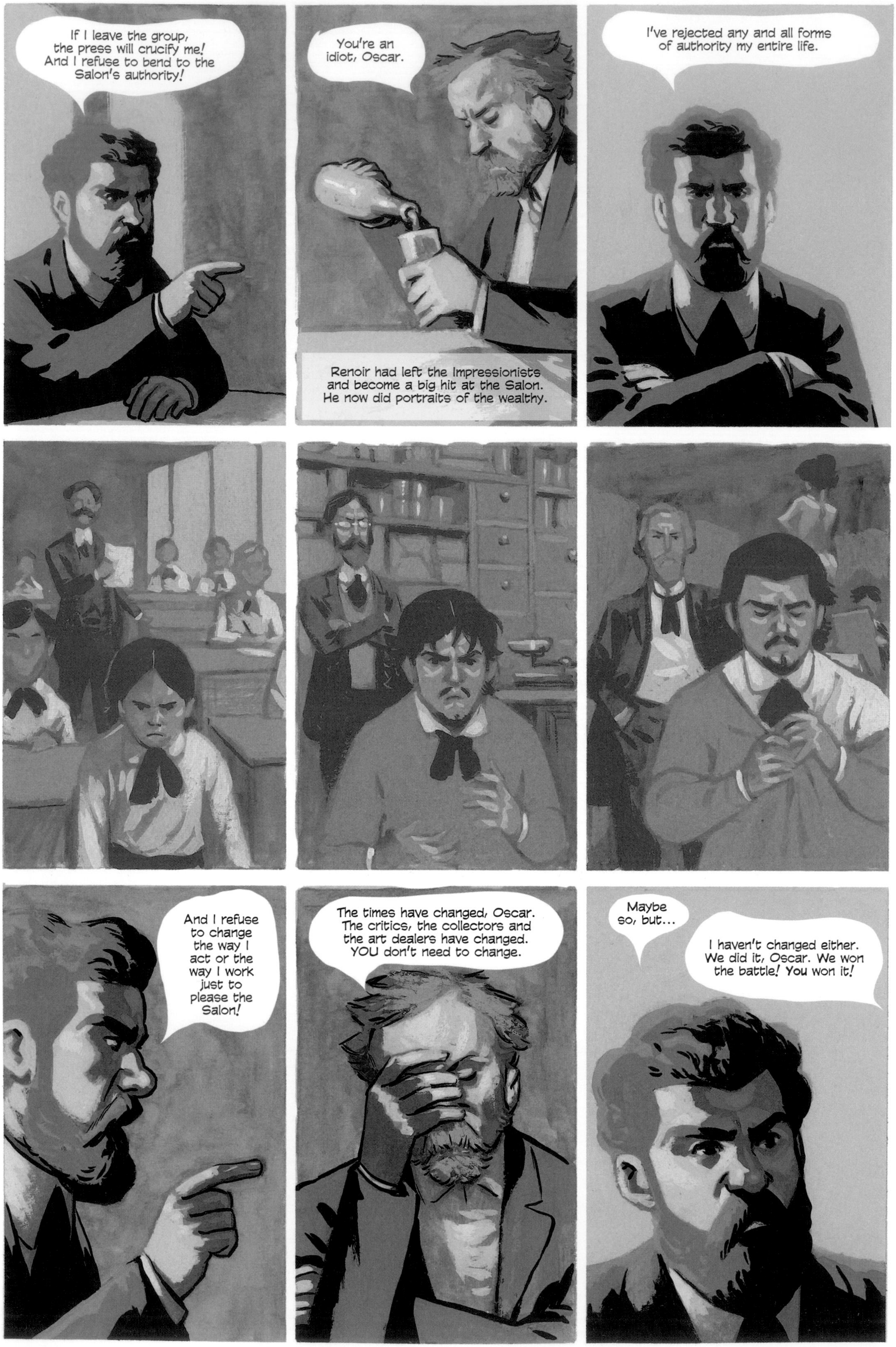
If I leave the group, the press will crucify me! And I refuse to bend to the Salon's authority!
You're an idiot, Oscar.
Renoir had left the Impressionists and become a big hit at the Salon. He now did portraits of the wealthy.
I've rejected any and all forms of authority my entire life.
And I refuse to change the way I act or the way I work just to please the Salon!
The times have changed, Oscar. The critics, the collectors and the art dealers have changed. YOU don't need to change.
Maybe so, but...
I haven't changed either. We did it, Oscar. We won the battle! You won it!

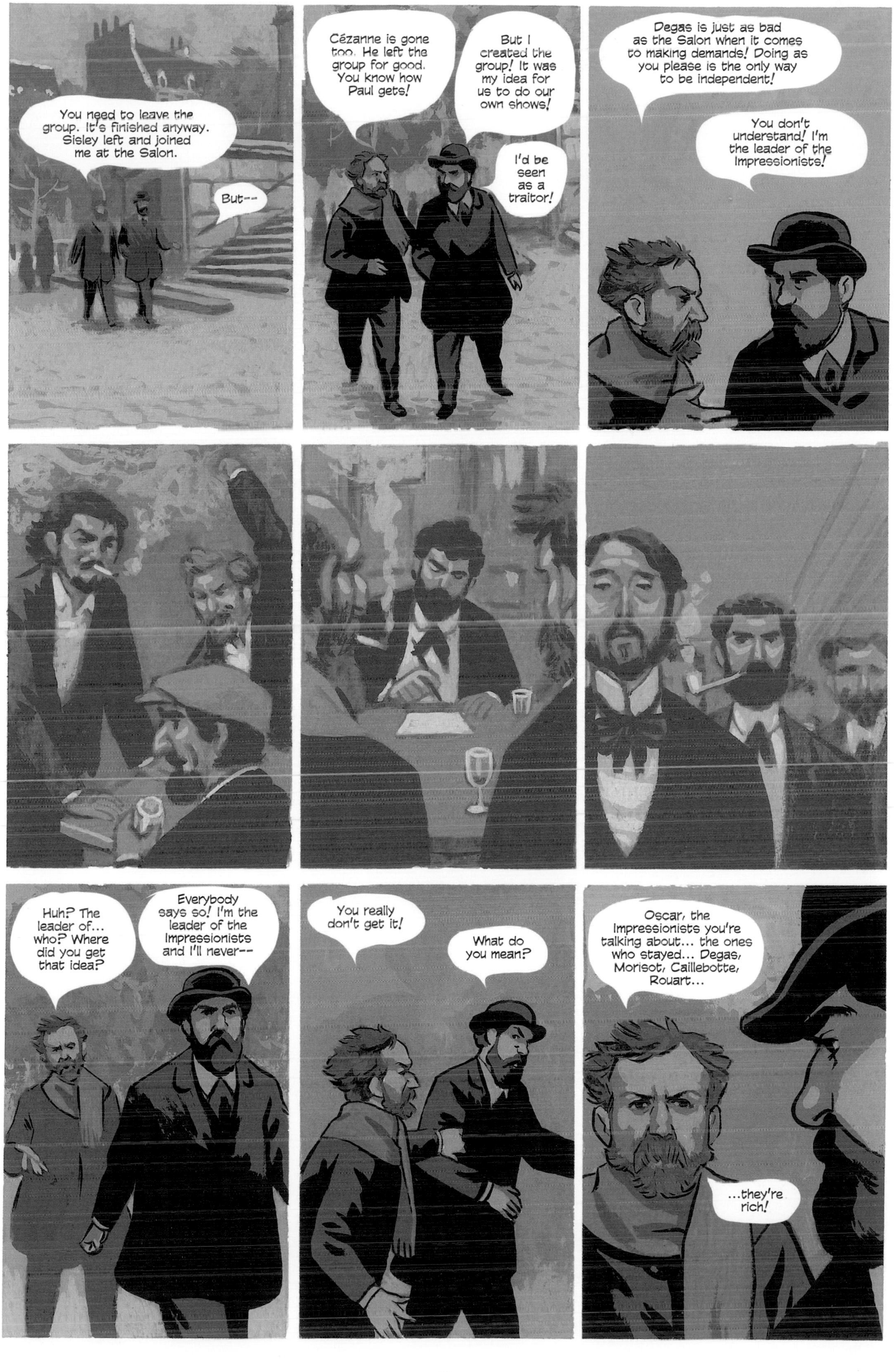
You need to leave the group. It's finished anyway. Sisley left and joined me at the Salon.
But--
Cézanne is gone too. He left the group for good. You know how Paul gets!
But I created the group! It was my idea for us to do our own shows!
I'd be seen as a traitor!
Degas is just as bad as the Salon when it comes to making demands! Doing as you please is the only way to be independent!
You don't understand! I'm the leader of the Impressionists!
Huh? The leader of... who? Where did you get that idea?
Everybody says so! I'm the leader of the Impressionists and I'll never--
You really don't get it!
What do you mean?
Oscar, the Impressionists you're talking about... the ones who stayed... Degas, Morisot, Caillebotte, Rouart...
...they're rich!

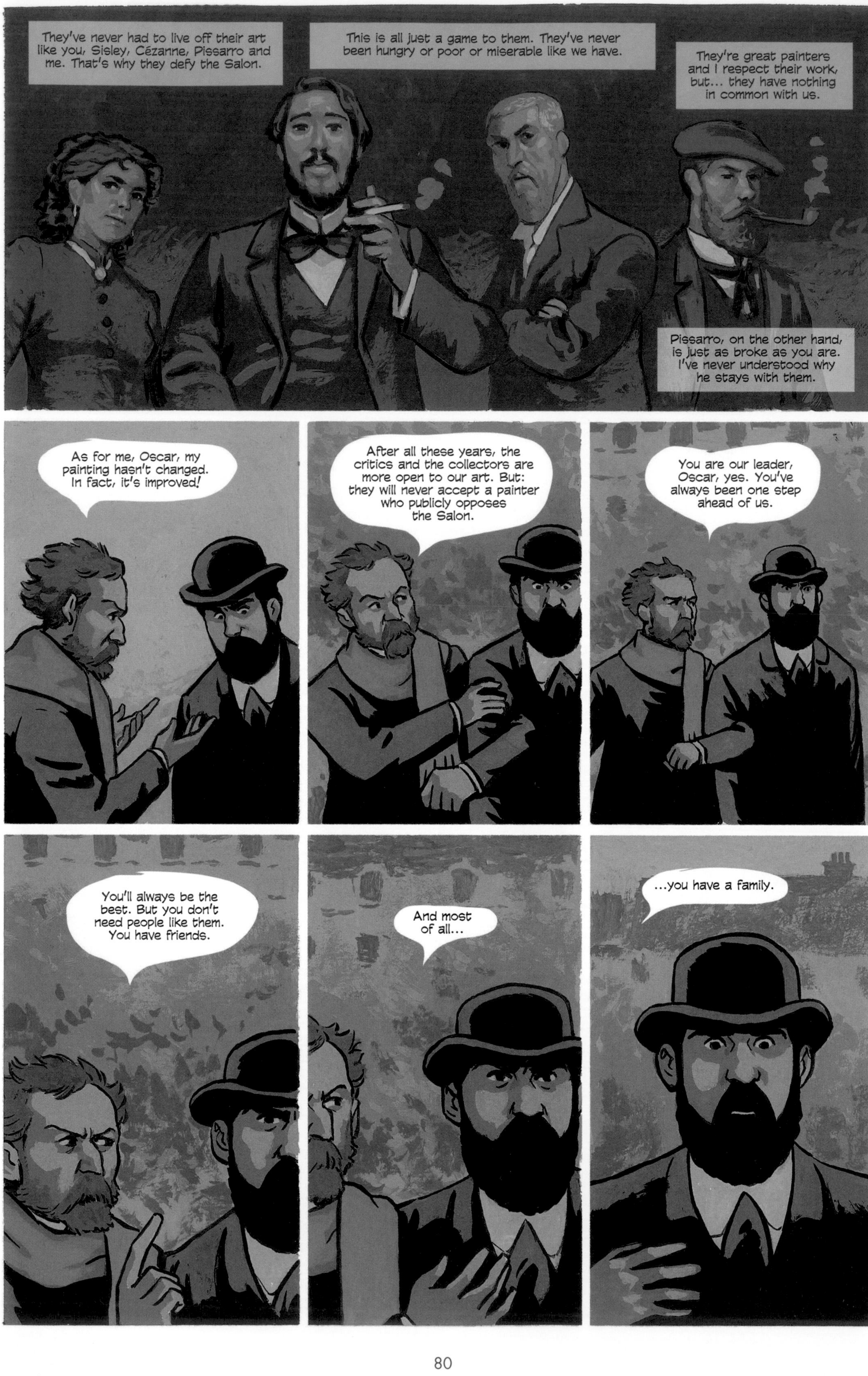
They've never had to live off their art like you, Sisley, Cézanne, Pissarro and me. That's why they defy the Salon.
This is all just a game to them. They've never been hungry or poor or miserable like we have.
They're great painters and I respect their work, but... they have nothing in common with us.
Pissarro, on the other hand, is just as broke as you are. I've never understood why he stays with them.
As for me, Oscar, my painting hasn't changed. In fact, it's improved!
After all these years, the critics and the collectors are more open to our art. But: they will never accept a painter who publicly opposes the Salon.
You are our leader, Oscar, yes. You've always been one step ahead of us.
You'll always be the best. But you don't need people like them. You have friends.
And most of all...
...you have a family.

You're always so removed, Oscar, except from the light you love so much. You could probably live that way for the rest of your life, but your loved ones deserve better.

You've lived with them for years but you act like you're alone.

Do you intend to force this lifestyle on them until the day they die?

If that's the case, then leave them. They don't deserve to be treated this way.

Or you could try giving back what they've given you: love, attention, and support.

They've remained at your side all these years.

You spend so much time staring at landscapes and oceans and rivers that I wonder if you've ever even noticed your loved ones were there.

Don't you think you deserve to succeed... if only for them?

Forget about the Impressionists, Oscar. Join us! Send the Salon your best work! It's high time you reaped what you've sewn.

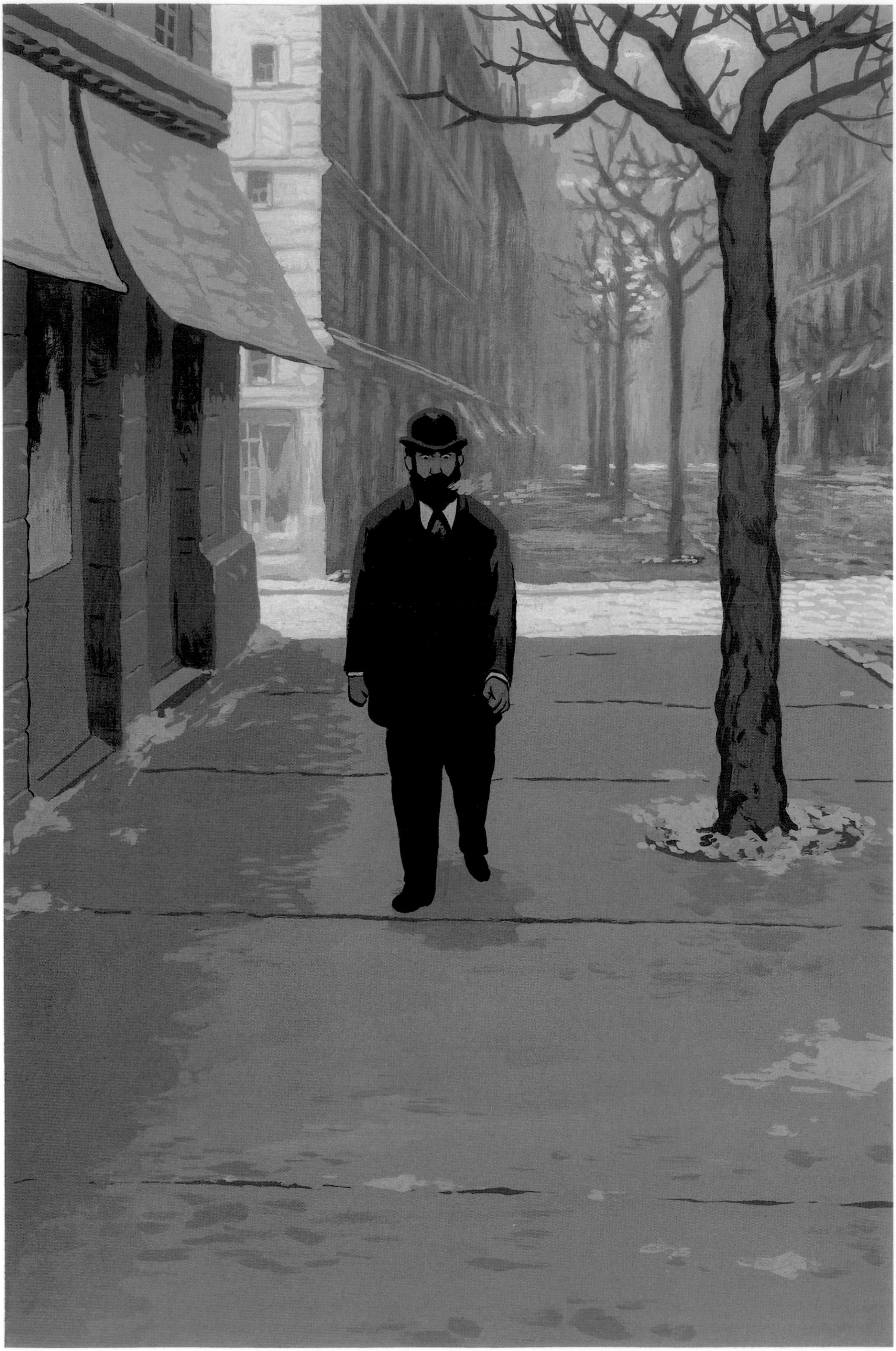

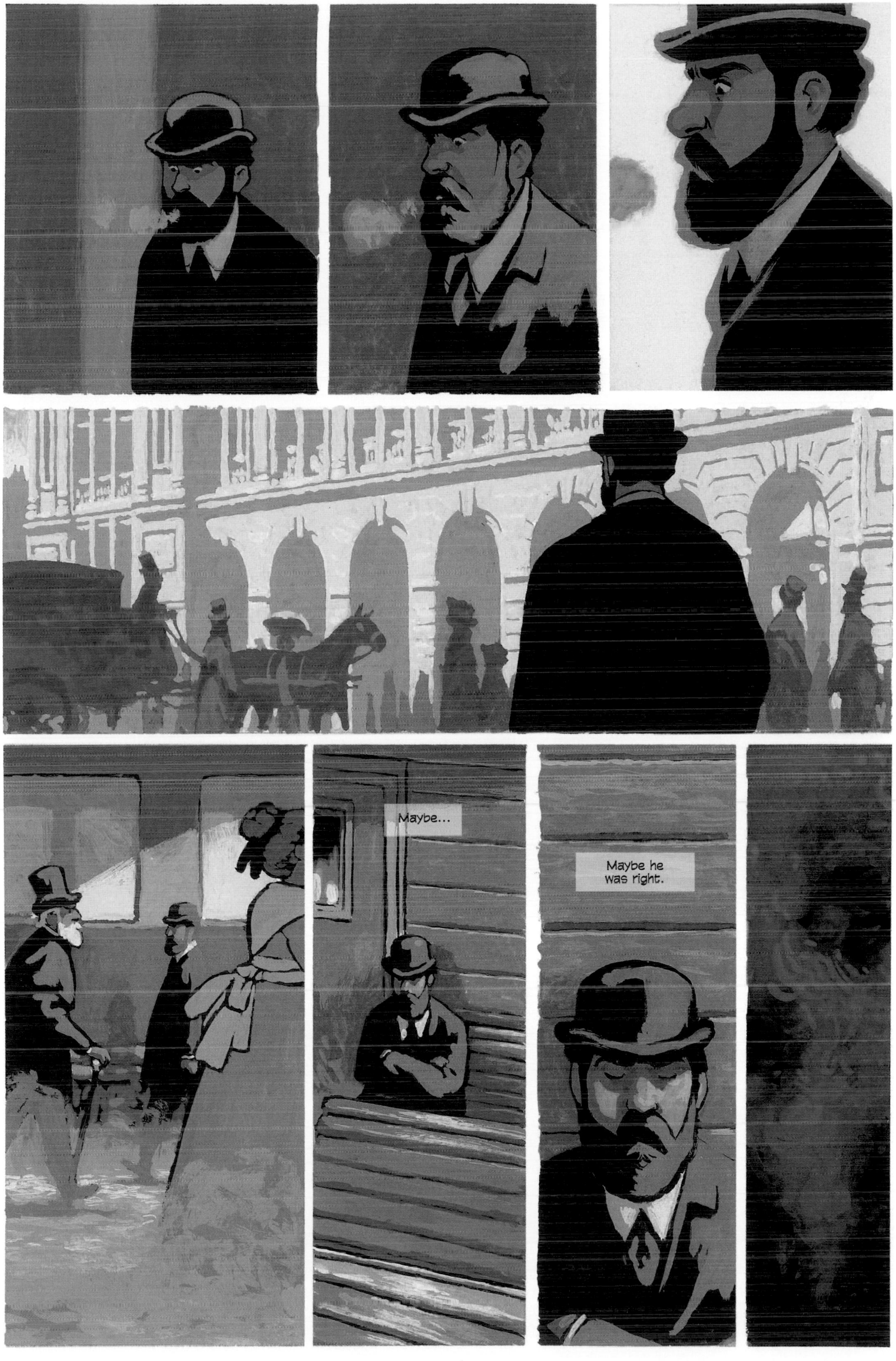
Maybe...
Maybe he was right.

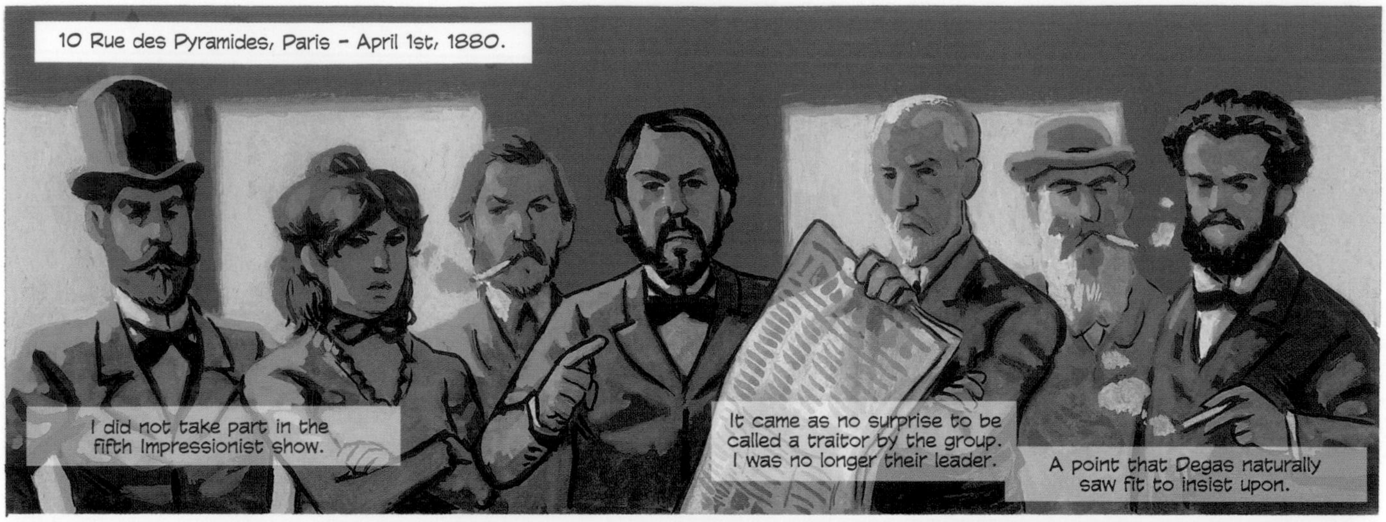
10 Rue des Pyramides, Paris - April 1st, 1880.
I did not take part in the fifth Impressionist show.
It came as no surprise to be called a traitor by the group. I was no longer their leader.
A point that Degas naturally saw fit to insist upon.

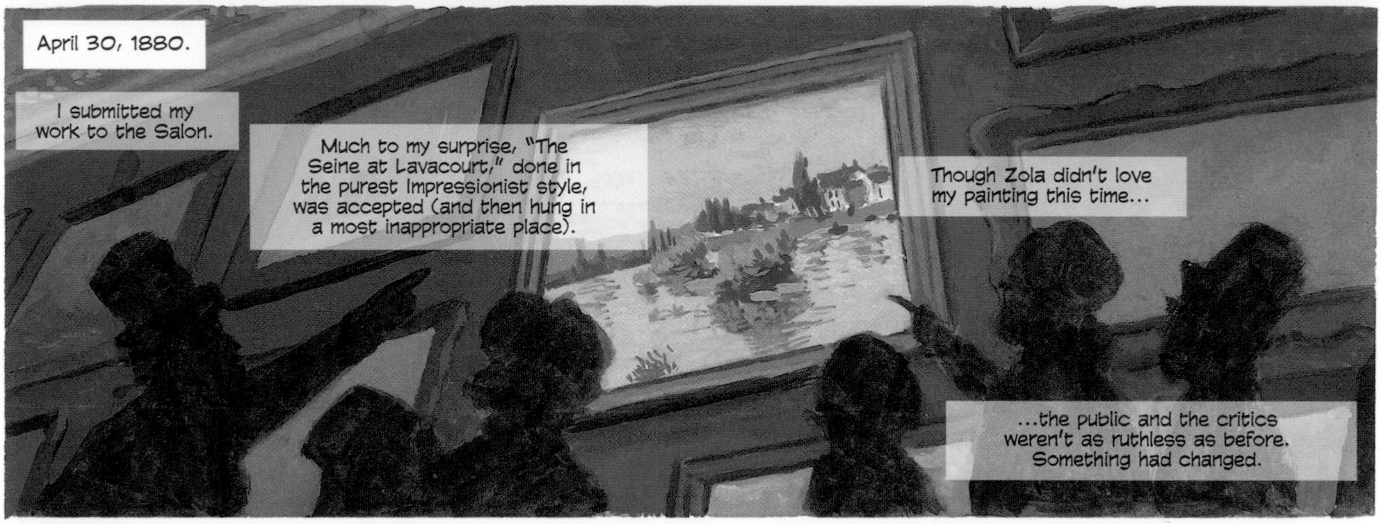
April 30, 1880.
I submitted my work to the Salon.
Much to my surprise, "The Seine at Lavacourt," done in the purest Impressionist style, was accepted (and then hung in a most inappropriate place).
Though Zola didn't love my painting this time...
...the public and the critics weren't as ruthless as before. Something had changed.

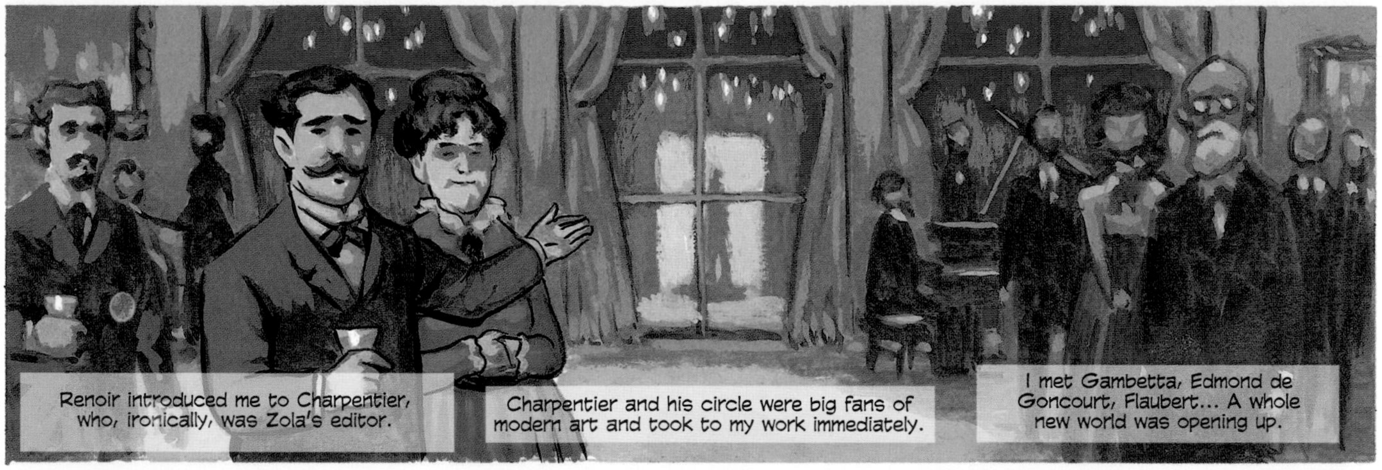
Renoir introduced me to Charpentier, who, ironically, was Zola's editor.
Charpentier and his circle were big fans of modern art and took to my work immediately.
I met Gambetta, Edmond de Goncourt, Flaubert... A whole new world was opening up.

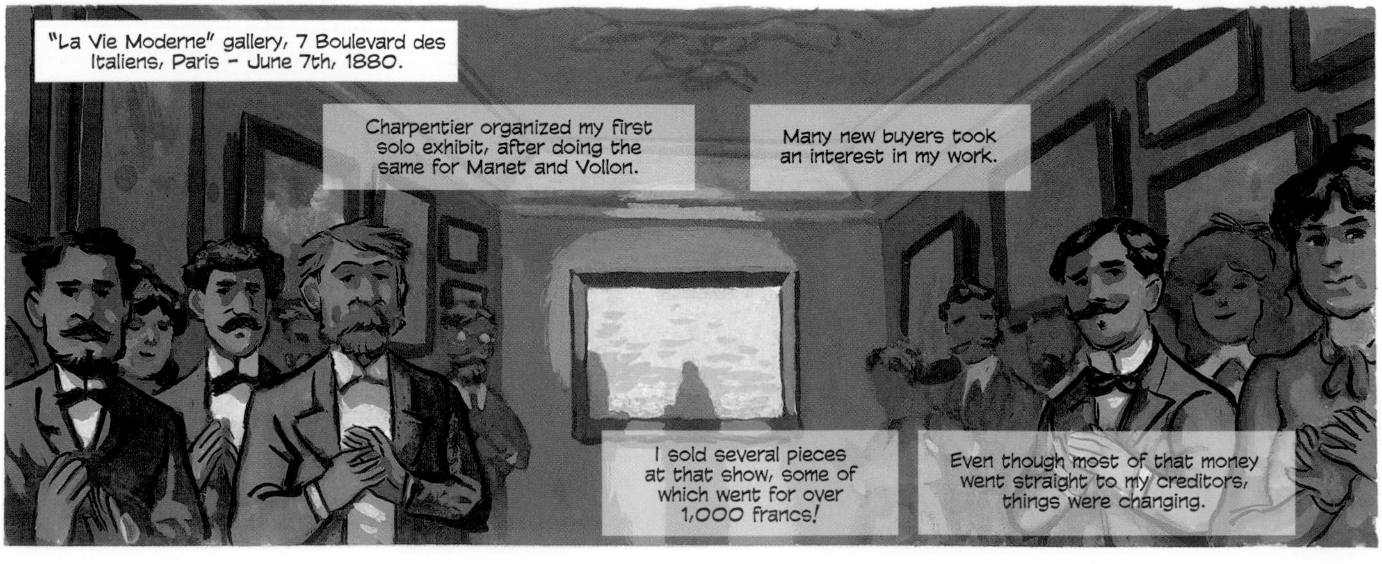
"La Vie Moderne" gallery, 7 Boulevard des Italiens, Paris - June 7th, 1880.
Charpentier organized my first solo exhibit, after doing the same for Manet and Vollon.
Many new buyers took an interest in my work.
I sold several pieces at that show, some of which went for over 1,000 francs!
Even though most of that money went straight to my creditors, things were changing.

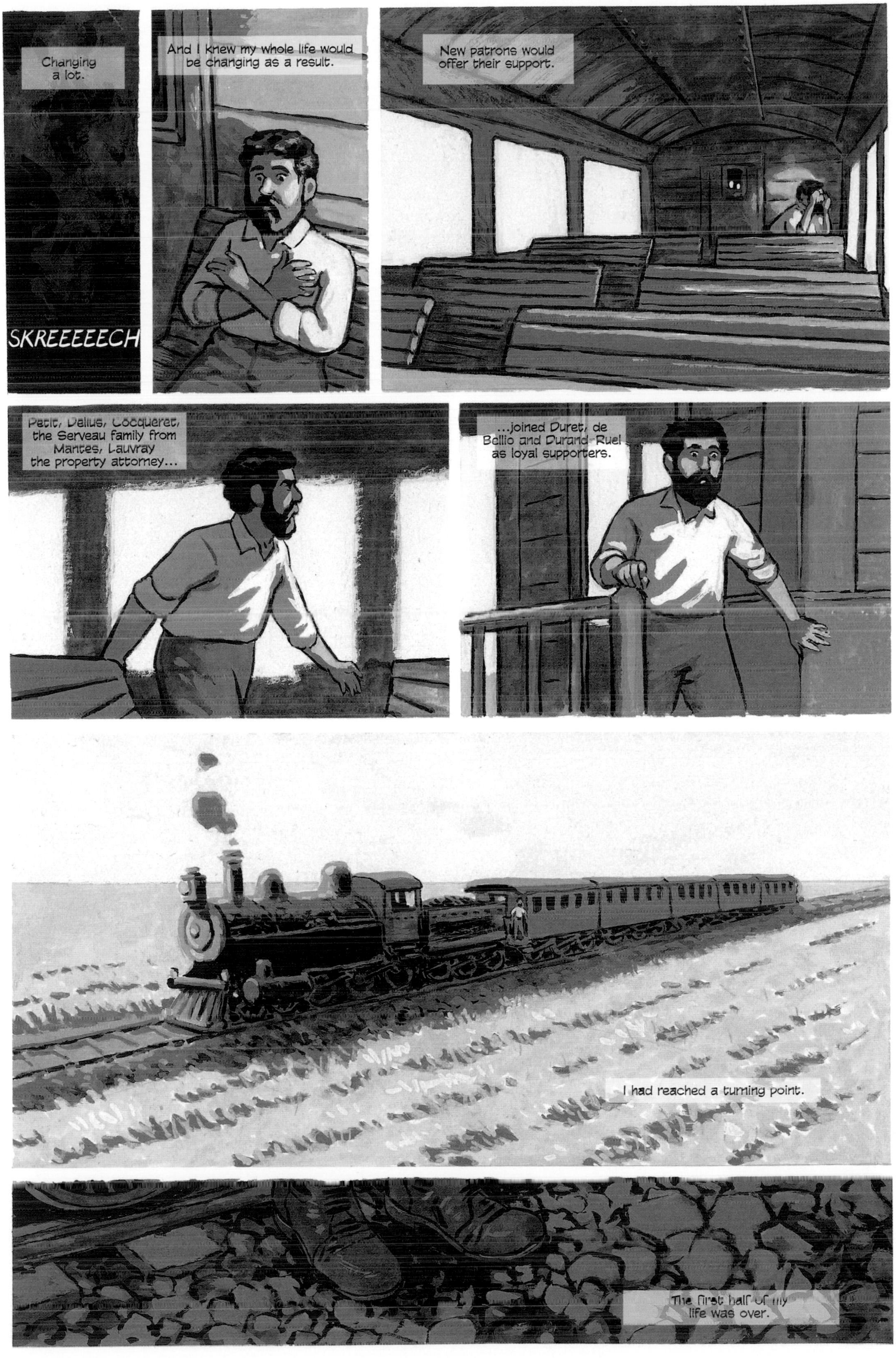
Changing a lot.
SKREEEEECH
And I knew my whole life would be changing as a result.
New patrons would offer their support.
Petit, Dalius, Cocqueret, the Serveau family from Mantes, Lauvray the property attorney...
...joined Duret, de Bellio and Durand-Ruel as loyal supporters.
I had reached a turning point.
The first half of my life was over.

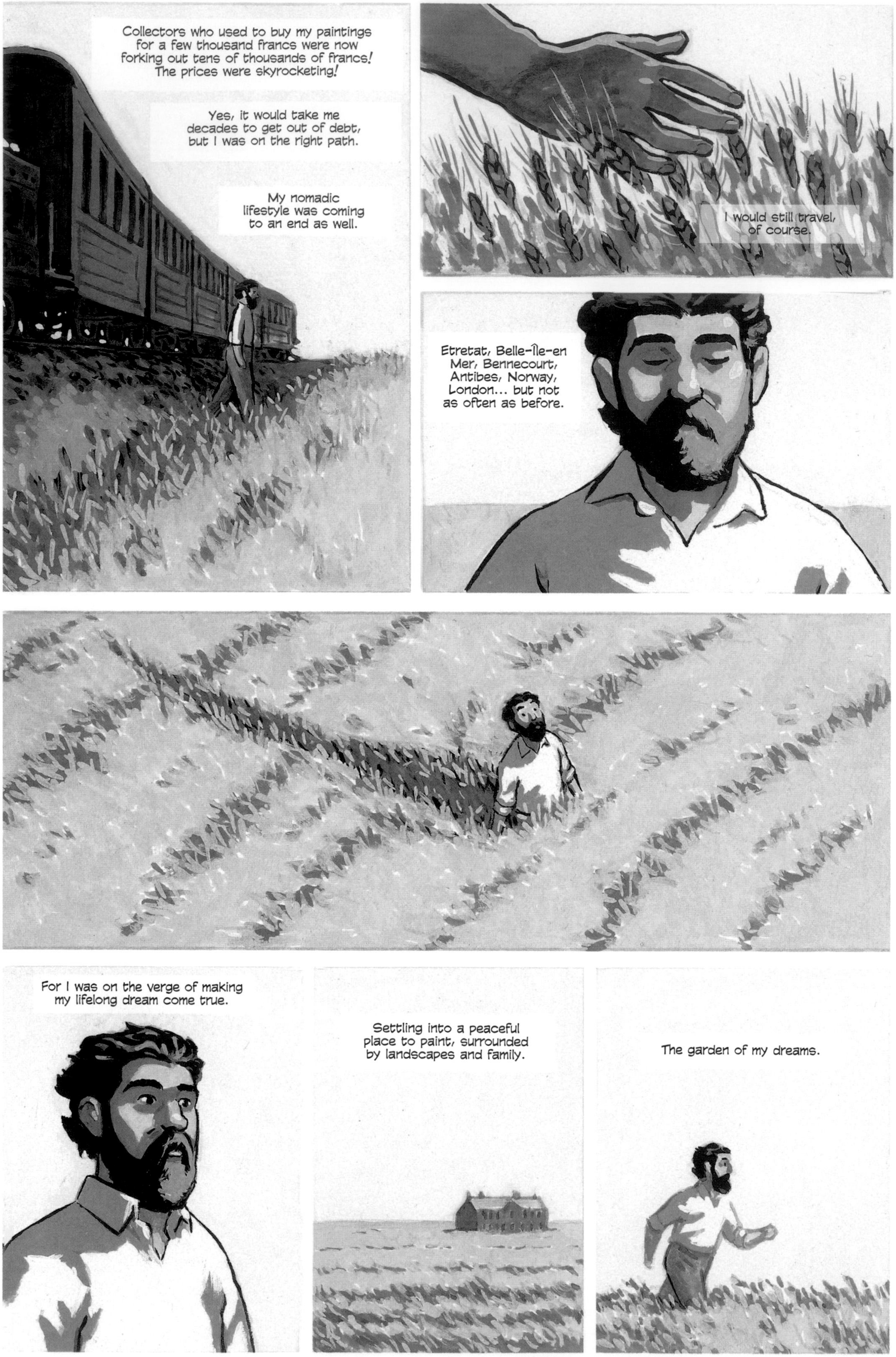
Collectors who used to buy my paintings for a few thousand francs were now forking out tens of thousands of francs! The prices were skyrocketing!
Yes, it would take me decades to get out of debt, but I was on the right path.
My nomadic lifestyle was coming to an end as well.
I would still travel, of course.
Etretat, Belle-Île-en Mer, Bennecourt, Antibes, Norway, London... but not as often as before.
For I was on the verge of making my lifelong dream come true.
Settling into a peaceful place to paint, surrounded by landscapes and family.
The garden of my dreams.

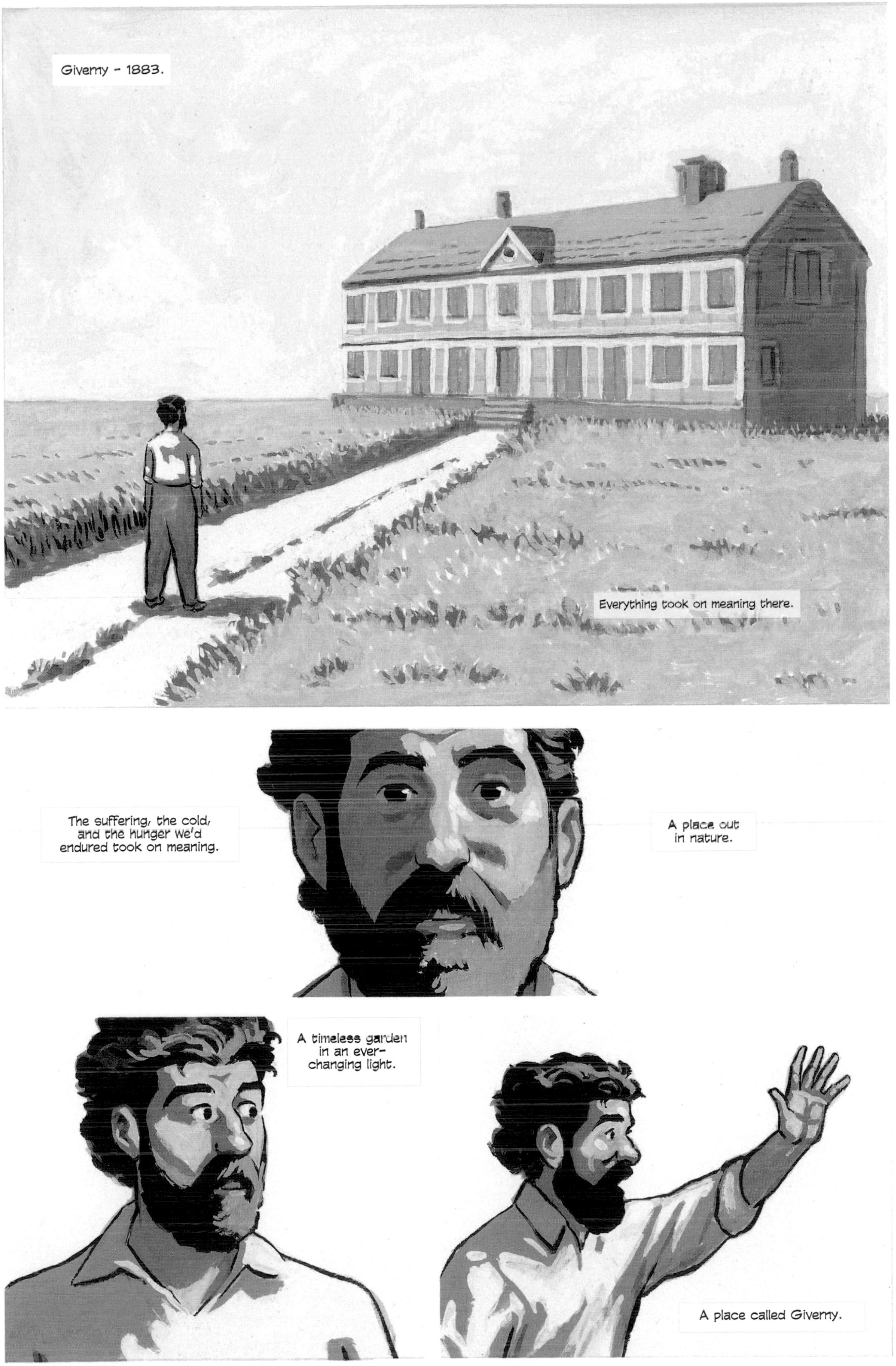
Giverny - 1883.
Everything took on meaning there.
The suffering, the cold, and the hunger we'd endured took on meaning.
A place out in nature.
A timeless garden in an ever-changing light.
A place called Giverny.

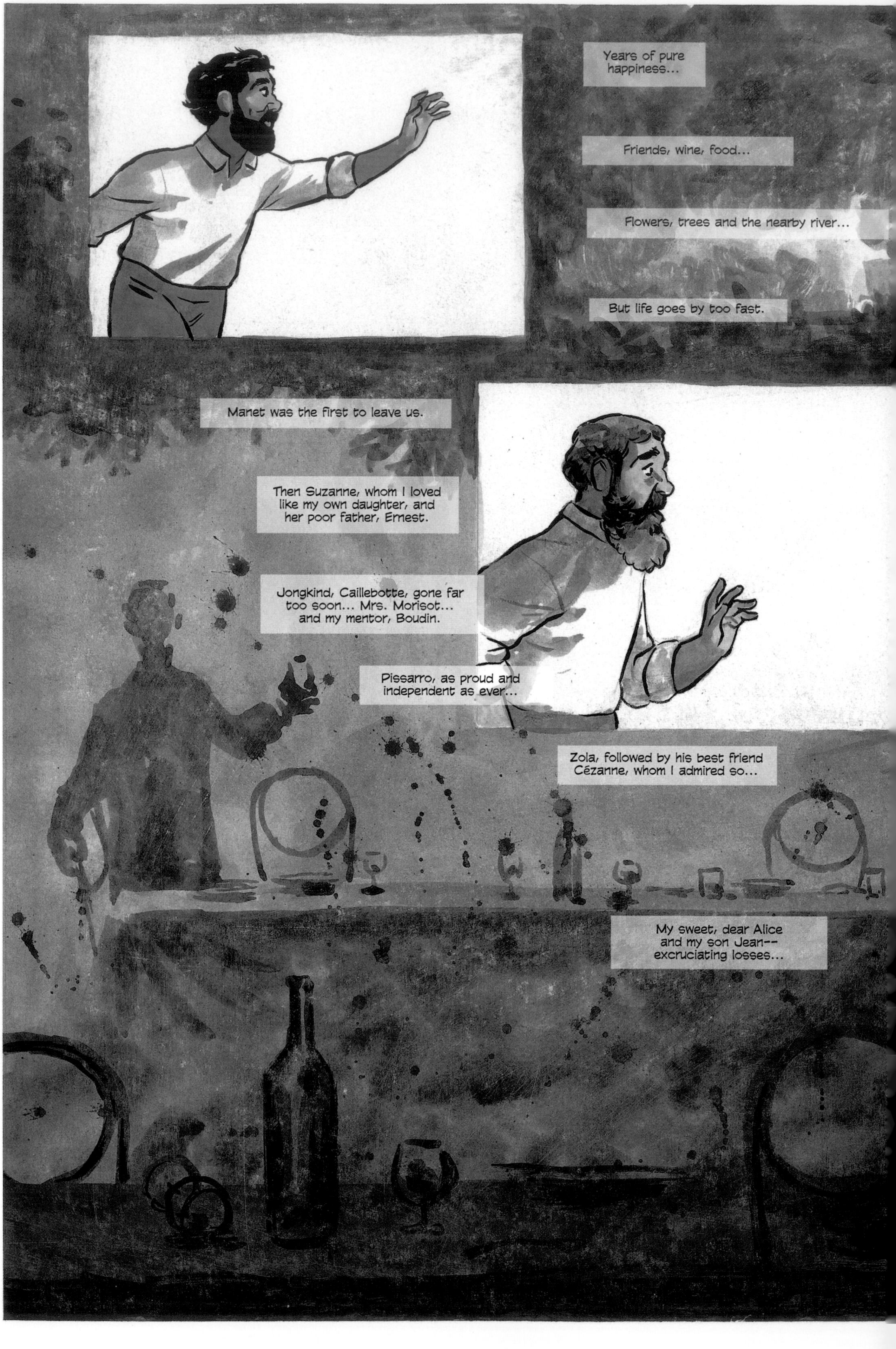
Years of pure happiness...
Friends, wine, food...
Flowers, trees and the nearby river...
But life goes by too fast.
Manet was the first to leave us.
Then Suzanne, whom I loved like my own daughter, and her poor father, Ernest.
Jongkind, Caillebotte, gone far too soon... Mrs. Morisot... and my mentor, Boudin.
Pissarro, as proud and independent as ever...
Zola, followed by his best friend Cézanne, whom I admired so...
My sweet, dear Alice and my son Jean-- excruciating losses...

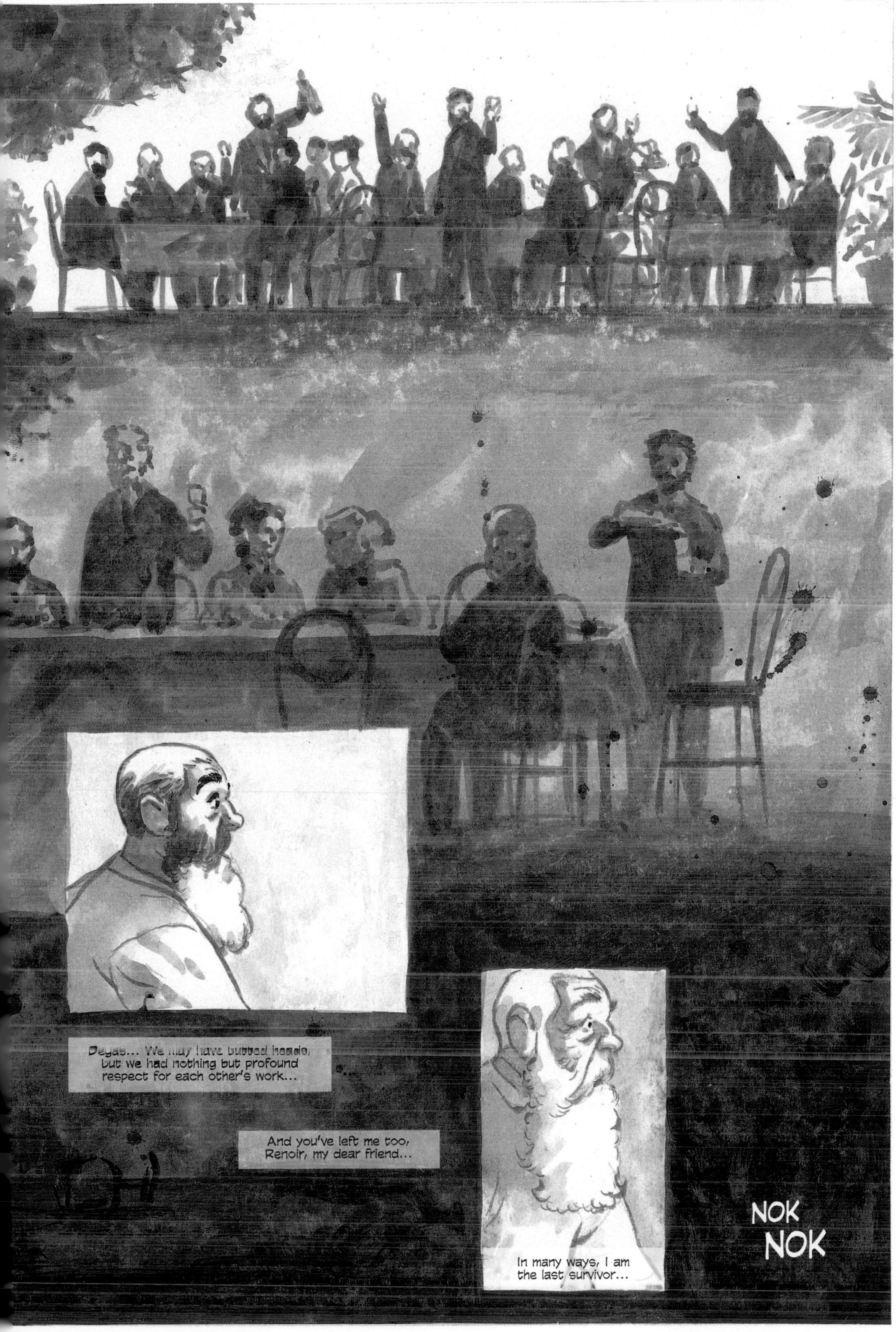
Degas... We may have butted heads, but we had nothing but profound respect for each other's work...
And you've left me too, Renoir, my dear friend...
In many ways, I am the last survivor...
NOK NOK

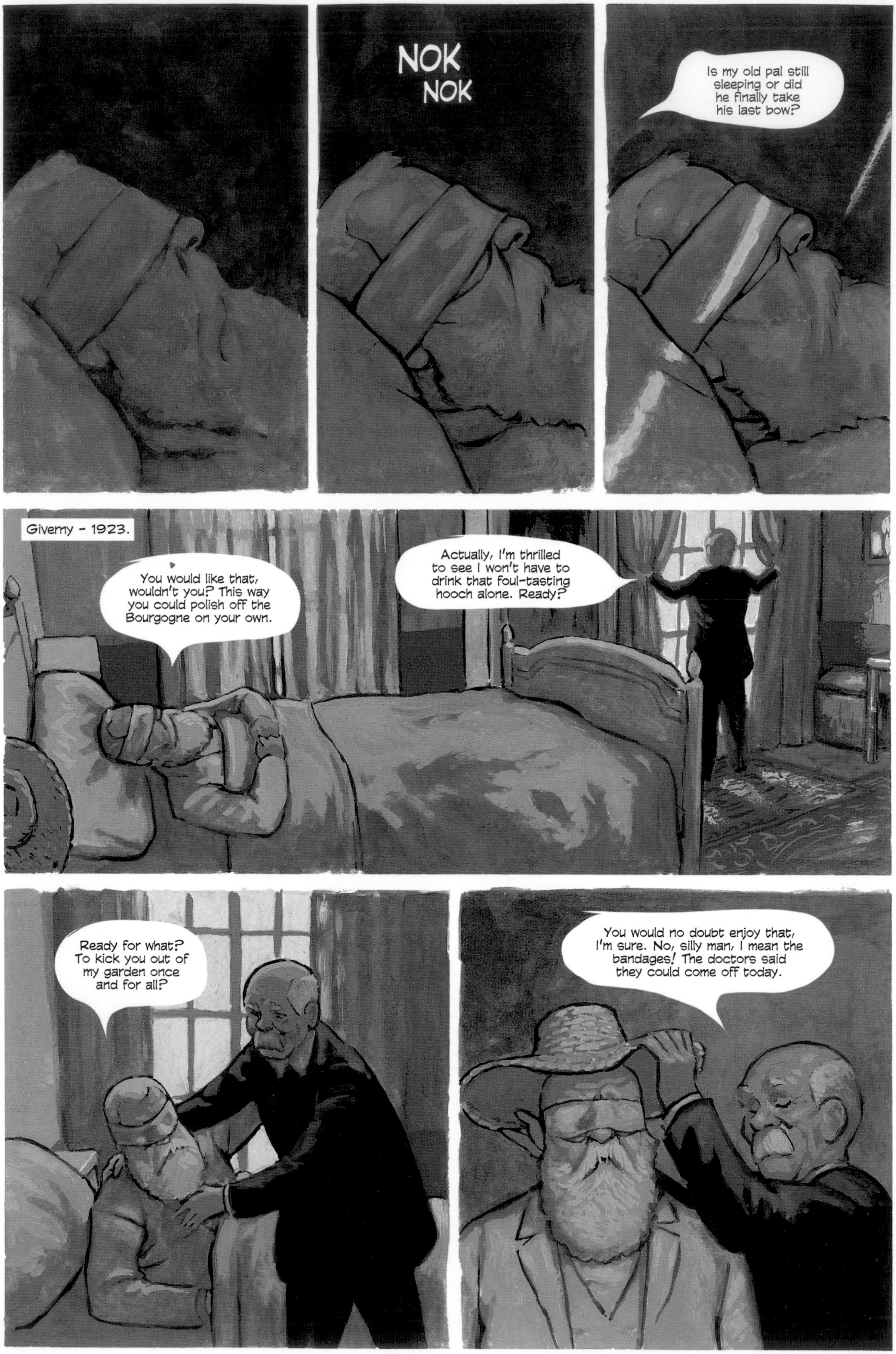
NOK
NOK
Is my old pal still sleeping or did he finally take his last bow?
Giverny - 1923.
You would like that, wouldn't you? This way you could polish off the Bourgogne on your own.
Actually, I'm thrilled to see I won't have to drink that foul-tasting hooch alone. Ready?
Ready for what? To kick you out of my garden once and for all?
You would no doubt enjoy that, I'm sure. No, silly man, I mean the bandages! The doctors said they could come off today.

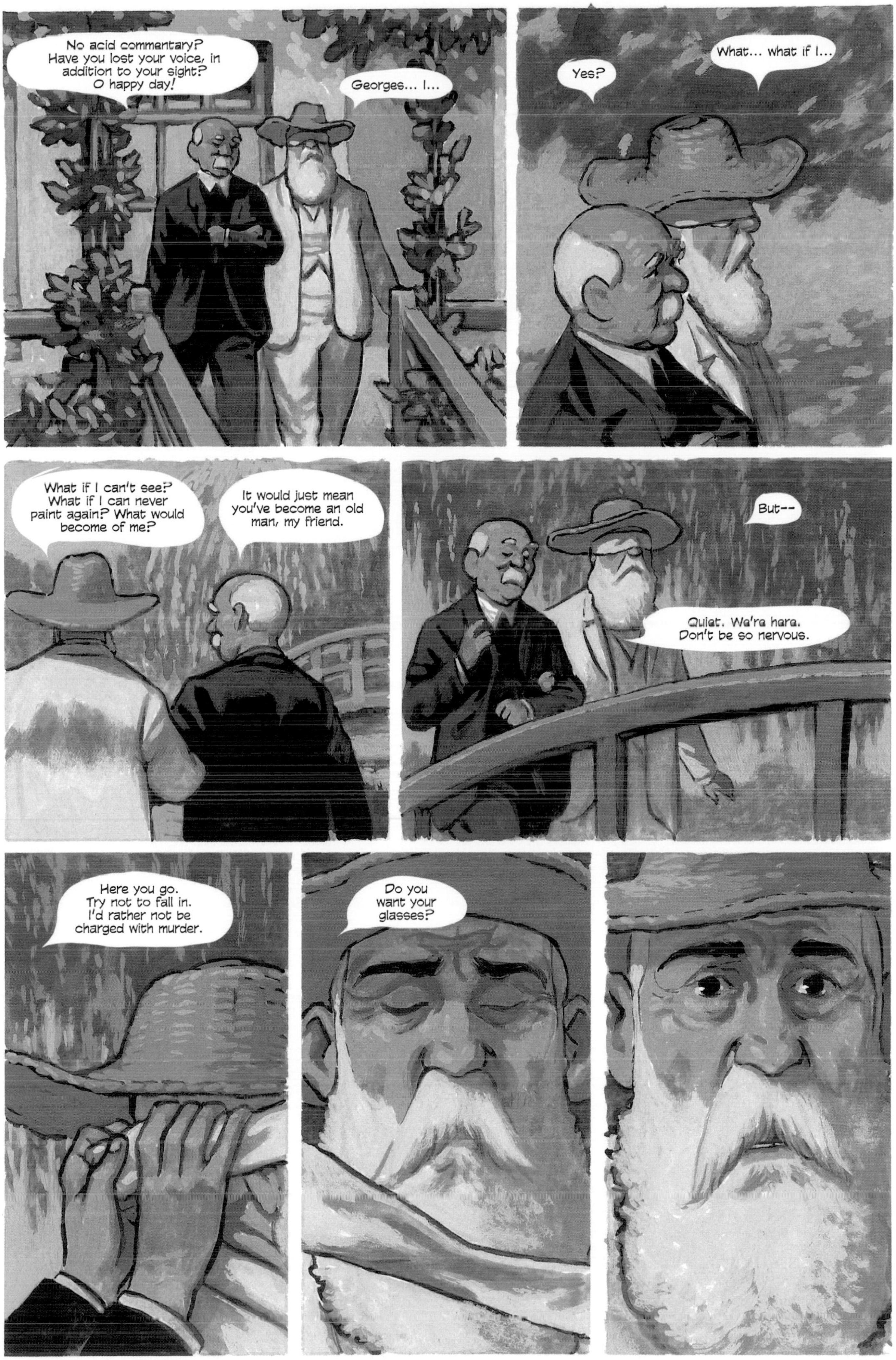
No acid commentary? Have you lost your voice, in addition to your sight? O happy day!
Georges... I...
Yes?
What... what if I...
What if I can't see? What if I can never paint again? What would become of me?
It would just mean you've become an old man, my friend.
But--
Quiet. We're here. Don't be so nervous.
Here you go. Try not to fall in. I'd rather not be charged with murder.
Do you want your glasses?

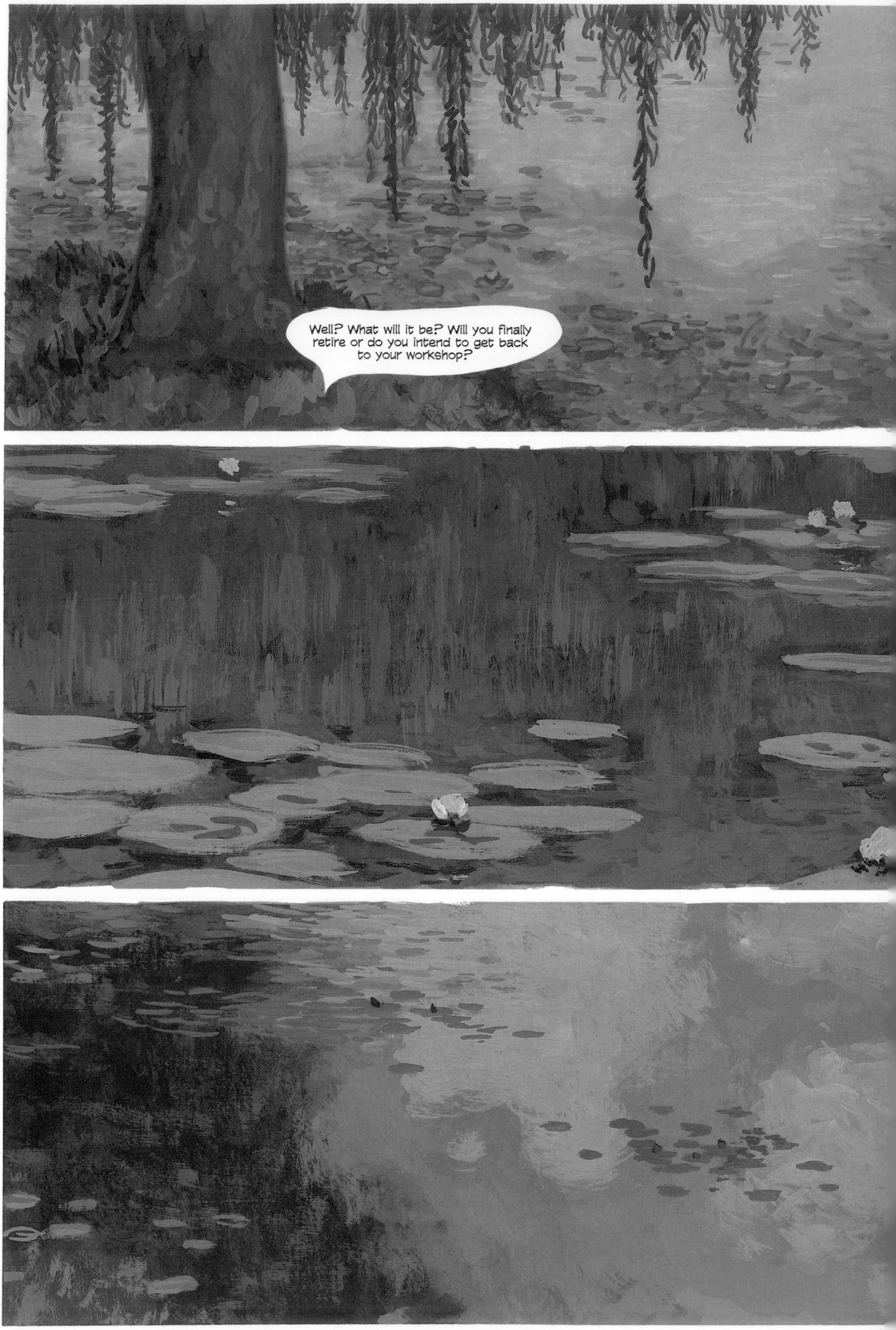
Well? What will it be? Will you finally retire or do you intend to get back to your workshop?

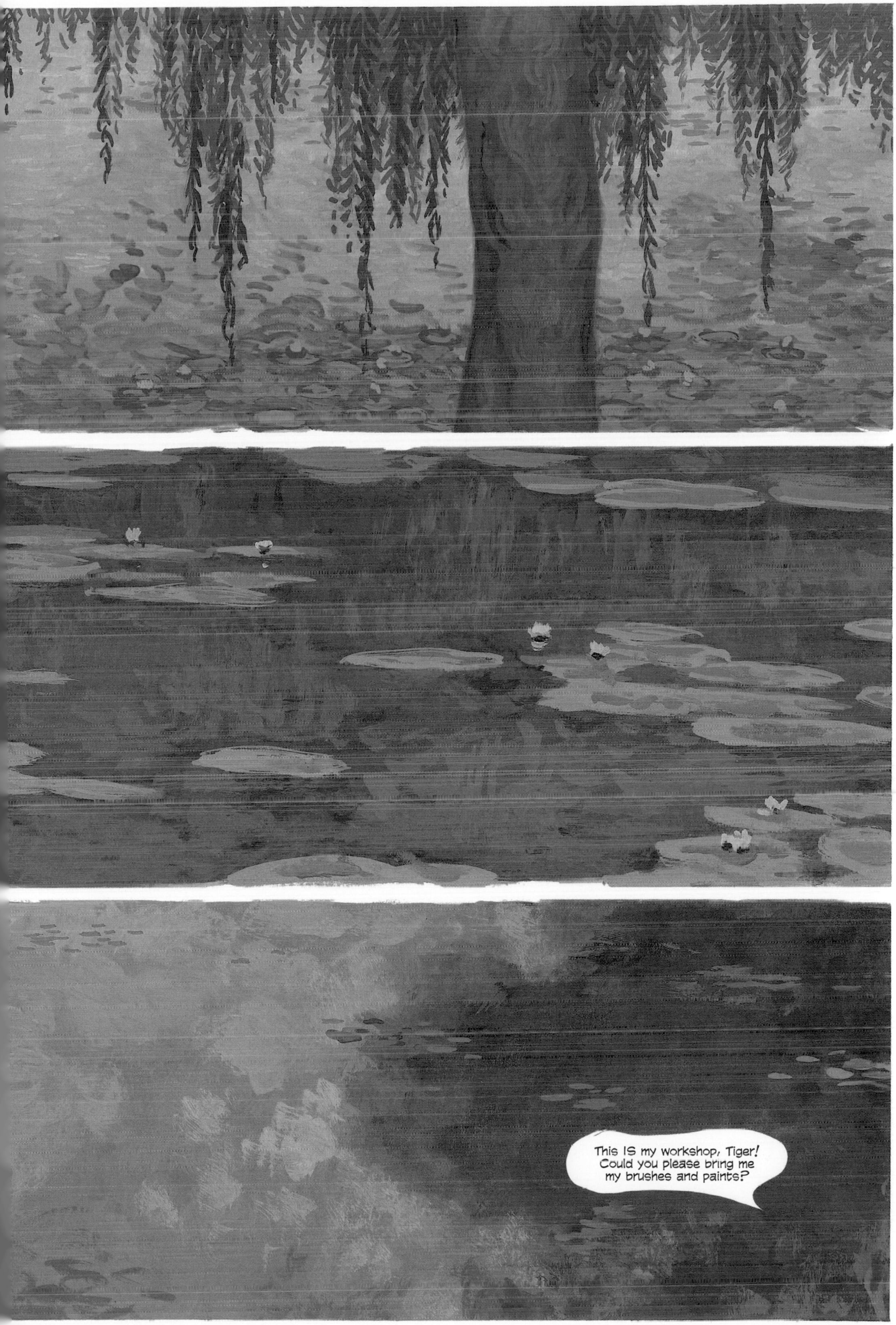
This IS my workshop, Tiger! Could you please bring me my brushes and paints?

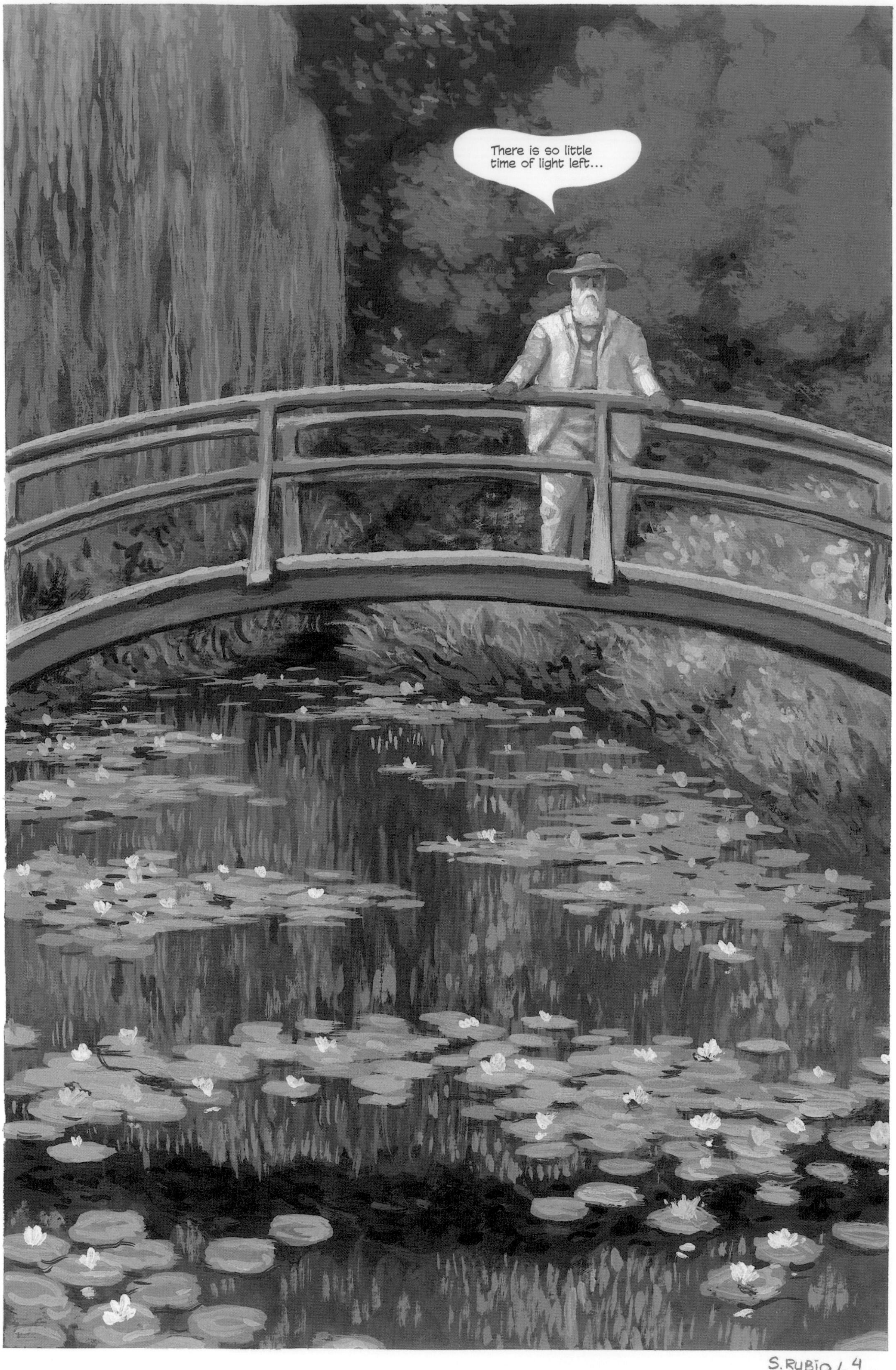
There is so little time of light left...

S. RUBIO + R. EFA / 4 JUNY 2016

Monet's Mirror: Behind the Canvas

Madrid, 2002. As an art history student at the University of Complutense, I was supposed to be studying for my exams, but I was completely engrossed in a fascinating book I was reading: *The History of Impressionism* by John Rewald. Structured like a novel, the book uses a dynamic, journalistic style to recount the captivating adventures of a group of young rebels rising up against the status quo. Essential reading for a young man of twenty-three!

One of the artists in Rewald's book clearly had all the qualities required for my recently discovered calling as a writer: inspiration, determination, and passion. I remember thinking: "Why hasn't Monet's life story ever been the subject of a film or comics?" Fifteen years later, I am grateful for the opportunity to tell that story myself in graphic novel form.

Naturally, this book is an adaptation that uses poetic license and the usual process of developing characters. Much like a film is not a documentary, this graphic novel is not a history book.

However, my training as a historian compels me to list the works referenced in the pages that follow. Readers should keep in mind that those works by Monet chosen for the book are not always presented in the chronological order in which they were created. In many cases, the paintings were selected for the emotional dimension they lend to the narrative.

Furthermore, several passages and monologues have been taken verbatim from various sources.

This graphic novel includes facts and anecdotes presented without any explanation: mysteries that inquisitive readers will enjoy trying to solve.[1]

It is time to shed some light on Monet's life.

Salva Rubio

BIBLIOGRAPHY

Bonafoux, P. (2010) : *Monet (1840-1926)*, Perrin, Paris.

Clemenceau, G. (2010) : *Claude Monet "intime"*, Parkstone Press International, New York.

Heinrich, C. (2000) : *Monet*, Taschen, Köln.

Lobstein, D. (2002) : *Monet*, Éditions Jean-Paul Gisserot, Paris.

Rewald, J. (1973) : *Historia del impresionismo*, Seix Barral, Barcelona.

Roe, S. (2006) : *The Private Lives of the Impressionists*, HarperCollins, New York.

Sagner-Düchting, K. (2006) : *Monet*, Taschen, Köln.

Walther, I. F. (2010) : *Impressionism*, Taschen, Köln.

Wildenstein, D. (2014) : *Monet ou le Triomphe de l'impressionnisme*, Taschen, Köln.

Zambianchi, C. (2008) : *Monet et la Peinture en plein air*, Le Figaro, Paris.

---

1 : For reasons of layout, the dimensions of some of the paintings are not an accurate representation of the real dimensions. Additionally, since some of the sources we used were contradictory, the book may contain errors, for which we apologize and for which, as the writer, I take full and sole responsibility.

PAGE 10 : The overall mood of this page was inspired by the many paintings Eugène Boudin did of the Trouville beach, most notably the *Beach Near Trouville* with the blue sky and the one with the cloudy sky (1890), on display at London's National Gallery.

Beach Near Trouville, Eugène Boudin, 1864

© *Beach Near Trouville,* 1864 (oil on canvas), Boudin, Eugene Louis (1824-98) / Art Gallery of Ontario, Toronto, Canada / Anonymous gift, 1991 / Bridgeman Images

PAGE 12 : We thought it would be a good idea to place Monet in his first famous landscape, *View at Rouelles* (Le Havre, 1858). As suggested by the position of the easel, this view is exactly the one Monet is about to paint.

View at Rouelles, Claude Monet, 1858

© *View at Rouelles,* 1858, Monet, Claude (1840-1926) / Private Collection / Noortman Master Paintings, Amsterdam / Bridgeman Images

PAGE 14 : This image of Paris was inspired by Van Gogh's *Rooftops in Paris* (1886). We got carried away by our enthusiasm and love for the famous Dutch painter and didn't hesitate to place this painting... 24 years before it was actually painted! We hope our readers will forgive us for this anachronism.

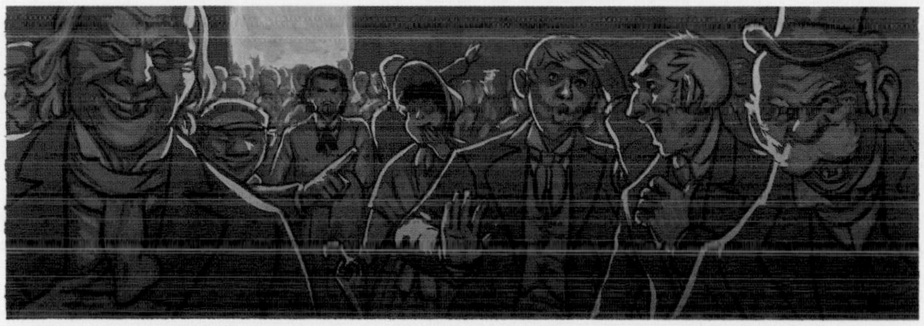

PAGE 18 : For the many attitudes, expressions and faces of the visitors, Ricard Efa drew his inspiration not only from the statuettes and caricatures of one of Monet's contemporaries, but also from Louis Léopold Boilly's *Group of Thirty-Five Heads* (circa 1823).

The Luncheon on the Grass, Édouard Manet, 1863

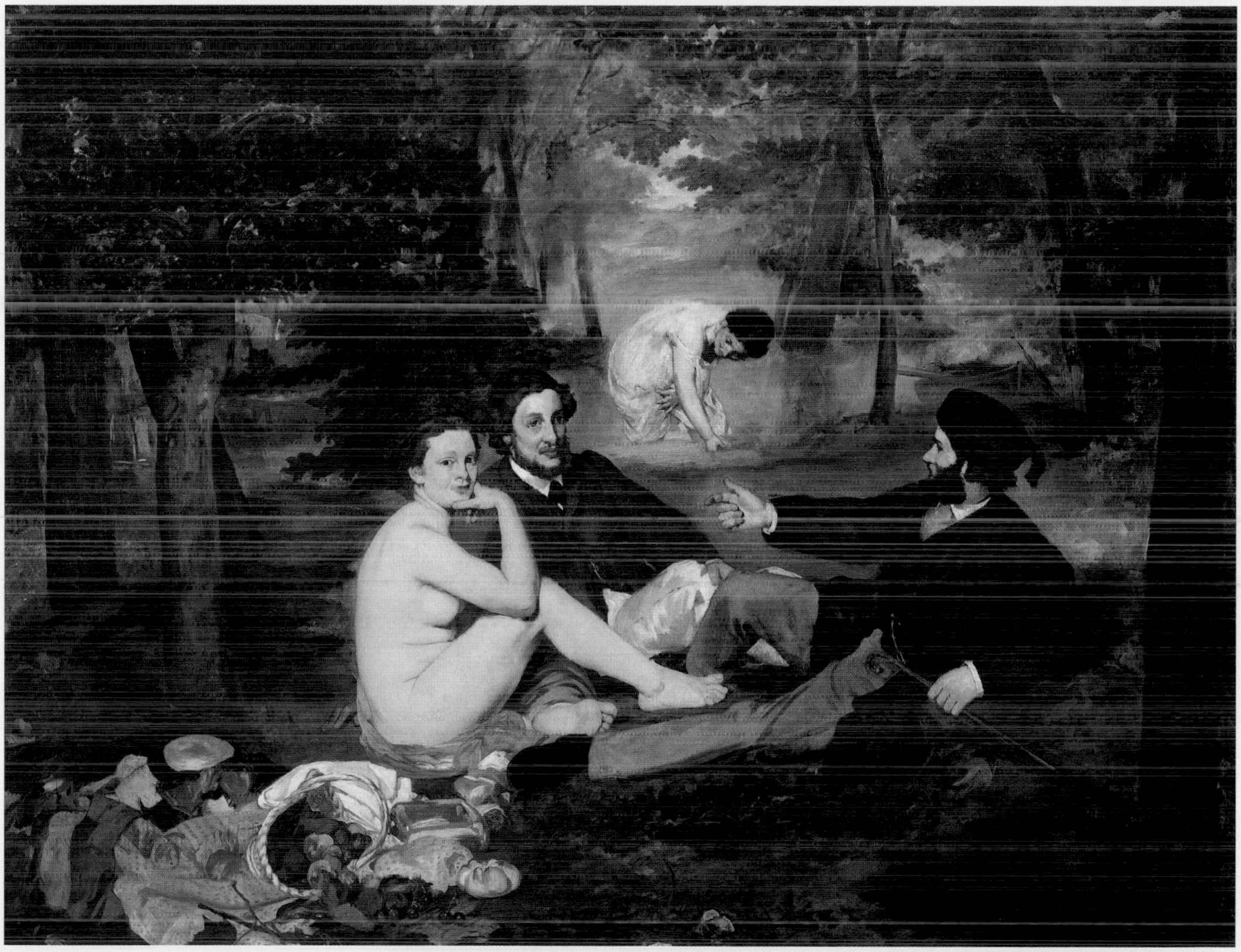

PAGE 19: Though it needs no introduction, the painting Monet is admiring is Édouard Manet's *The Luncheon on the Grass*. This work, which caused a huge scandal at the time, was a key source of inspiration for Monet and his friends.

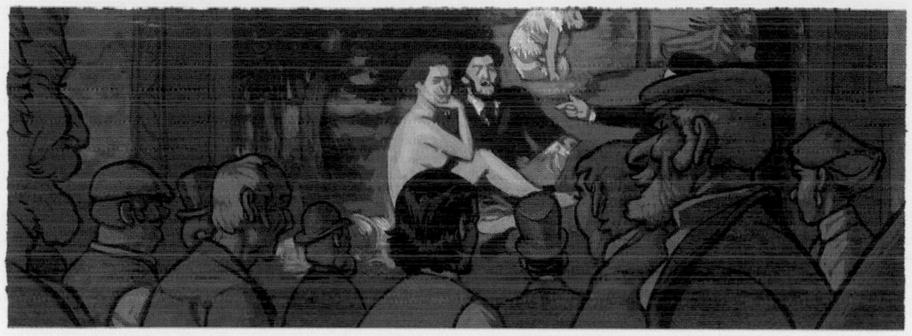

PAGE 23 : As alert readers will have no doubt observed, the painting the group is working on is none other than Monet's *The Road from Chailly to Fontainebleau* (1864).

The Luncheon on the Grass,
Claude Monet, 1865-1866

© THE LUNCHEON ON THE GRASS, 1865-1866 (OIL ON CANVAS), MONET, CLAUDE (1840-1926) / PUSHKIN MUSEUM, MOSCOW, RUSSIA / BRIDGEMAN IMAGES

PAGES 24-25 : This two-page spread reproduces one of Monet's most ambitious works, which was an homage but also a challenge to Manet, because of the dimensions and the subject matter. Monet's *Luncheon on the Grass* brings together several of his friends, including Bazille, whom he used as a model for several of the characters, and Camille, who makes her first appearance in the graphic novel here. This huge painting was damaged and cut into different pieces, so we drew from the étude of it that belongs to Moscow's Pushkin State Museum of Fine Arts. Putting Monet inside the painting while he's metaphorically—or perhaps for real—painting his friends is a mirror effect inspired, it goes without saying, by Velázquez's *Las Meninas.*

PAGE 26 : Another mirror effect. The accident Monet was involved in gives his friend Frédéric Bazille the opportunity to paint a work titled *The Improvised Field Hospital.* We thought it would be interesting to show the scene from the opposite point of view.

PAGE 27 : Readers will have no doubt recognized one of Monet's most famous paintings, *Camille, or The Woman in the Green Dress* (1866), in a version that's probably more realistic and romantic.

Camille, or The Woman in the Green Dress, Claude Monet, 1866

© CAMILLE, OR THE WOMAN IN THE GREEN DRESS, 1866 (OIL ON CANVAS), MONET, CLAUDE (1840-1926) / KUNST-HALLE, BREMEN, GERMANY / BRIDGEMAN IMAGES

PAGE 30 : The first panel is a reference to a beautiful painting by Corot, *Little Chaville* (circa 1823, i.e. one of the artist's first works), belonging to the Ashmolean Museum at Oxford. The next page is another famous painting by Monet, *Women in the Garden* (1866). Camille is thought to be have been the model for most of the characters. Like many other authors, we had fun trying to guess the identity of the redhead, who was probably one of Monet's ex-lovers.

Women in the Garden, Claude Monet, 1866

© WOMEN IN THE GARDEN, 1866 (OIL ON CANVAS), MONET, CLAUDE (1840-1926) / MUSÉE D'ORSAY, PARIS, FRANCE / BRIDGEMAN IMAGES

PAGE 37 : In yet another mirror effect, Monet is getting ready to paint *The Luncheon* (1868) and is asking his models to strike a pose. The canvas should be bigger: the work, which belongs to the Städel Museum in Frankfurt, measures 231.5 x 151 cm. We reduced the size to make it look like Monet is doing an étude. This page also features a reference to another work by Monet, *On the Seine at Bennecourt* (1868), whose open, peaceful mood is a perfect reflection of that time in his life.

PAGE 40 : This is another famous painting by Monet, *Bain à La Genouillère* (1869). We chose it because it represents one of the key moments in Monet's evolution towards a purely impressionist style, and also because it embodies the close bond between Claude Monet and Pierre-Auguste Renoir.

Bain à la Grenouillère, Claude Monet, 1869

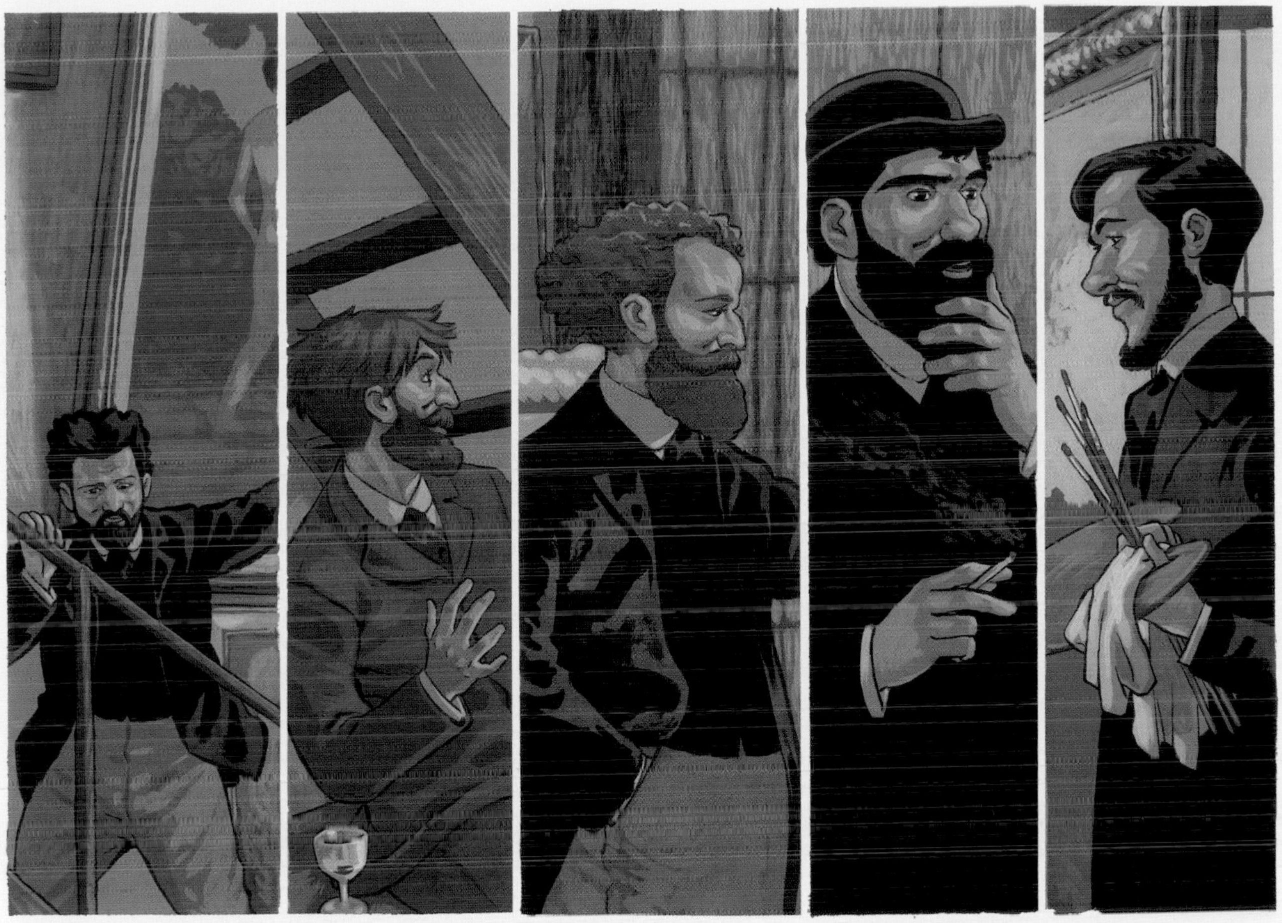

PAGE 42 : An homage to Bazille's most famous painting, *Bazille's Studio* (1870) and a tribute to the friendship and mutual admiration between the different members of the group. This work also portrays one of the last peaceful moments before the war broke out.

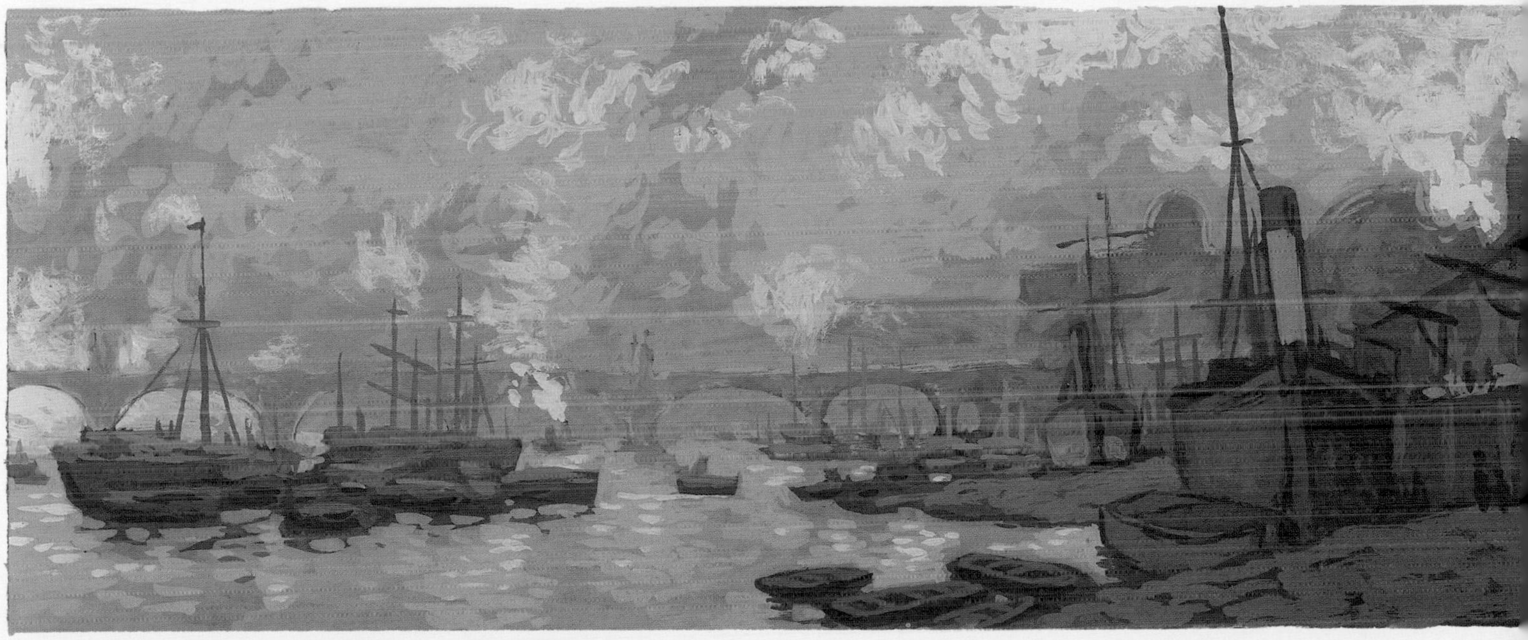

PAGE 44 : The cold, misty and humid atmosphere of London is a perfect illustration of that particular period in Monet's life. We found the best representation of that atmosphere, as well as the typical boats and docks, in *Boats in the Port of London* (1871), a work that is nothing like the more famous foggy and enchanting images the artist painted in the 1890s.

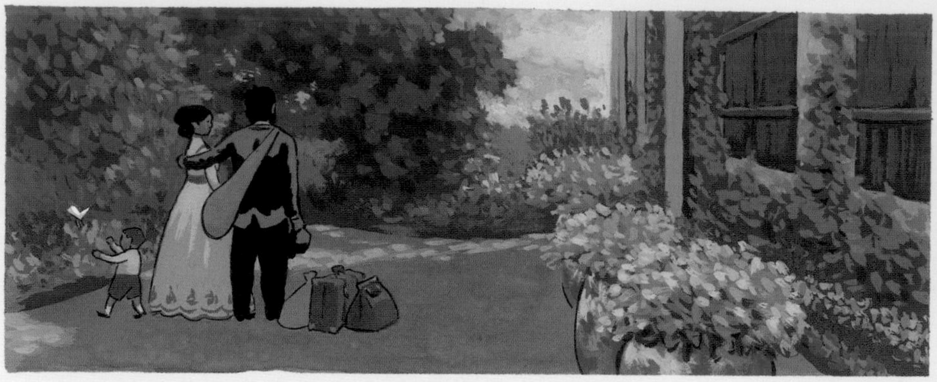

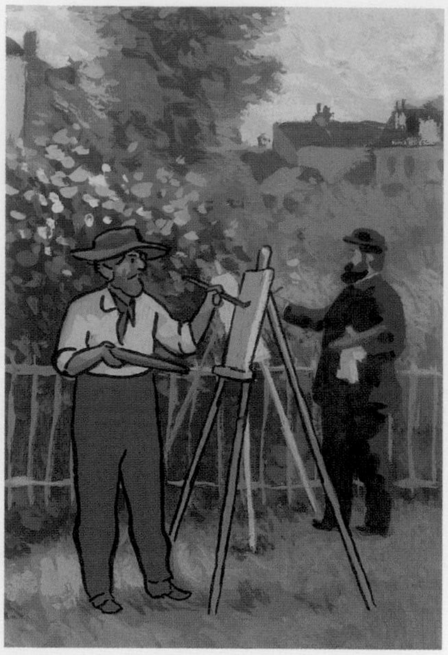

PAGE 47 : The first panel is a reference to *The Artist's House at Argenteuil* (1873). The other panels present another mirror effect, this one inspired by the influence Monet and his friends had on each other during the Argenteuil days: Monet is probably painting *The Artist's House at Argenteuil*, while Renoir is painting Monet in *Monet Painting in His Garden at Argenteuil*. Manet would later also paint his friend in *Monet in His Studio Boat*.

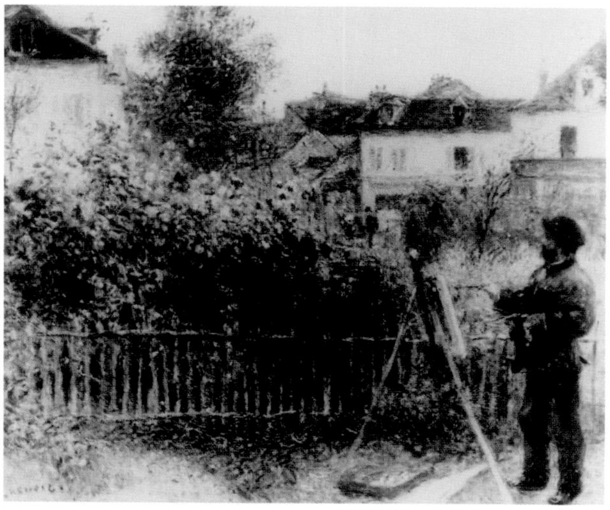

Claude Monet Painting in his Garden at Argenteuil,
Auguste Renoir, 1873

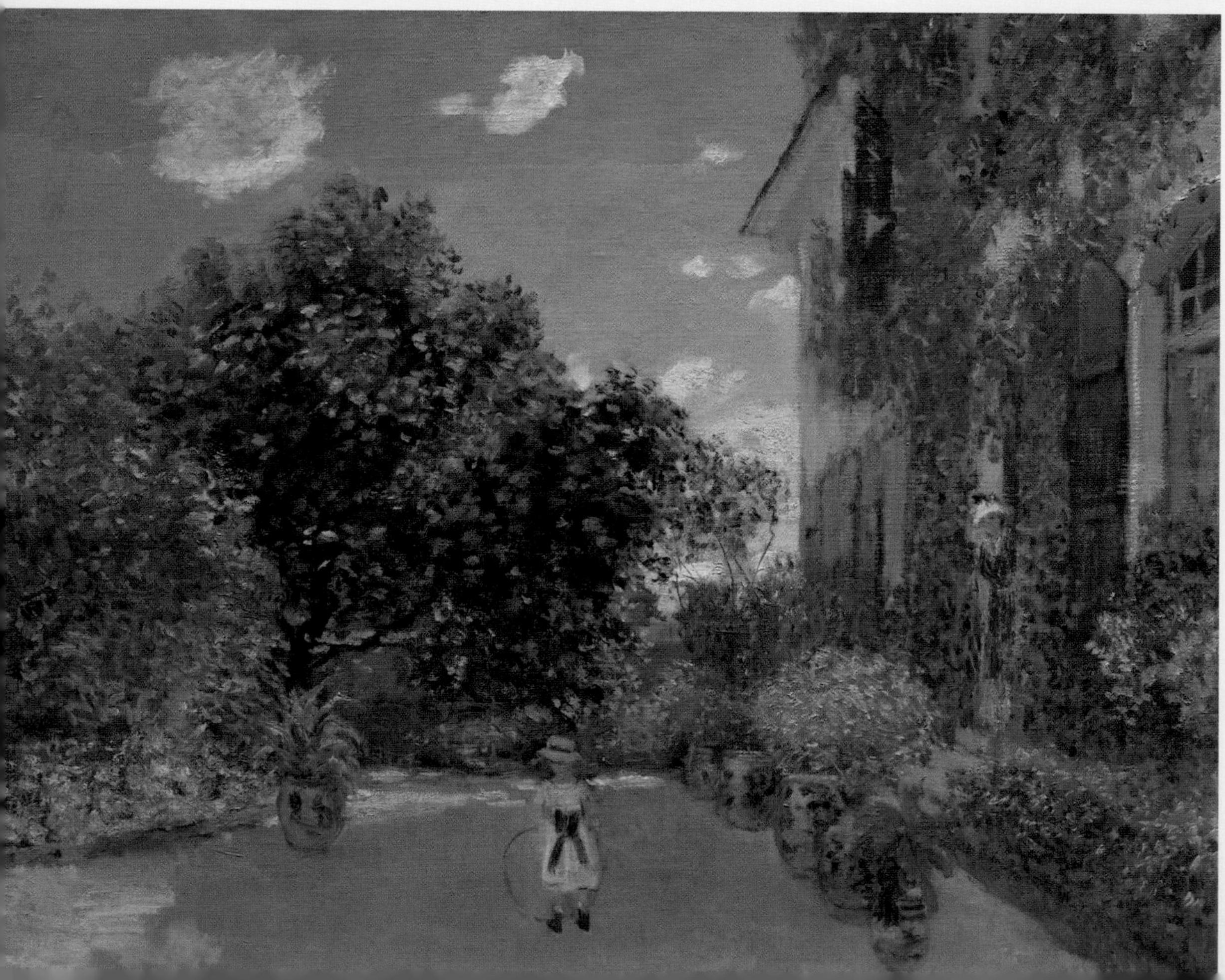

The Artist's House at Argenteuil,
Claude Monet, 1873

PAGE 48 : The days of happiness and productivity Monet experiences in Argenteuil inspired most of the scenes on this page: *The Reader* (1872); *Lilacs, Grey Weather* (1872-1873); *Jean Monet on His Hobby Horse* (1872); *Camille Monet at the Window* (1873); *The Monet Family in the Garden*, by Manet (1874); *Wild Poppies, near Argenteuil,* (1873); and of course *Impression: Sunrise*, a view of Le Havre dated 1872.

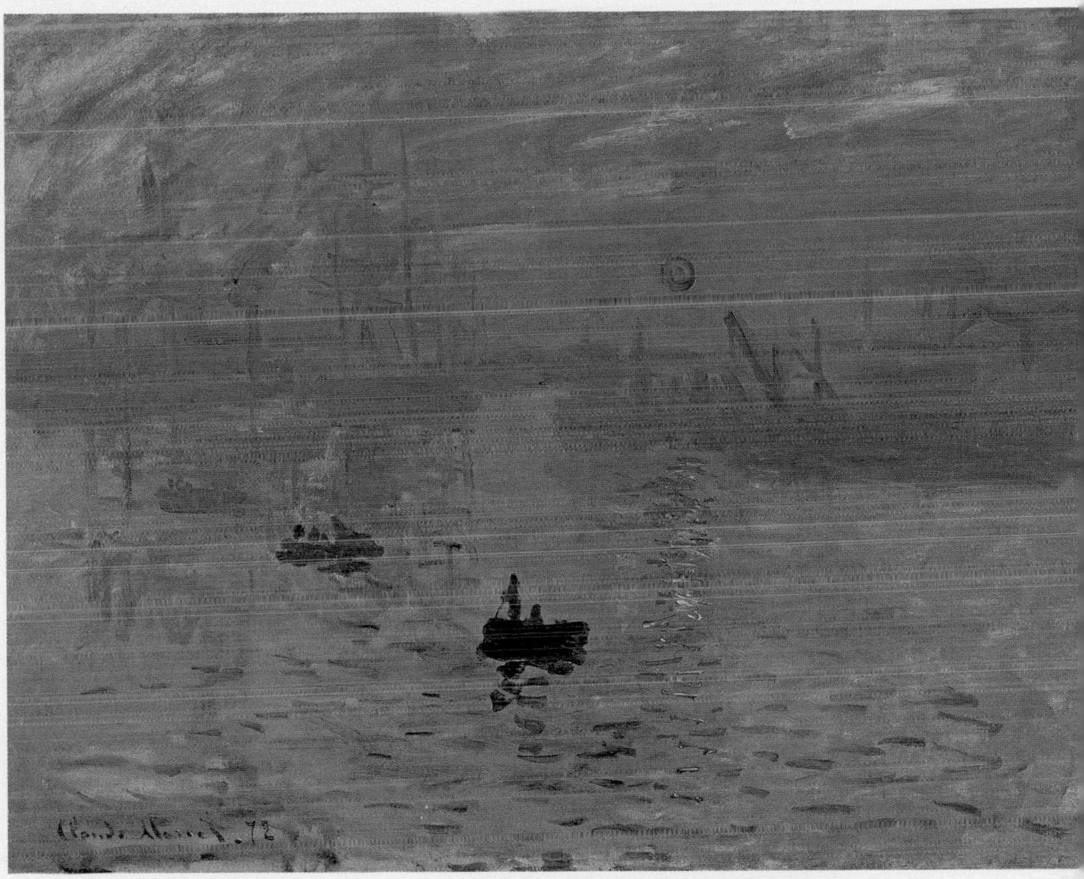

Impression: Sunrise
Claude Monet, 1872

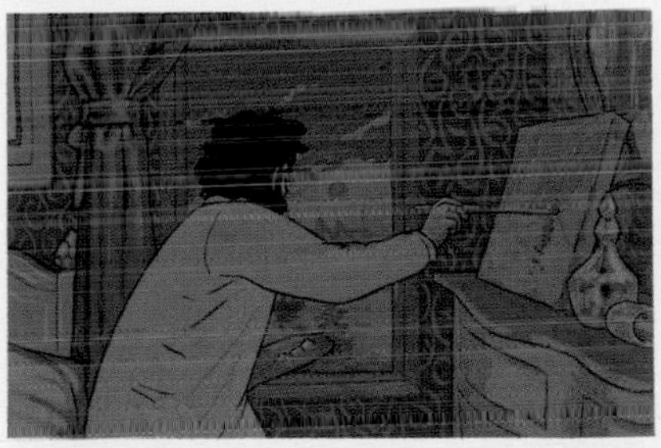

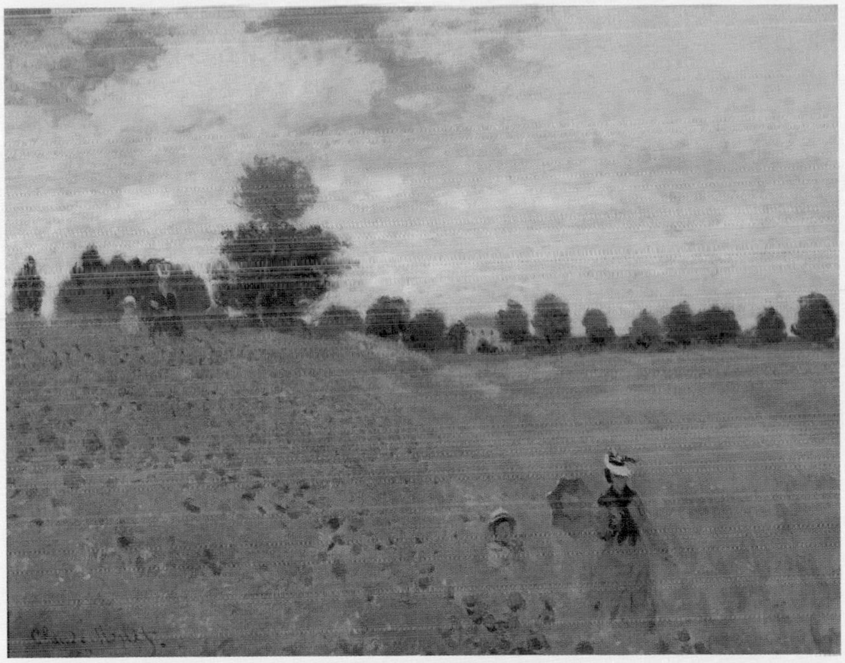

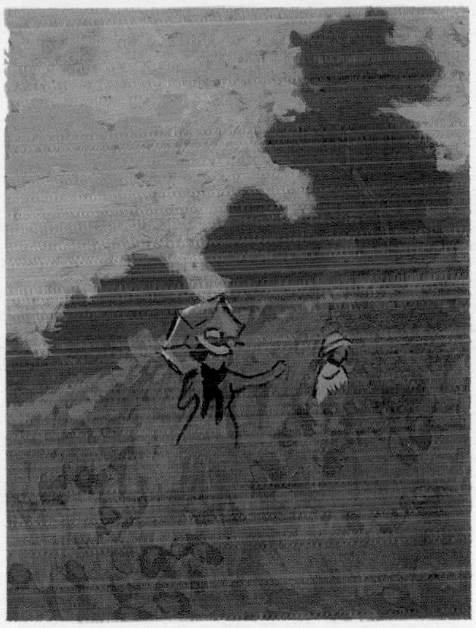

Wild Poppies, near Argenteuil,
Claude Monet, 1873

PAGE 49 : The inside of the Café Nouvelle Athènes is borrowed from a work by one of our fellow Spaniards, Santiago Rusiñol, from 1890, i.e. a few years after the scene shown here.

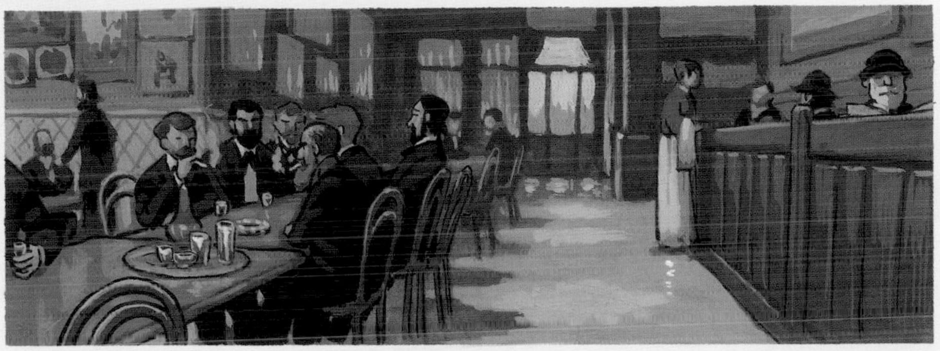

The Magpie, Claude Monet, 1869

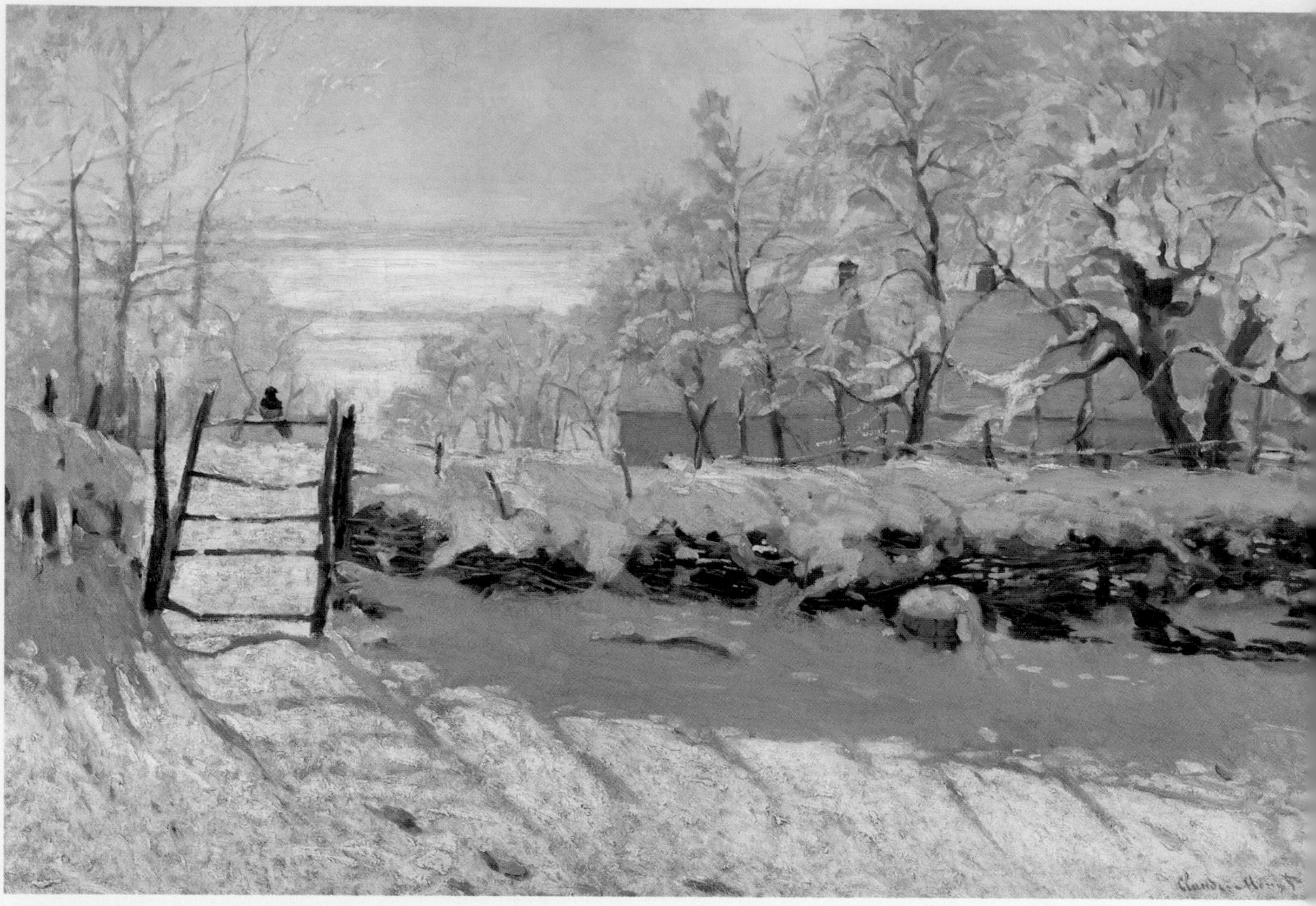

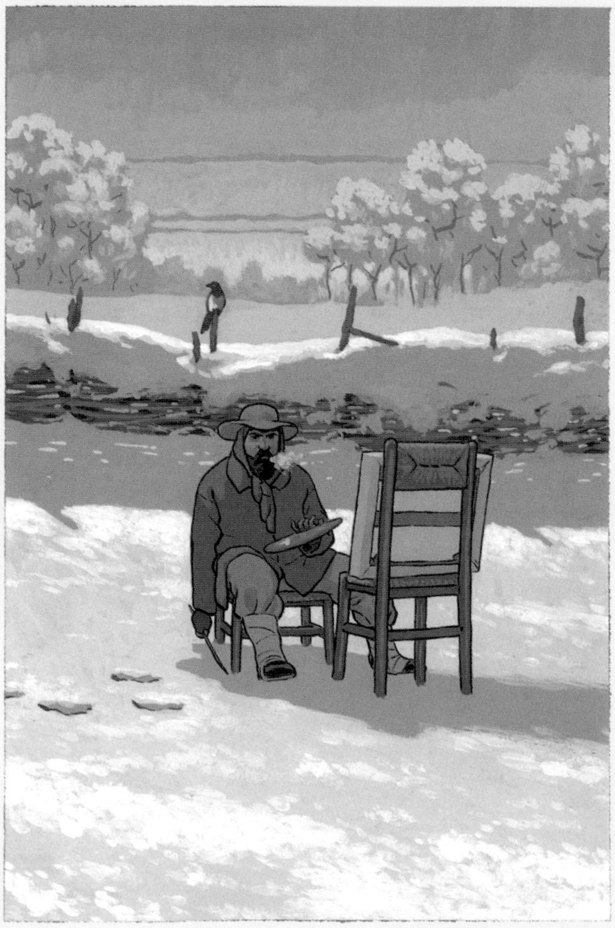

PAGE 53 : The reference here is obvious; it's an homage to *The Magpie*. Though this work was actually done a few years earlier (1869), we couldn't resist the temptation to include it here. We hope our dear readers won't hold it against us.

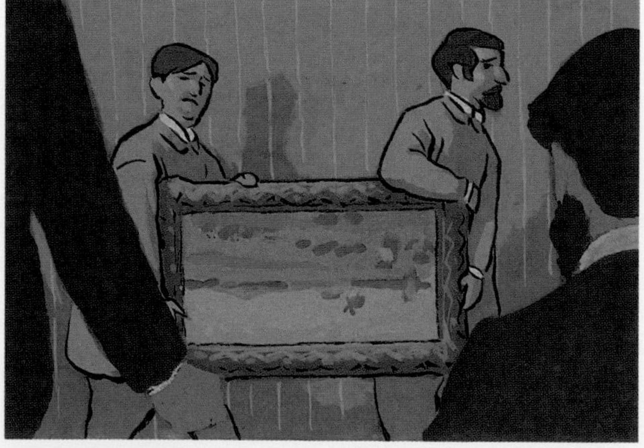

PAGE 54 : The painting here, being shown upside down (a true anecdote, apparently), is none other than Berthe Morisot's *The Little Windmill at Gennevilliers* (1875).

Camille Monet in Japanese Costume, Claude Monet, 1876

PAGE 56 : The painting referred to indirectly in the last few panels is *Camille Monet in Japanese Costume* (1876). Regarding Camille's health problems, "Monet believes she has an "ulcerated uterus." The conclusion was that Camille suffered from a botched abortion. (...). It appears as if the surgical procedure being planned was avoided, possibly following Dr. de Bellio's intervention."[1].

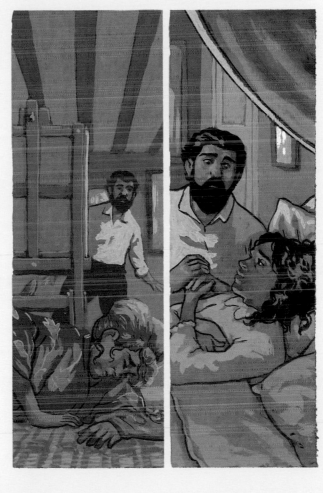

PAGE 58 : The paintings shown in the first three panels are, respectively, *Turkeys* (1977), *The Pond at Montgeron* (1877), and *The Avenue* (1878).

1 : Wildenstein, D. (2014) : *Monet ou le Triomphe de l'impressionnisme*, Taschen, Köln, p. 131.

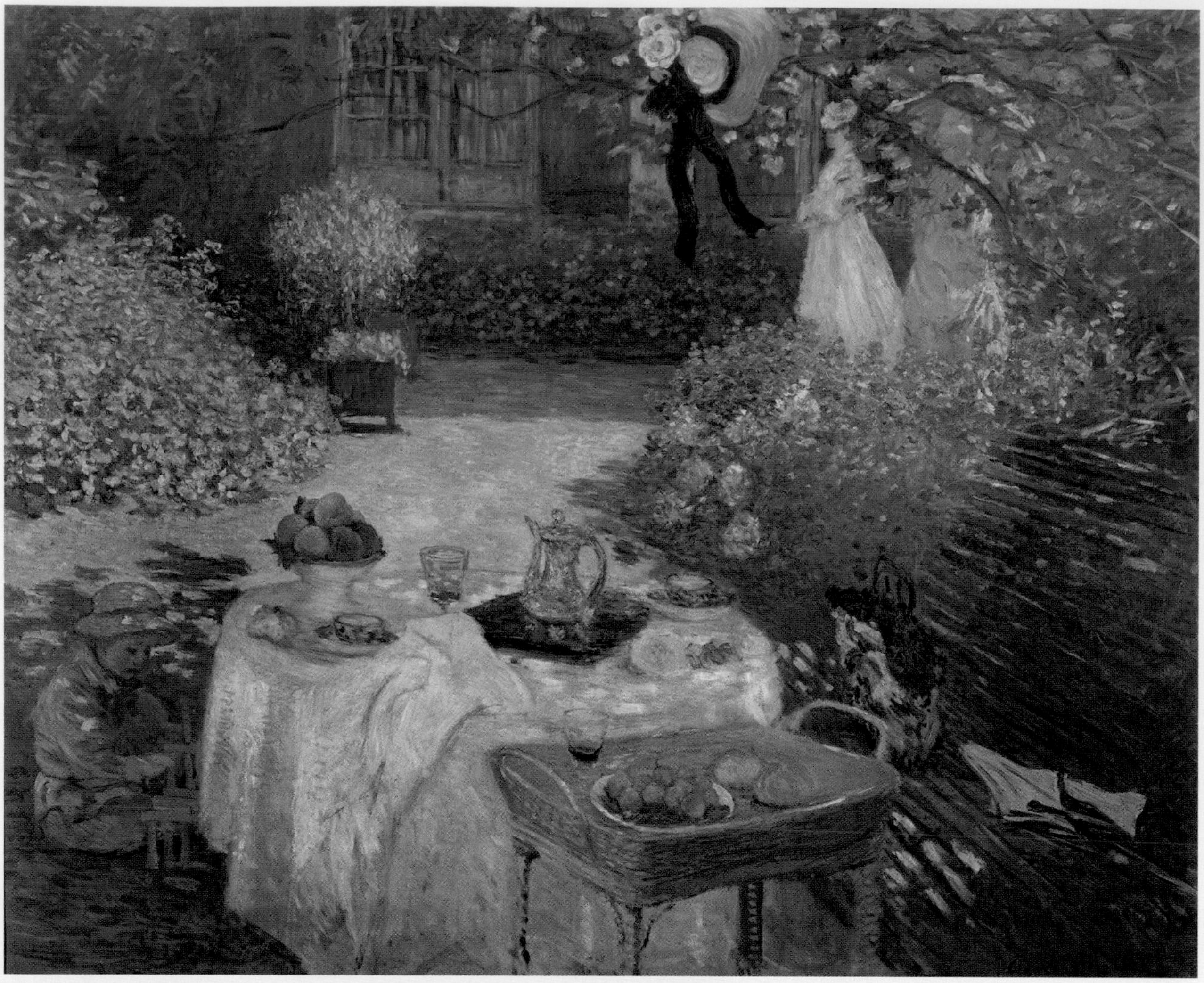

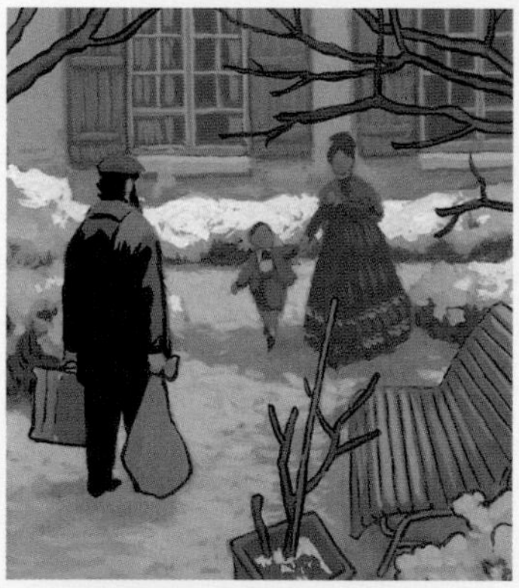

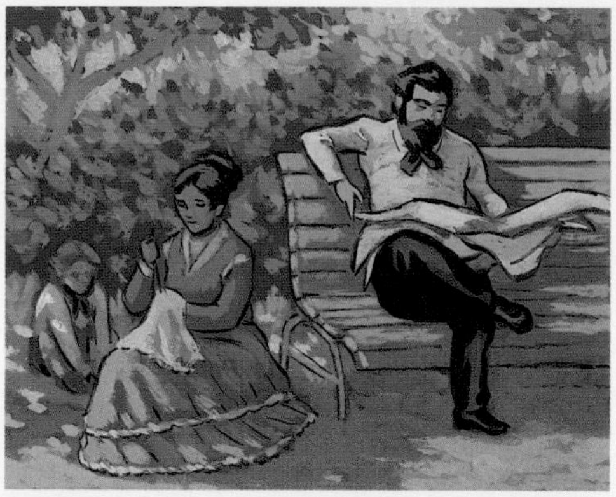

The Luncheon, Claude Monet, 1873

PAGE 60 : Though it's winter here and the similarity isn't obvious, the first panel is inspired by The Luncheon, from 1873. The fifth panel is a reference to *Camille Monet with a Child in the Artist's Garden* (1875).

PAGE 63 : This page features several references to the amazing painting Monet did in 1878, *The Rue Montorgueil.*

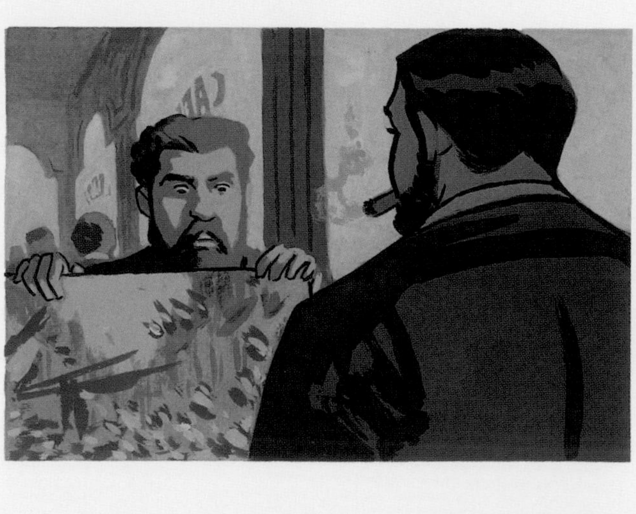

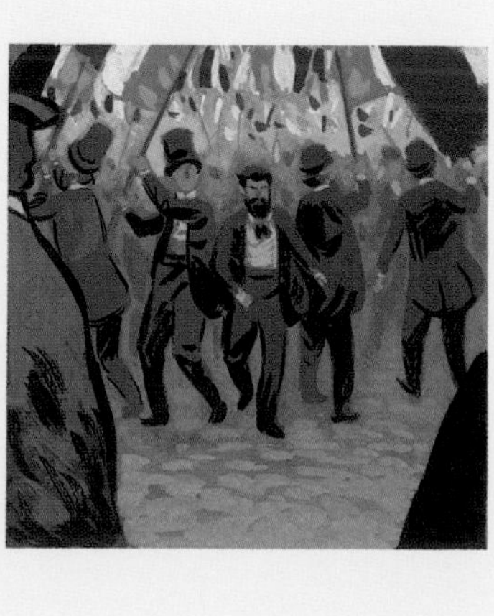

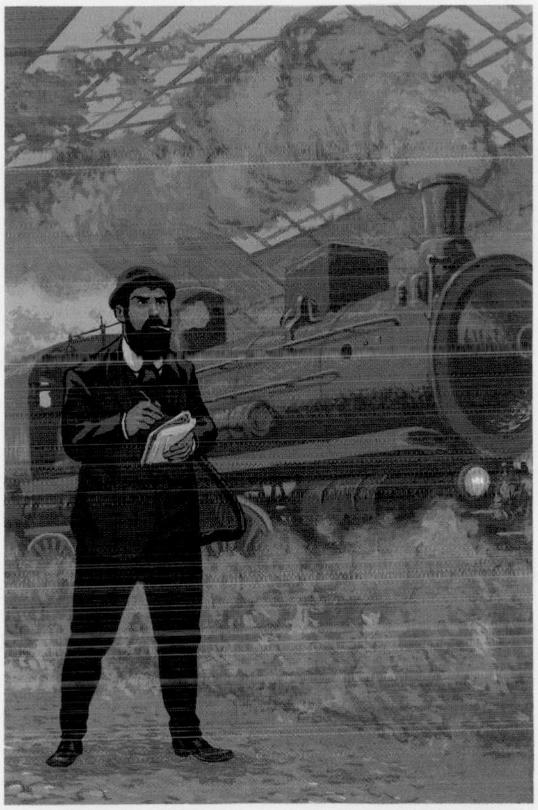

PAGE 61 : This page is obviously inspired by the series of paintings on the Paris Saint-Lazare train station. When we learned Monet had done a bunch of preliminary sketches, we couldn't resist the temptation to show him working on them.

The Gare Saint-Lazare: Arrival of a Train, Claude Monet, 1877

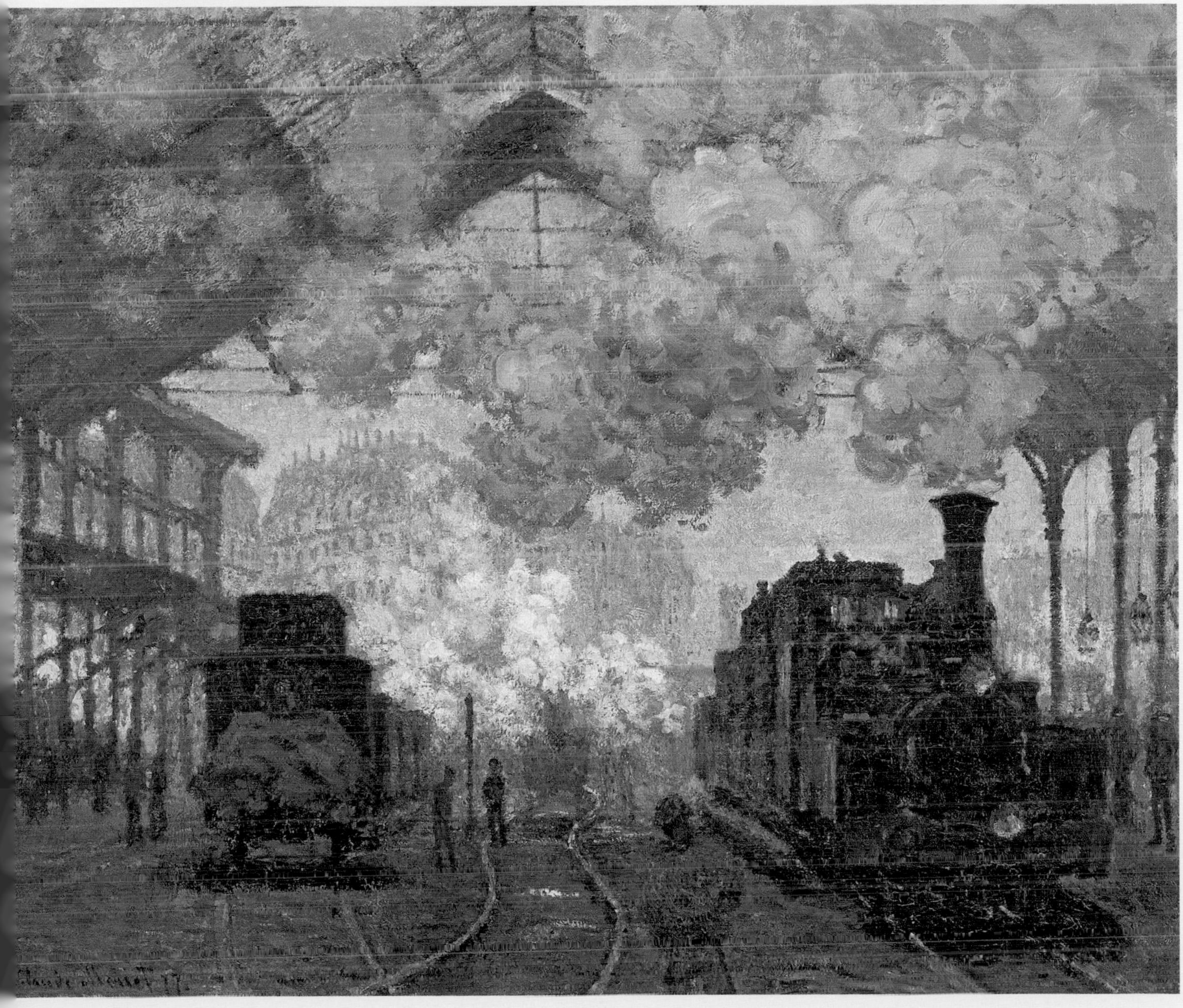

PAGE 65 : The paintings showing the rivalry between Camille and Alice are, respectively, *Michel Monet as a Baby* (1878-1879) and *Jean-Pierre Hoschedé, called 'Bebe Jean'* (1878).

Michel Monet as a Baby, Claude Monet, 1878-1879

© MICHEL MONET (1878-1966) AS A BABY, 1878-79 (OIL ON CANVAS), MONET, CLAUDE (1840-1926) / MUSÉE MARMOTTAN MONET, PARIS, FRANCE / BRIDGEMAN IMAGES

PAGE 68 : The garden in panel 3 was inspired by several of Monet's works on the garden at Vétheuil. Though no doubt different than the real life version, the door to the house is nevertheless easy to recognize.

PAGES 70-71 : One of Monet's most peculiar paintings. These two pages are an homage to *Camille on Her Deathbed* (1879), a work that embodies the artist's grief. The text on these pages corresponds to the author's own words almost verbatim, and we wanted to include the whole passage right here :

"You can't imagine," Monet replied to me, "how true everything you just said really is. It's what obsesses me, torments me, and fills my days with joy. To such an extent that one day, having found myself at the bedside of a dead woman who had been and still was very dear to me, I caught myself, as I stared down at her tragic face, casually wondering about the pattern, about the gradual loss of color that death had brought to her lifeless features. Hues of blue, yellow, grey? That's how low I had stooped. It's a natural reflex to want to reproduce the last image of the one who has just left us forever. But before the idea came to paint the features I was so deeply attached to, my natural instinct was to react to color first, and my reflexes were leading me, in spite of myself, to subconscious rote behavior that swallows up my day-to-day life. Like a beast grinding at the mill. Feel sorry for me, my friend."[3]

3 : Clemenceau, G. (2010) : *Claude Monet "intime"*, Parkstone Press International, New York, p.24.

Camille on her Deathbed,
Claude Monet, 1879

© CAMILLE MONET (1847-79) ON HER DEATHBED, 1879 (OIL ON CANVAS), MONET, CLAUDE (1840-1926) / MUSÉE D'ORSAY, PARIS, FRANCE / BRIDGEMAN IMAGES

Ice Floes on the Seine at Bougival, Claude Monet, 1868

© Ice floes on the Seine at Bougival, c.1867-68 (oil on canvas), Monet, Claude (1840-1926) / Musée d'Orsay, Paris, France / Bridgeman Images

PAGE 75 : This image drew its inspiration from *Ice Floes on the Seine at Bougival,* which Monet painted in 1868.

PAGE 84 : As we can see in panel 2, the painting exhibited at the Salon is *The Seine at Lavacourt* (1880).

The Seine at Lavacourt, Claude Monet, 1880

© The Seine at Lavacourt, 1880 (oil on canvas), Monet, Claude (1840-1926) / Dallas Museum of Art, Texas, USA / Munger Fund / Bridgeman Images

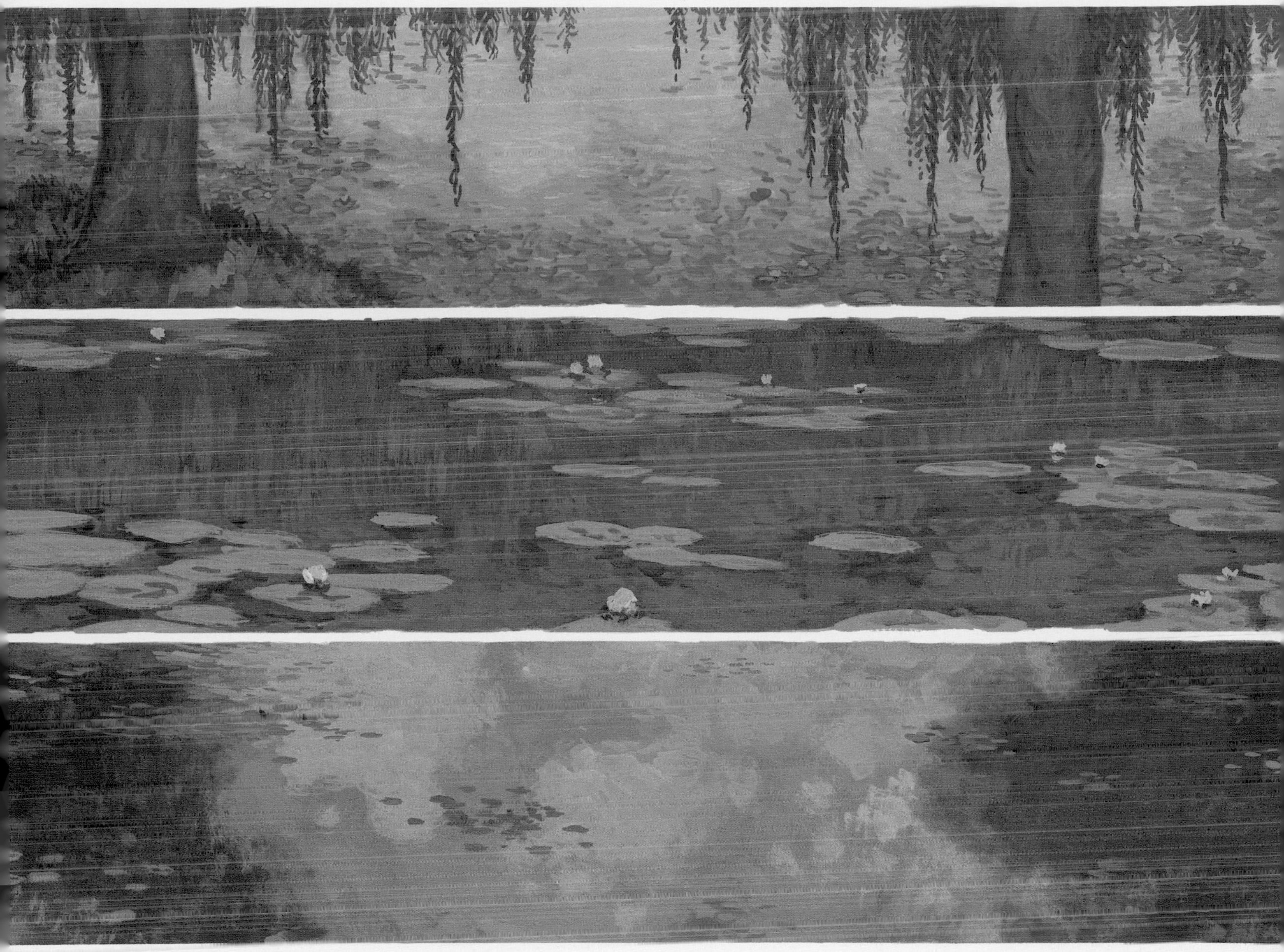

PAGES 92–93 : The last reference shows, through Monet's eyes and in all their glory, the garden and the lake at Giverny in a composition titled *The Set of the Orangerie*, made up of *Water Lilies: Clear Morning with Willows*, *Water Lilies: Green Reflections*, and *Water Lilies: The Clouds.*

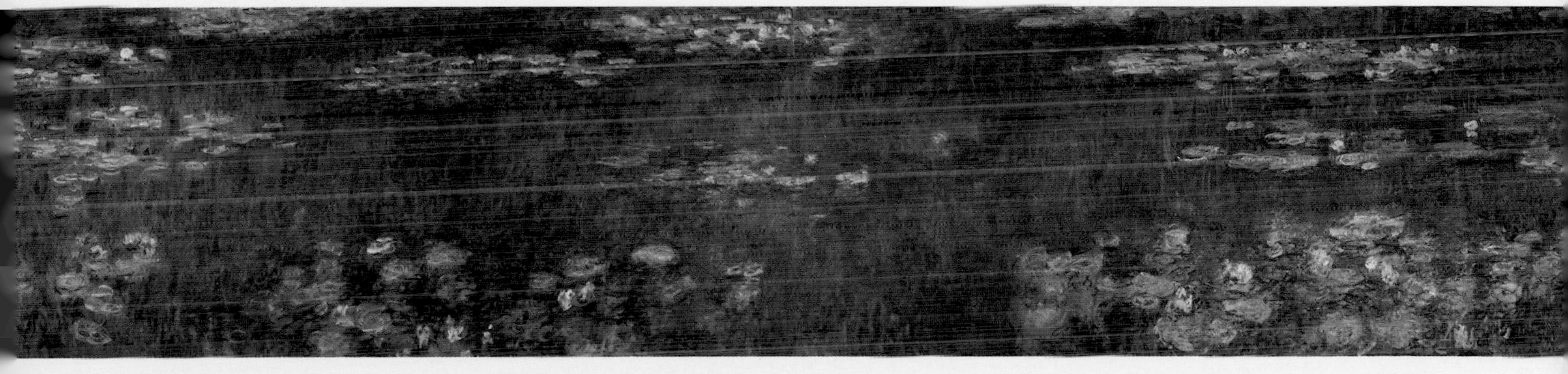

Water Lilies: Green Reflections, Claude Monet, 1914–1918

SALVA RUBIO

A screenwriter, novelist and historian specializing in projects with historical themes, Salva Rubio was a finalist in the prestigious SGAE Julio Alejandro awards and has won many awards as a screenwriter. En 2010, one of his short films was shortlisted for a Goya (the Spanish Oscars). He holds a Masters in screenwriting for film and television (University Carlos III in Madrid) and has written scripts for several short films as well as for film projects for various Spanish production companies, including the animated feature film Deep (2016). He is the author of several novels, works of non-fiction and essays, and he also teaches creative writing. *Monet: Itinerant of Light* is his first graphic novel. He is currently working on *Le Photographe de Mauthausen*. A painter and amateur illustrator, Salva Rubio somehow has found time to pick up the trumpet.
WWW.SALVARUBIO.INFO

EFA

Ricard Fernandez dropped out of school at sixteen to pursue his life's passion. After founding his first fanzine, *Realitat Virtual*, he worked for an animation studio and became a freelance illustrator. He collaborated with Toni Termens on *Les Icariades*, then released a solo work titled *Rodriguez*. Meanwhile, he became Efa, and then there was no stopping him. He created *L'Âme du vin* (The Soul of Wine), then began working with Virginie Ollagnier and Oliver Jouvray on the series *Kia Ora*. He followed that up with *Alter Ego*, in collaboration with Denis Lapière and Pierre-Paul Renders, then *Yerzhan*, penned by Régis Hautière. He teamed up with Olivier Jouvray again on *Le Soldat* (The Soldier), released as part of Le Lombard's "Signé" collection. In 2014, he met Salva Rubio. As they both share a passion for art history and painting, the idea of working together on books such as *Monet* came naturally to them. More projects are sure to follow!